ARE YOU PREPARED FOR A DISASTER?

MITIGATION AND MANAGEMENT OF DISASTERS

Rajni Sekhri Sibal

BLOOMSBURY
NEW DELHI • LONDON • OXFORD • NEW YORK • SYDNEY

BLOOMSBURY INDIA
Bloomsbury Publishing India Pvt. Ltd
Second Floor, LSC Building No. 4, DDA Complex, Pocket C – 6 & 7,
Vasant Kunj, New Delhi 110070

BLOOMSBURY, BLOOMSBURY INDIA and the Diana logo are
trademarks of Bloomsbury Publishing Plc

First published in 2020

Maps contained in the book are source maps drawn prior to August 2019

ISBN: 978-93-89351-92-7

2 4 6 8 10 9 7 5 3 1

Typeset by Fortune Graphics, New Delhi
Printed and bound in India by Sanat Printers, Kundli, Sonepat

To all those bravehearts
who lost their lives
during disasters while saving
the lives of those who survived

and for
Lakshi and Pushan
with love

Contents

Author Note

Disasters happen. And, they happen to people like us. They happen because we are often not prepared and do not know how to reduce risk or what to do in the event of a calamitous event. Often hazards like earthquakes, cyclones, tsunamis or even fire incidents are something we see from afar—in the newspapers and via the electronic media, where clips relating to the hazard and its aftermath are played and replayed for a few days—and then forget. To us it may seem like a faraway incident that doesn't affect us so, we continue to read the news, watch the TV coverage, lament about the mishap, post comments on the social media, and then put our concern away—until the next disaster happens. However, the fact is that disasters happen and they happen to people like us.

Hazards become disasters when they cause extreme disruption in the functioning of a vulnerable society. A disaster leads to human, economic, and environmental losses that exceed the coping ability of the affected community. In common parlance, the words disaster, calamity, hazard and catastrophe are often used interchangeably. They have different connotations for different people depending on their life experiences.

For me, the word 'disaster' brings forth an image of vacant eyes searching devastated homes for their loved ones—lost forever—along the tsunami-ravaged coastline of Tamil Nadu in December 2004. I recall sitting on the edge of the Bay of Bengal near Nagappatinam two days after the calamitous event and staring at the vast, serene ocean at sunset in disbelief. The sea looked so placid and innocent—hardly capable of the savage onslaught and destruction it had caused two days earlier on the shore behind me.

Some moments in life leave behind such a strong impression that they live on forever...

The memories associated with the 2004 tsunami have stayed with me over the years, as have the memories of an incredibly tragic day in June 1999. I was posted as the Deputy Commissioner of Rewari, a district in Haryana that borders Rajasthan in North India. The kharif crop had been harvested, and the post-harvest crop residue was still lying in stacks in the farmers' fields. The haystacks in the fields were at a considerable distance from habitation but were a favourite for children to play in. On a sweltering day, when the atmospheric temperature was 46°C at noon, a stray spark caused havoc. The stack of hay in which four children were playing, caught fire. The children were aged between 5–7 years and were caught unawares. They must have screamed in fear and shouted for help before being burnt to cinders. However, they were too far away to be heard or assisted. Hapless, they clung to each other in fright and died a dreadful death. The deceased had to be cremated together, for even the distraught parents could not tell one child apart from the other. The image of four children clinging to each other as the flames engulfed them continues to haunt me even after two decades.

From a small village to the capital of the nation, the tragedy associated with a disaster is just as poignant. Two years before the Rewari incident, the Uphaar Cinema tragedy took place in Delhi in 1997 and shook the nation. Fifty nine people died while watching a movie in a theatre, mostly due to suffocation, while a hundred and three were grievously injured in the resulting stampede.

In crowded and packed movie theatres of Delhi, I often look for the mandated fire equipment and am not sure whether my fellow cinemagoers remember this incident. We have short memories, and we often unwittingly blank out the unpleasant ones. Despite the Uphaar Cinema tragedy, the average cinemagoer, even in Delhi, is not aware of the procedures that should be followed in the event of a fire.

Recently, I was dismayed to see the lack of awareness regarding hazards and the essential preparedness and responses during a capacity building exercise for schoolteachers. More so since these teachers are the guardians of vulnerable children at school. The informal 'training needs analysis' conducted at the beginning of the session revealed that none of the fifty schoolteachers could respond correctly to multiple-choice questions regarding what they would do to assist the children in their care in the event of a thunderstorm or if tremors were felt during a class. It is frightening to think that children during school hours are at risk because their guardians are unaware of how to reduce risk in the event of a hazard.

India is disaster-prone and vulnerable and has experienced virtually all the natural and man-made disasters known to exist. The country has also witnessed CBRN (chemical, biological, radiation and nuclear) disasters, including several epidemics and one of the most tragic chemical hazard events—The Bhopal gas tragedy. Floods and droughts have become almost an annual feature in one part of the country or the other. A significant part of the country is earthquake-prone, and quakes have occurred in places, which were hitherto thought to be quake-safe. The extensive coastline is susceptible to several natural hazards like cyclones and tsunamis. The vastness of India with varied climatic zones admits the occurrence of avalanches, snowstorms, frost, and cold waves in some parts of the country and heatwaves, dust storms, and droughts in others, along with tropical storms, periodic floods and urban flooding.

The August 2018 deluge in God's own country, Kerala, which had not seen a natural disaster in almost a century is a reminder of the fact that disasters can strike anywhere. Kerala was taken completely unawares by the floods which shook the state in 2018. The last time the state witnessed a hydro-meteorological disaster was in 1924 when the Periyar River got flooded. In terms of the havoc it created, the cataclysmic event in 1924 was no match to the 'Great Kerala Flood' in August 2018. Around 1/6th of the state's population (around 5.4 million people) were affected, and 655,000 houses got destroyed. Even as 280,679 people were rescued and evacuated to safer locations, the floods left behind a trail of disaster with hundreds dead, and many physically injured and rendered homeless. All the affected suffered some form of psychosocial trauma.

There were essential lessons to be learnt from the Kerala rescue and relief operations, which I helped coordinate alongwith a dedicated team of officers and officials of the Ministry of Home Affairs, the National Disaster Management Authority other organisations of the central and state governments, and the brave rescue teams of the National Disaster Response Force (NDRF), as well as the rescue efforts of the Indian Army, Navy, the Coastguard, and the Air Force. The community's lack of awareness with regard to handling a disaster was evident as Kerala had not witnessed a natural disaster for over a century.

In the future, due to climate change, and also due to the socioeconomic interface of communities with the environment, natural disasters are likely to become more frequent. They can also occur at locations that were hitherto assumed less vulnerable to a particular hazard based on historical data. It is not safe to exist in a bubble of false belief that one is safe simply because the area they live in has not witnessed a hydro-meteorological or a seismic calamity in over 50 years or more.

A visit to the millennium city Gurugram, which has developed rapidly in the last decade and a half, with its multi-storied buildings and glass facades, worries me. Gurugram falls in seismic zone-IV, and I often wonder if the inhabitants of the apartment on the 17th floor or the offices on the 13th floor for instance know what to do in the event of an earthquake. This lack of awareness is compounded, in some cases, by an attitude that can only be best described as that of an ostrich that hides its head in the sand in the event of impending danger. The mindset is effectively: 'Hazards do not affect me for I am safe in my own little glass house; – they affect other less fortunate people'. Furthermore, 'If something doesn't affect me', the argument goes, 'I don't need to bother myself with knowing about it!'

It took a great deal of convincing and the involvement of the local administration for the National Disaster Response Force (NDRF) to conduct a mock earthquake and fire drill in the swanky offices of Gurugram's Cybercity in February 2019. It was only after the exercise began that the 5,000 odd participants understood how crucial it was for them to know these procedures. Disasters can occur anytime. It is common sense to ensure the survival of oneselves, family, wards, colleagues, neighbours and the community in the event of a disaster.

There is a nebulous apprehension about disasters, even if a subconscious one and that is evident from the fact that you, have picked up this book on disaster management. There is also a desire to know more and to take responsibility for your safety along with the safety of your family and loved ones into your own hands.

Disaster risk reduction is a matter of global concern, as highlighted in the Sendai framework. The National Disaster Management Authority (NDMA), the Government of India, and the capacity building institutes and risk mitigation agencies within the government have documented several manuals and advisories for the state governments, rescue and response agencies, and other stakeholders responsible for managing disasters. Several advisories on individual calamities are also issued and circulated from time to time. However, a comprehensive manual or compendium about multiple hazards for individuals, families, schools, colleges, offices and the community at large is not available. Drawing upon my experience of handling disasters on the ground as a field functionary as well as working on policy and coordinating the rescue and relief operations at the national level, I decided to write a handbook for individuals, families and the community about preparedness and reducing risk concerning the multiple hazards that beset us.

This book seeks to provide the reader with information about the major hazards, risks associated with them and the vulnerability profile of different geographies and communities. This book also endeavours to establish the last link, which is critical in ensuring disaster risk reduction. It seeks to help to enhance the coping capacities of individuals, families, schools, institutions, offices, and communities in the event of a disaster. The first chapter of the book provides information regarding the nature of hazards, disaster risks and their management, and the second chapter, the specific vulnerability of India to multiple hazards. Each chapter after that gives in-depth information about a particular natural or man-made hazard along with its cause, effects, and the risk involved while also providing an insight into what the affected community should do and not do, before, during, and after the specific calamitous event. Although the cataclysmic events depicted in this book are Indian Peninsula-centric, the information and verities are generic with a global application.

India is an appropriate geographic backdrop for a book on disaster management. The country's geo-climatic conditions make it vulnerable to almost all the natural calamities known to humans like avalanches, cyclones, cloudbursts, droughts, earthquakes, tsunamis, fires, floods, hailstorms, landslides, pest attacks, as well as heat and cold waves. Man-made disasters and events associated with chemical, biological, nuclear and radiation hazards have also occurred in the past. As the Additional Secretary, Disaster Management in the Ministry of Home Affairs, I was responsible for the disaster management policy and mitigation and response mechanisms during disasters of a severe nature that are beyond the coping capacity of the affected state. In this book, I have shared the insights and the lessons that I learned while coordinating rescue and relief operations of several cataclysmic events like the 2018 Kerala floods, the *Titli*, *Gaja*, *Fani* and *Bulbul* cyclones, droughts, landslides, hailstorms, flash floods, and other severe disasters. My experience in coordinating rescue and relief operations has imbued a more personal touch to the book. The chapter on tsunami includes a few verses I wrote in 2004 on the tsunami-ravaged shores of coastal Tamil Nadu. At the end of the book, there is a section on case studies, response operations and information regarding agencies that can be contacted to obtain more details about early warnings, shelters and evacuation plans. All information in this book is factual. Any views and opinions that have been expressed over and above the factual statements are entirely my own and not of the government.

Acknowledgements

Are You Prepared for a Disaster?: Mitigation and Management of Disasters is a book that is very close to my heart. The book represents all that I have seen and learnt while preparing for and responding to disasters: mainly floods, drought, fire and agrarian disasters like hailstorm, pest attack and frost as a field level officer in Haryana (a land locked agrarian state in North India) besides managing relief efforts in natural disasters and man-made calamitous events like riots. The book also shares all I experienced and learnt during my posting as Additional Secretary in the Ministry of Home Affairs in the Government of India. It was a period of immense learning, both in policy making and managing disaster response and relief across the country. It also gave me the opportunity to see how some of the States had grown over the years in their capacity to handle disasters learning from their past experiences. The State of Gujrat, having suffered major loss of life and property in the Bhuj earthquake put in institutions and processes that have proved extremely robust over the years. The story of disaster risk reduction in Odisha is a fascinating case study. Cyclones are almost an annual feature in the coastal state of Odisha in the Bay of Bengal. The intensity and periodicity of hydro-metrological disasters like cyclones has increased over the years due to climate change. Odisha lost about 10,000 precious human lives in the Super Cyclone of 1999 – a tragedy that the State refused to forget and one that proved to be a turning point for the State to get its act together. The Odisha State Disaster Management Authority was set up, capacities built, institutions, processes and procedures put in place. The State is remarkable in its ability to reduce risk, prepare for and manage disasters, conduct massive evacuations timely to save lives even in the worst cyclonic storms. My stint as Additional Secretary Disaster Management also gave me the opportunity to study the disaster risk reduction efforts in the international arena first hand. The sing-song manner in which an entire class of Japanese Junior School children can recite the procedure to be adopted as soon as a tremor is felt is reminiscent of School children in India reciting their Math tables. Seeing toddlers neatly evacuate and follow the laid down guidelines without alarm, on hearing an emergency bell is fascinating. Even as I share my experiences and learnings in this book, I would like to thank providence for giving me this wonderful opportunity to work in this area.

I need to acknowledge the assistance of many persons who have helped make this book a reality. My gratitude to Paul Kumar and Jyoti Mehrotra of Bloomsbury Publications in realizing the value of this book when I outlined my idea and their encouragement was a source of inspiration. I conscientiously woke up early each day and wrote for a couple of hours every morning before I left for office for almost a year.

I would like to thank my daughter Lakshi for the title of the book. It was suggested by her and selected by Paul of Bloomsbury from a number of other suggestions. Thank you Lakshi. Your title is definitely more appropriate and attractive as against the prosaic one I had suggested: 'A Handbook on Disaster Management – For Families, Offices Institutions and the Community.' The latter sounds rather matter-of-fact and mundane and merely describes what this book is all about.

I owe a great deal to my senior colleagues who shared their wisdom and taught me all I know, way beyond the books I read on the subject, about Disaster Risk Reduction: Dr P.K. Mishra, now the Principal Secretary to the Prime Minister of India, Mr Kamal Kishore, Member National Disaster Management Authority (NDMA), Lt. General Marwaha, Member NDMA and Mr R.K. Jain, and the then Secretary and Member NDMA. I have learnt all I know about Chemical Biological Radiation related and Nuclear Disasters from Dr D.N. Sharma, Member NDMA and would also like to thank him for the photographs that I have used in the two chapters on CBRN disasters.

My gratitude to Director General National Disaster Response Force (NDRF) and his team for their support and for sharing pictures and permitting me to use them for this book. I also thank him for arranging several meetings with the brave 'men in orange' for them to share their personal experiences in rescuing disaster victims. Mr Ravi Joseph, the then second in command, at the NDRF needs special mention for his timely support and for sharing his own personal experiences and photographs of various rescue operations as well as mock drills.

I would like to express my gratitude to Professors of the National Institute of Disaster Management (NIDM) for sharing their experiences and for permitting me to use some of the photographs they shared with me when I held the charge of Executive Director NIDM. I need to thank Sanjeev Jindal Joint Secretary (Disaster Management) MHA for sharing photographs and information regarding State Disaster Management Authorities and the State Emergency Operation Centres (SEOCs). For fire related photographs I need to thank Mr Nalin. I would also like to place on record my gratitude to all the Secretaries responsible for Disaster Management and Relief Commissioners of the State Governments, specially the RCs of Gujrat, Odisha, Kerala, Andhra Pradesh, Karnataka, Tamil Nadu, Manipur, Assam, Nagaland, Maharashtra and Bihar for their support and for sharing photographs of disaster and rescue and relief operations that I have used in this book.

Last, but not the least I would like to thank a group of school teachers I spoke to who were attending an awareness generation workshop about natural disasters. It came as a shock to me that, at the beginning of the workshop, not a single one could correctly answer a question I asked of them: 'what will you do to save the children under your care if you feel a tremor during school hours?' This despite the fact that I gave them four options to choose from. I shared this experience with a friend who works in a senior management position in a multinational and was surprised by her response – for she too asked: 'So what *should* they do? In fact, I also don't know – what should *I* do in such an event?'

And that was the day I decided to write this book…

ONE

Hazards and Disaster Risk Reduction

Hazards have been known to occur since time immemorial and can be traced back to 430 BC when an epidemic of Typhus was reported in Athens. The earliest recorded cataclysmic event in the world dates back to January 1556, when an earthquake in the Shaanxi province of China caused loss of innumerable lives. Over the years, disasters have now increased in magnitude, frequency, complexity and economic impact.

The word 'disaster' is derived from the French word *désastre*, which in turn has an affinity with the Old Italian word *disastro*. Section 2(d) of India's Disaster Management Act 2005 defines a disaster as a 'catastrophe, mishap, calamity or grave occurrence in any area, arising from natural or man-made causes, or by accident or negligence which results in substantial loss of life or human suffering or damage to, and destruction of, property, or damage to, or degradation of, environment, and is of such a nature or magnitude as to be beyond the coping capacity of the community of the affected area.'

The United Nations defines a disaster as 'the occurrence of sudden or major misfortune which disrupts the basic fabric and normal functioning of the society or community'. The Sendai Framework for Disaster Risk Reduction 2015–2030 promotes: (a) understanding disaster risk; (b) strengthening disaster risk

Figure 1.1 Tsunami

Figure 1.2 Forest fire

Figure 1.3 Cyclone

Figure 1.4 Earthquake

Figure 1.5 Flood

Figure 1.6 Avalanche

Natural Disasters

governance; (c) investing in disaster risk reduction for resilience; (d) enhancing disaster preparedness for effective response and (e) 'building back better' in recovery, rehabilitation and reconstruction.

DISASTERS SANS BORDERS

Disasters and their impact have no borders in a global world. The international community comes together to assist each other in rescuing and providing aid to disaster-affected communities. Rescue teams of the NDRF and the Indian Armed Forces played a crucial role during the Nepal earthquake, and in Japan and Indonesia, for instance. Countries also share best practices in preparedness, response, relief, recovery, and rehabilitation. The early warning system of the Indian Meteorological Department (IMD) issues warnings of impending disasters across India and also provides 'early warnings' to 12 other nations under an international treaty. Of all the disasters that have occurred in the world in the last few decades, 43 per cent have occurred in Asia, 23 per cent in America, 16 per cent in Africa, 15 per cent in Europe and the remaining 4 per cent in Oceania. The loss of human lives because of disasters is disproportionately high in Asia and stands at 68 per cent of all lost human lives in the world due to disasters. Although the occurrence of disasters is about 23 per cent in America, the percentage of lives lost is lower and stands at 14 per cent—the same as in Africa with fewer hazard events. The total lives lost in Europe and Oceania stands at 3 per cent and 1 per cent respectively.

DISASTERS: NATURAL AND MAN-MADE

Disasters are traditionally classified into natural and man-made. Natural disasters are those that are associated with natural hazards like floods, cyclones, droughts, tidal waves, thunderstorms, flash floods, heat and cold waves, tsunamis, and earthquakes.

Figure 1.7 Fire in an oil and gas plant

Figure 1.8 Train accident in Assam

Figure 1.9 CBRN

Figure 1.10 Flyover collapse (Kolkata)

Figure 1.11 Tunnel rescue

Figure 1.12 Capsized boat

man-made Disasters

Amongst all the natural hazards, earthquakes are the major killers. Furthermore, about 90 per cent of the death toll in an earthquake is attributable to accidents relating to the collapse of built-up structures. Anthropogenic or man-made disasters include political unrests, stampedes, accidents and disasters which are associated with chemical, biological, radiation and nuclear hazards. The distinction between natural and man-made disasters is somewhat artificial. Natural calamities are often precipitated by human actions or inactions and have complex causal factors. Floods, for instance, are traditionally treated as natural disasters. Over time, with environmental degradation, rapid urbanisation and ill-planned construction over dry riverbeds and drainage channels, floods have become a complex phenomenon, and the causal factors are a combination of both natural and induced elements.

ELEMENTS OF DISASTER RISK

A *hazard* is an event that has the potential to cause damage to life and property; such as a Category IV Cyclone. The 1737 Cyclone left behind a trail of 300,000 deaths in and around Kolkata. Events counted amongst the most tragic hazards of the 20th century include the Great Chinese Famine of 1958–1961 during which millions died, and the 1970 Bhola Cyclone in Bengal with 50,000 casualties.

Disaster is an extreme disruption of the functioning of a society associated with a hazard that causes widespread human, material, and environmental losses, which exceed the ability of the affected society to cope with the help of its resources.

Disaster Risk is a function (f) of Capacity, Hazard, Exposure, and Vulnerability. R = (f) CHEV.

Vulnerability is the susceptibility of the community, its assets, regular economic activity and livelihoods vis-á-vis the hazard.

Exposure refers to the number of people, value of assets and the value of the economic activities that are likely to be affected by a hazard.

Capacity is a combination of the strengths, attributes and resources available within a society to manage and reduce disaster risk and strengthen its resilience.

Preparedness and risk mitigation go a long way in enabling a community to enhance its capacity to deal with a hazard and to reduce risk and vulnerability through specific actions. Not all hazards result in disasters. Effective preparedness, risk mitigation, and reduction measures can reduce the loss of lives and economic losses associated with a disaster.

RISK ASSESSMENT AND REDUCTION

Risk assessment helps to quantify and predict the probability of occurrence of a disaster. It also delineates its possible impact. The process of assessing risk involves analysis of historical data regarding hazards and the effect it has on the exposed and vulnerable population. Risk assessment enables governments, response and relief agencies, and communities to enhance their preparedness.

Communities are placed in situations of higher risk when they degrade their environment or overpopulate urban centres. Communities often settle down in vulnerable seismic zones or on steep landslide-prone mountainsides on account of their socio-economic conditions. Disaster risk can be reduced through specific interventions.

The Land of the Rising Sun, Japan, like India, is inherently prone to multiple hazards. The word tsunami is Japanese. Besides being at risk to natural hazards, the Japanese have faced the most tragic man-made hazards. The bombing of Hiroshima and Nagasaki has left behind a trail of sorrow, and several generations of this nation have been impacted by the worst man-made disaster in our history. Having been exposed to such tragic natural and man-made disasters, the Japanese are proactively involved in reducing disaster risk. Japan has judiciously invested in quake resilient infrastructure, for instance, to reduce risk.

VULNERABILITY AND THE CYCLE OF POVERTY

A community's vulnerability or its susceptibility to hazards often increases because of human behaviour. The poor are disproportionately vulnerable to disasters. They typically emerge the worst off in any cataclysmic event. Besides being more at risk, they lack adequate resources for coping. Risk and poverty are inextricably linked and mutually reinforcing. Poverty compels the poor to migrate and live in physically vulnerable locations, often in unsafe shelters in disaster-prone locations: on dry riverbeds and in low-lying flood-prone areas, on steep landslide-prone mountainsides and along fault lines that are prone to seismic activity. The situation is further aggravated by the economic compulsion of the poor to exploit environmental resources for their survival, which, in turn, increases their risk and exposure to disasters.

Post-disaster, the breakdown of limited essential services leads to significant morbidity, which affects the poor disproportionately. Inadequate provision of water supply, sanitation, and transport in more impoverished neighbourhoods enhances their vulnerability. Loss of life is often higher in these neighbourhoods. In Haiti, after the 2010 earthquake, the post-disaster period adversely affected the more impoverished neighbourhoods to a more significant extent than the actual seismic event. An outbreak of cholera due to limited sanitation and lack of clean water resulted in immense morbidity and mortality. This was compounded by the difficulty faced by relief agencies in transporting emergency water supplies to these impoverished neighbourhoods due to poor connectivity.

The 'Great' Kerala Flood of August 2018 caused immense havoc, especially amongst the more deprived communities and fisherfolk. Post-rescue, the lessons learnt from the Haiti earthquake formed the basis for post-disaster operations for the response agencies, especially in these poorer neighbourhoods. Clearing the debris, treating and burying dead animals, spraying and cleaning the flood-ravaged districts and inoculating the affected, especially in the flood shelters, to ensure that an epidemic did not break out, was of paramount importance. Besides the loss of life and property during a hazard, the loss of livelihoods can push poorer households further into abject poverty and make them more vulnerable to future disasters. It is a vicious cycle and ultimately traps the poor into a cycle of poverty.

LOSS OF LIVES AND LIVELIHOODS

Disasters cause massive human and economic losses across the world. The United Nations International Strategy of Disaster Reduction (UNISDR), in its Global Assessment Report on Disaster Risk Reduction, estimates that disasters have affected 1.7 billion people and 0.7 billion individuals have been killed during the decade 2005–2015. Hydro-meteorological and climatological disasters caused more than 70 per cent of the losses during this period.

Globally, disasters caused economic losses worth US$2–US$2.5 trillion as per UNISDR estimates. It has been estimated that the economic losses on account of disasters, as a percentage of the gross domestic product (GDP), are 20 per cent higher in developing countries. The World Bank estimates that disasters account for economic losses of up to 2 per cent of the GDP in India. The Government of India assists state governments in coping with disasters through financial mechanisms like the State Disaster Relief Fund, which is at the disposal of the state

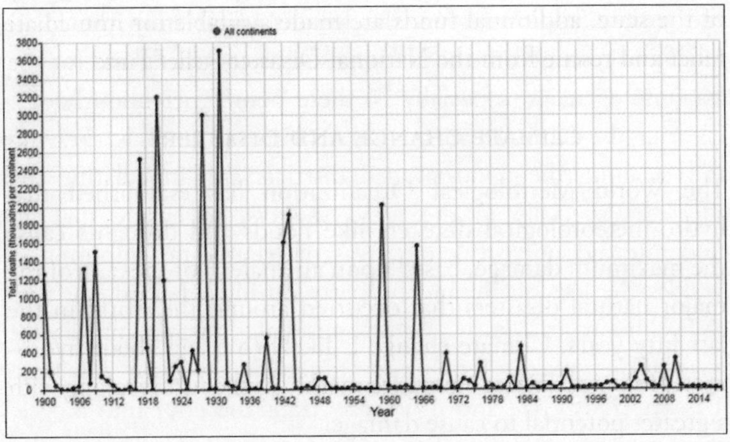

Loss of Human Lives

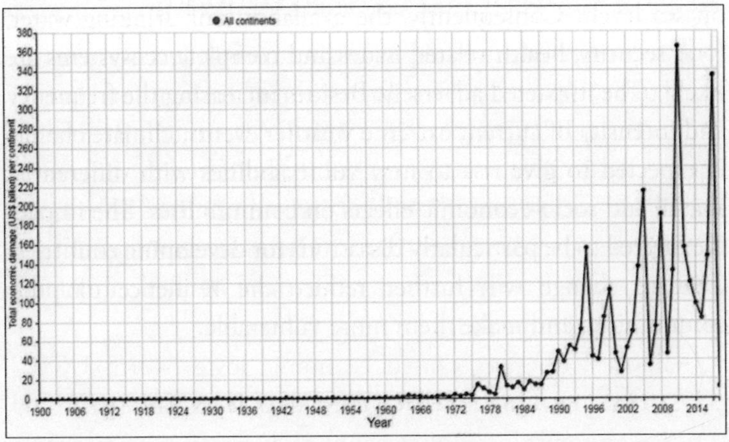

Economic Losses

Source: EM-DAT

Global Disaster Losses (1900–2018)

governments for providing immediate relief. In the event of a disaster of a severe nature, that is beyond the coping capacity of the state, additional funds are made available for immediate relief and rescue from the National Disaster Relief Fund.

CLIMATE CHANGE AND DISASTERS

The World Metrological Organization has established that hydro-meteorological disasters like floods and droughts cause the maximum damage, based upon an analysis of the data of the major natural disasters that occurred around the world in the last fifty years. Climate change is likely to bring about hydro-meteorological hazards more frequently in the future, along with a greater potential to cause damage.

Climate change is expected to have a more deleterious effect on the hydrological cycle, especially on droughts and floods and on sea levels. Consequently, the availability of drinking water, food security, health-related issues and complete ecosystems are likely to be impacted adversely. Besides increasing the frequency and intensity of current extreme weather events, climate change is expected to give rise to new vulnerabilities with differential spatial and socio-economic effects on communities. The impact is expected to be particularly disastrous for developing countries. Climate change will further reduce the resilience of poor communities and make them more vulnerable.

DISASTER RISK REDUCTION AND MANAGEMENT

Disaster Management is the enhancement of the capacity of a population to cope with hazards, and aims at managing and reducing risk through risk mitigation measures, better coping mechanisms and planned preparedness. Since a disaster is a calamitous event which is beyond the coping capacity of the affected community, the efficient and effective response to a disaster requires a holistic and proactive strategy, which is

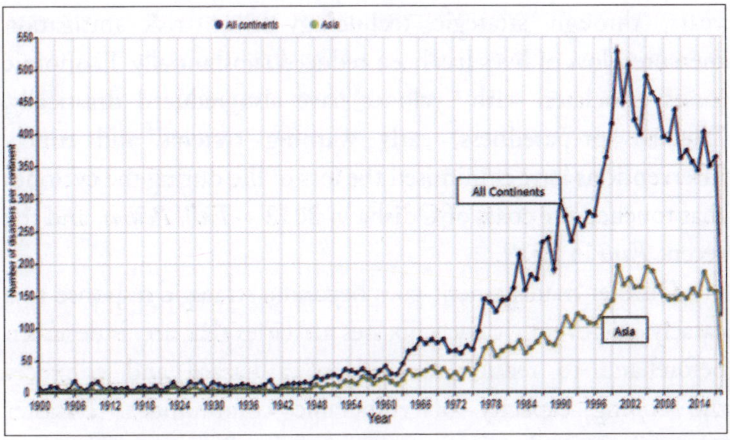

Source: EM-DAT

Increasing due to factors like climate change, population, concentration of assets, urbanization.

Global Natural Disasters (1900-2018)

technology-driven. In recent times, disaster management as a means of enhancing preparedness and risk reduction, rather than a response to the occurrence of a hazard, has received increasing attention globally.

In Japan, preparedness and disaster risk reduction are an integral part of the DNA of individuals, families and the community at large. Recently during a disaster risk reduction workshop in Japan, it was a pleasure to witness the awareness and preparedness levels of the community. Even children in primary schools responded with a standard drill to an alarm indicating that an earthquake was imminent. Primary school children can rattle off the drill to be followed in the event of a hazard—just like a child of the same age can recite a multiplication table in an Indian school.

Cyclones are almost an annual feature of the lives of communities residing in the coastal states of India. The 1999 'Super'Cyclone of Odisha, for instance, brought with it immense destruction and caused a loss of about 10,000 lives. Over the years, through strategic technology-driven risk mitigation measures, loss of lives has been reduced substantially. Economic losses associated with cyclones have also reduced drastically. Effective preparedness, early warning systems and timely interventions have minimised the loss of life during the cyclones that touched the coast of Odisha in 2018—*Titli, Pethai,* and the recent *Fani* in 2019.

Disaster management goes beyond a strategic response to a cataclysmic event. It encompasses activities that are undertaken beforehand to reduce the risk of a hazard and enhances the coping capacity of vulnerable communities. Disaster management embraces every stage of the disaster management cycle: enhanced preparedness and expedient risk mitigation, prompt rescue with minimal reaction time, timely relief to meet the immediate needs of the affected population and constructive rehabilitation measures to build back a safer and a more disaster-resilient world.

TWO

India: Disasters and their Management

This book has been written against an Indian backdrop, sharing personal experiences in disaster management policy and its implementation. During the early years of my career, I was responsible for coordinating rescue and relief operations in the event of a disaster at the subdivision and district levels. In this book, I have drawn upon my first-hand experience of putting together disaster management plans at district levels, and in handling natural and man-made disasters at the cutting edge. The book also includes policy interventions for disaster risk reduction, as well as strategies for rescue, relief, and rehabilitation in India based upon my first-hand experience in handling policy interventions and coordinating of response operations of severe disasters in the Government of India. This section of the book is designed to provide necessary information about the geo-climatic conditions and India's vulnerability to disasters, as well as highlighting the institutional mechanisms for preparedness, risk reduction, and response in the country.

Although the instances and events described in the book are Indian, the verities and information provided about hazards, risks, vulnerabilities and disaster response mechanisms have a global application.

HAZARD PROFILE AND VULNERABILITY

India's geo-climatic conditions, its topography and the high degree of socio-economic vulnerability make it one of the ten most disaster-prone countries in the world. Demographic pressures and their socio-economic impact on the environment exacerbate the situation further. Factors like rapid urbanisation, industrialisation, climate change and environmental degradation have enhanced the vulnerability profile of India. The country

Figure 2.1 Tsunami

Figure 2.2 Earthquake

Figure 2.3 Drought

is especially vulnerable to twelve natural calamities that have been notified by the Government of India as hazards. These hazards include avalanches, cyclones, cloudbursts, droughts, earthquakes, tsunamis, fire, floods, hailstorms, landslides, pest attacks, and cold wave. India's vulnerability to natural disasters is attributable to its unique geographic and geological situation. Out of the thirty-five states and union territories in the country, twenty-seven are vulnerable to disasters. Almost 59 per cent of the landmass is prone to earthquakes ranging from moderate to very high intensity. 12 per cent is prone to flood and river erosion. In addition to the notified hazards, different regions are vulnerable to state-specific hazards like forest fires, snowstorms, heatwaves, and lightning.

The Himalayan region is prone to seismic activity and hazards like water erosion, landslides, forest fires, and avalanches. The geotectonic features of the Himalayas and the adjacent alluvial plains of Indus, Ganges, and Brahmaputra make the region susceptible to earthquakes. Significant parts of the Himalayan region are incredibly vulnerable, lying in seismic zone-V. Parts of North India, including Delhi and the National Capital Region (NCR) are in seismic zone-IV and are vulnerable to earthquakes. The tectonic movements in the ocean floor make the coastal region of India Tsunami-prone.

The river basins of India, especially of the Indo-Gangetic plain, are flood-prone. Tropical thunderstorms, and flash floods, as well as lightning and hailstorms, are common hydro-meteorological hazards. Extreme weather conditions and massive quantities of ice and snow stored in the glaciers are other natural factors, which enhance India's vulnerability to various forms of natural disasters like floods, landslides, and avalanches. With a vast coastline of 8,118 km, a large portion of the coastline, about 5,700 km, is prone to cyclones and storms because of the disturbance in the atmospheric pressure over oceans and tidal waves. Urban flooding is a complex, recent phenomenon, which occurs year after year in metropolitan cities like Mumbai; and in Chennai, where urban floods in 2015 caused immense damage and loss.

The western part of the country, especially the region in and around the Thar Desert, is drought-prone and is vulnerable to dust storms. The northwestern and western parts of the country are prone to heatwaves. More than 68 per cent of the cultivable agricultural land in India is vulnerable to droughts. Natural calamities like droughts, cold waves, frost, hailstorms, and pest attacks make a sizable proportion of India's population, which is dependent upon agriculture extremely vulnerable to agro-climatic and agrarian disasters. India is vulnerable to man-made and induced hazards too. Fire incidents, industrial accidents and other man-made disasters involving chemical, biological, radioactive, and nuclear materials are hazards which owe their occurrence to the action or inaction of the community. The economically and socially weaker sections of the community are both vulnerable and incapable of coping in the event of a natural or man-made disaster. Women, the elderly, children, and differently-abled people are amongst the most vulnerable and require special attention by the family and the community in the event of a calamity.

DISASTER MANAGEMENT: INDIA'S INSTITUTIONAL FRAMEWORK

The prime minister of India heads the National Disaster Management Authority, the NDMA, given the risk profile and vulnerability of the country. The Ministry of Home Affairs is responsible for framing policies for disaster management. The existing policy framework in the country determines the structures, institutions, and mechanisms that are responsible for ensuring risk mitigation and measures for enhancing preparedness and effective response, relief, rehabilitation, and rebuilding in the event of a disaster.

"Forgive me O Lord—but *my* god came in orange!"

The Disaster Management Act 2005 is a watershed. The 2005 Act has heralded a new era in the manner in which the government manages disasters. The erstwhile policy perspective of improving the manner, effectiveness and reaction time of response to a disaster event has been made more comprehensive and proactive. There is greater emphasis on preparedness and disaster risk reduction. The Act mandates the creation of a multi-tiered institutional system comprising of the NDMA, the State Disaster Management Authorities (SDMA) headed by the respective chief ministers, and the District Disaster Management Authorities (DDMA) headed by the collector. The National Institute of Disaster Management (NIDM) assists the NDMA in building capacity.

Twelve specialised battalions of NDRF deployed across the country are capable of conducting specialised rescue operations, like search and rescue during floods, in collapsed structures and during CBRN emergencies. The NDRF is also trained to conduct mountain rescues, rescue operations requiring deep-sea diving, as well as canine and technical search, and animal disaster responses. The NDRF men are also trained as medical first responders. Some states also have State Disaster Response Forces (SDRF).

The 2009 Disaster Management Policy promotes a culture of prevention, preparedness, and resilience. It aims at enhancing preparedness and risk mitigation to reduce the vulnerability and risk of the affected population, efficient response and immediate relief in the event of a disaster along with rehabilitation and reconstruction to build better after. The National Disaster Management Plan (NDMP) formulated in 2016 lays down the roadmap for the development of contemporary forecasting and early warning systems backed by responsive and fail-safe communications to reduce risk. The Plan also provides direction for all the phases of the disaster management cycle, including prevention and risk reduction as part of mitigation, preparedness, response, and recovery.

EARLY WARNING

The Government of India has a robust system of providing 'early warnings' on a real-time basis for impending disasters to all agencies like the State Emergency Operation Centers (SEOC).

The Indian Meteorological Department (IMD) is the nodal agency for all meteorological hazards and provides multi-hazard warnings concerning heavy rainfall, snowfall, fog, heat and cold waves, thunder, frost, hailstorms, and cyclones. Besides providing forecasts regarding Indian weather, IMD provides early warnings to a large number of countries in the region. Forecasts made by IMD include seven-day city and tourist forecasts, five-day forecasts at sub-division level, and colour-coded forecasts and warnings for districts. The colour codes represent the severity of risk: yellow represents moderate risk and a 'watch' mode, orange symbolises an 'alert' indicating the need for readiness and red is for a 'warning', requiring immediate action. Recently the Metrological Department has been able to provide three hourly 'nowcasts' regarding potential climatic and meteorological hazards.

The early warning system of the IMD and the Central Water Commission (CWC) issues alerts which help in risk reduction. CWC is the nodal agency for issuing alerts related to floods. IMD provides meteorological support to CWC for issuing flood warnings. The Indian National Centre for Ocean Information Services (INCOIS) is an autonomous body under the Ministry of Earth Sciences. INCOIS provides ocean information and advisories to the marine sector, fisherfolk, governments, scientific community, and society at large. Tsunami early warnings are issued by INCOIS to help minimise loss due to oceanographic disasters. The Centre also provides storm surge warnings and

Region	*10 October (Rainfall till 0830 IST of next day)*	*11 October (Rainfall till 0830 IST of next day)*	*12 October (Rainfall till 0830 IST of next day)*	*13 October (Rainfall till 0830 IST of next day)*
Odisha	Very heavy rainfall at a few places and extremely heavy rainfall on the coast.	Very heavy rainfall in most places and extremely heavy rainfall in isolated places.	Rainfall in many places with heavy rainfall in isolated places over north Odisha.	Nil
North Coastal Andhra Pradesh	Rainfall in many places with heavy to very heavy rainfall in isolated places.	Rainfall in many places with heavy to very heavy, and extremely heavy rainfall in isolated places.	Nil	Nil
Gangetic West Bengal	Many places with heavy to very heavy rainfall in isolated places over coastal West Bengal.	Rainfall in most places with heavy to very heavy rainfall in isolated places.	Rainfall in many places with heavy to very heavy rainfall in isolated places.	Nil
Assam & Meghalaya	Nil	Rainfall in most places with heavy falls in isolated places.	Rainfall in most places with heavy to very heavy rainfall in isolated places.	Rainfall in many places with heavy rainfall in isolated places.
Mizoram & Tripura	Rainfall in most places with heavy rainfall in isolated places.	Rainfall in most places with heavy to very heavy rainfall in isolated places.	Rainfall in most places with heavy to very heavy rainfall in isolated places.	Rainfall in many places with heavy rainfall in isolated places.

Legend: Red: Take action; Orange: Be prepared; Yellow: Watch and update; Green: No warning

Heavy rain: 64.5–115.5 mm/day; Very heavy rain: 115.6–204.4 mm/day; Extremely heavy rain: more than 204.4 mm/day

A typical IMD rainfall forecast

information regarding tidal waves besides giving ocean state forecasts in the form of a nowcast as well as a forecast of coastal parameters.

PREPAREDNESS AND RISK REDUCTION

The Ministry of Home Affairs is responsible for formulating policy for reducing risk, enhancing preparedness and for effective response in the event of a disaster on the advice of the National Disaster Management Authority, NDMA. In the arena of preparedness and risk reduction for communities, a multi-hazard approach is more resilient. The NDMA formulates plans and guidelines in the field of disaster management. The Authority is also responsible for building the capacity of volunteers and rescue personnel, conducting mock exercises, and risk mitigation programs, strengthening disaster management authorities in the state, and in enhancing awareness through workshops and conferences. The Flood Management Program and Cyclone Risk Mitigation Project, overseen by the Authority provide focused risk reduction in the case of specific hazards. A National School Safety Programme (NSSP) in 8,600 schools enhances the preparedness of children and their guardians. *Aapda Mitra* is a training programme for training community volunteers in flood-prone districts.

RESPONSE AND RELIEF MECHANISMS

The nature of response has evolved over the years to one that is more proactive rather than reactive. Advanced preparedness and mitigation measures are an integral part of the response mechanism. The primary responsibility of rescue, relief, and rehabilitation rests with the concerned state where the hazard occurs. State agencies prepare area-specific rescue and relief plans and evacuation plans, which also include evacuation routes for pre-identified shelters well in advance. State agencies

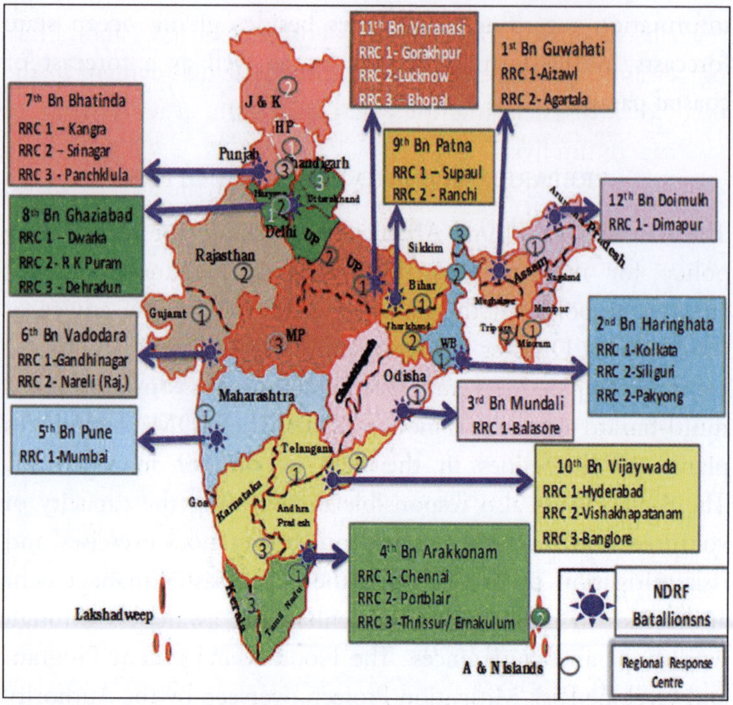

Figure 2.7 India rescue and relief: National Disaster Response Force

being the first responders to a disaster event, undertake extensive operations, which among other things include the evacuation of people to safer places, setting up relief camps, providing gratuitous relief, distribution of food packets and safe drinking water, and measures to prevent an outbreak of an epidemic.

In the event of a severe disaster, the Ministry of Home Affairs responds immediately and assists the concerned state in conducting a timely and effective rescue operation. The Ministry of Home Affairs coordinates the rescue operations and mobilises specialist teams of NDRF and military personnel of the Indian army, navy, Coast guard, air force and central paramilitary forces. Based on the vulnerability profile of different regions, specialist NDRF battalions and teams are stationed in readiness at strategic locations. Government of India keeps aircraft, boats, specialist teams of Indian Armed Forces, Central Paramilitary Forces and NDRF personnel for immediate deployment in the event of a disaster situation, with minimum reaction time to save maximum lives.

Agencies like the IMD, INCOIS, and the CWC are in constant touch with the coordinating disaster management team in the Ministry of Home Affairs. During the rescue and relief operations, the Ministry interacts closely with the states through their relief commissioners and the state control and emergency offices, as well as the Collectors, Deputy Commissioners of the affected districts. The control room in the Ministry functions round the clock on a 24/7 basis. Essential commodities, including medical stores and provision of immediate relief materials, are arranged for a severe disaster. The Government of India assists in the restoration of critical infrastructure and facilities, including communication network, and any other assistance as required by the affected states to meet the disaster situation effectively.

There are institutionalised financial mechanisms for effective management of disasters. Affected state governments are provided financial assistance from the State Disaster Response Fund and the National Disaster Response Fund. The State Government undertakes necessary relief measures in the wake of a disaster from the SDRF placed at its disposal each year. When the financial resources of states are inadequate, additional assistance is extended from the National Disaster Response Fund for disasters of a severe nature for providing relief to the affected.

REHABILITATION: BUILDING BACK BETTER

Post-disaster rehabilitation measures go beyond the immediate relief provided to affected communities. They are long term and more capital intensive. Rehabilitation provides an opportunity to reduce risk, relocate affected communities to safer places and

Combined rescue teams save lives in a disaster

to rebuild disaster-resilient infrastructure. India has taken the lead in building a coalition of nations to share technologies and exchange best practices regarding disaster resilient infrastructure. In the spirit of the Sendai framework, it is prudent to build back better.

Advisories regarding reconstruction are better received by the affected after a disaster rather than advisories and warnings given to a community before a calamitous event. A community that has suffered the ravages of a tsunami would be more amenable towards rebuilding further away from the shoreline and at higher height above the sea level. Similarly, the necessity of strong, resilient foundations and structural designs that are earthquake resistant in built-up structures for a population, which has suffered a shattering seismic event is more acceptable and an intrinsic part of the rehabilitation plan. In India, HUDCO, the Housing and Urban Development Corporation, provides both technical and financial assistance in the form of soft loans, technology transfer, retrofitting, and reconstruction of damaged housing stock with disaster-resistant features for rehabilitation and construction of areas affected by natural disasters and calamities.

Rebuilding damaged infrastructure like roads, rails, disconnected power and water supply and the repair of telecommunication and community built structures is taken up on a war footing after the cataclysmic event. It is prudent to appreciate that the post-disaster rehabilitation of an affected population is essentially about rebuilding lives and livelihoods. An important issue that sometimes gets overlooked in a rehabilitation plan is the psycho-social trauma caused by the cataclysmic event upon the affected community. The psychosocial effects of the hazard and rescue operations on the rescuers themselves are inadequately addressed in most rehabilitation plans.

Saving lives & beyond: Nepal Earthquake, 2015

THREE

Seismic Hazard: Earthquakes

An earthquake is quite literally an earth-shattering experience. People who have lived through an earthquake disaster or witnessed its aftermath genuinely experience the meaning of being vulnerable and feeling fragile. The tragic loss of loved ones, livelihoods, homes and an entire life's savings has traumatic psychosocial ramifications on the affected community.

One of the most devastating earthquakes in recorded history was the 1556 Shaanxi earthquake, which occurred in China and left behind a death toll of 830,000 people. While the Shaanxi quake was the most devastating in terms of the number of lives lost, the 1960 Chilean earthquake was the most massive quake that has been measured on a seismograph, reaching a magnitude of 9.5M. The energy released in the Chile quake was approximately twice than that of the next most potent seismic event, the Good Friday earthquake centred in Prince William Sound, Alaska. In terms of economic damage on country-levels, the 1995 earthquake in Japan with an economic loss of US$100 million and the 2011 Japan tsunami causing an economic loss of US$210 million were the costliest seismic events.

Around 500,000 earthquakes are estimated to occur each year which, are detectable with current instrumentation. Of these, only 100,000 tremors are felt in the form of vibrations or shaking of the ground. While massive earthquakes are less frequent, minor earthquakes occur regularly around the world particularly in El Salvador, Mexico, Guatemala, Chile, Peru, California and Alaska in the USA, the Azores in Portugal, India, Indonesia, Iran, Pakistan, Nepal, Japan, and New Zealand. 90 per cent of the world's earthquakes, including 81 per cent of the major ones, have occurred in the 40,000 km long horseshoe-shaped zone called the Circum-Pacific Belt, also known as the Ring of Fire, which bounds the Pacific Plate. Large magnitude earthquakes tend to occur along other plate boundaries like the Himalayan Mountains.

In areas of high seismic risk, especially with rapidly growing mega-cities like Mexico City, Tokyo, and Tehran, seismologists warn that a single quake in and around these cities may claim the lives of up to three million people. In India, rapid urbanisation in the National Capital Region, which lies in seismic zone-IV is a matter of concern. The recent construction of tall, non-earthquake-resilient, glass facade buildings in crowded areas has increased the risk and vulnerability of the community in the region.

EARTHQUAKES: GENESIS AND TYPES

Earthquakes, quakes or tremors are seismic events that generate seismic waves. Although most quakes are natural, they may also be induced by human intervention. Earthquakes are experienced in the form of shaking as well as ruptures in the ground, resulting in severe damage to rigid structures and buildings. The impact and severity of a quake depend upon a complex combination of the intensity and magnitude of the earthquake, the distance of the affected area from the epicentre and the amplification or dampening of seismic wave propagation due to local geological and geomorphological conditions. Some tremors are so weak that they are barely felt, while others are violent enough to toss people around and destroy entire cities.

Based on their genesis, there are two types of earthquakes: tectonic and induced. Most earthquakes are caused by the rupture of geological faults and are called tectonic earthquakes. Earthquakes caused by induced seismicity are fewer in frequency but have a similar impact as the more frequent tectonic quakes.

Tectonic Earthquakes

These earthquakes occur when energy associated with rapid movement on active faults is released. Tectonic quakes occur when there is sufficient elastic strain energy to drive fracture propagation along a fault plane—a plane that represents the fracture surface of a fault. A fault is a fracture or discontinuity in a volume of rock with significant displacement because of rock mass movement under the Earth's surface. Large faults within the Earth's crust result from the action of plate tectonic forces and can cause inter-plate earthquakes. Faults are of three types: normal, reverse, and strike-slip. Reverse faults are associated with the most powerful earthquakes or megathrust quakes of magnitude 8M or more. The 10 most massive earthquakes in the world to have been recorded have been megathrust earthquakes. Strike-slip faults can produce earthquakes up to a magnitude of 8M, while quakes associated with normal faults are generally less than magnitude 7M. It is estimated that only 10 per cent or less of the total energy of a tectonic earthquake is radiated as seismic energy. Most of it is used to power the earthquake fracture growth or is converted into heat generated by friction. For every unit increase in the magnitude of a quake, there is roughly a thirtyfold increase in the energy released. In relatable terms, a tectonic earthquake of magnitude 8.6M releases the same amount of energy as 10,000 atomic bombs of the type that were dropped on Hiroshima and Nagasaki during the Second World War.

Induced Seismicity

Induced seismicity is the phenomenon where an earthquake occurs due to human activity, unlike most earthquakes that are caused by the movement of tectonic plates. Induced earthquakes have either occurred or were exacerbated in the past due to human activities, which include storing large amounts of water behind dams, coal mining, and oil drilling. The largest earthquake in Australia's history occurred in Newcastle, which is built over a coal mining sector. The earthquake spawned from a fault that was reactivated due to the millions of tons of rock that was removed in the mining process. The 2008 Sichuan earthquake in China, which resulted in 69,227 deaths, has its genesis in induced seismicity. The Zipingpu Dam in Sichuan Province fluctuated the pressure of a fault 1,650 feet away, which probably increased the power of the earthquake and accelerated the rate of movement of the fault. The 1967 earthquake that struck Koynanagar in Maharashtra, India—an area that was hitherto considered quake-safe—near the site of the Koyna Dam, raised issues of induced seismicity related to human activity.

Hazardous events like volcanic activity, landslides, mine blasts, and nuclear tests can also cause earthquakes. In volcanic regions, quakes are caused both by tectonic faults and also due to the movement of the magma. Such earthquakes serve as an early warning of volcanic eruptions, as during the 1980 eruption of Mount St. Helens.

EARTHQUAKE: EFFECTS

Earthquakes manifest themselves on the Earth's surface by shaking, displacing, and rupturing the ground and causing severe damage to buildings and other rigid structures, which in turn results in economic losses and loss of life. In the past, about 90 per cent of the fatalities were caused more by the collapse of buildings, than the quake. Earthquakes can cause tsunamis and can trigger landslides, volcanic activity, floods, fires, and soil liquefaction.

Tremors or shaking of the ground is a result of the sudden release of energy in the lithosphere, which creates seismic waves. Every tremor produces different types of seismic waves, which travel through rock with different velocities: longitudinal P-waves (shock-pressure waves); transverse S-waves (both body waves), and surface waves. Seismic waves travel through the Earth's interior and can be recorded by seismometers placed at great distances.

Ground rupture is the other significant effect of an earthquake. It is a visible break and displacement of the Earth's surface along the trace of the fault. The rupture can be as large as several metres in the case of high magnitude earthquakes. While constructing large infrastructure projects, it is imperative to carefully map existing faults to identify if any faults are likely to break the ground surface during the structure's lifetime. Ground rupture is a risk for large structures like dams, bridges, and nuclear power stations.

The hypocentre or focus is the point of initial rupture of the ground by an earthquake, while the epicentre is the point

Figure 3.1 Ruptured ground

directly above the hypocentre on the surface. When the epicentre of a high magnitude earthquake is located offshore, the seabed can become displaced and cause a tsunami. Possible side effects of earthquakes include landslides, volcanic activity, floods, fires, and soil liquefaction. During the 1964 Alaska earthquake, soil liquefaction caused rigid structures, like buildings and bridges to tilt or sink into the liquefied soil deposits and collapse. Similarly, the fire that broke out during the 1906 San Francisco earthquake left a tragic trail of many deaths that were a result of the fire than by the quake itself.

SEISMICITY INTENSITY AND MAGNITUDE

Geophysicists, Gutenberg and Charles Francis Richter, coined the term seismicity. The Richter scale, a scale that measures the magnitude of a quake is named after them. Seismic activity or the seismicity of an area is the frequency, type, and size of the earthquakes experienced in that area over time. Seismicity encompasses quake events, mechanisms, intensity, and magnitude at a given location. The intensity and magnitude of an earthquake are terms that are used interchangeably in common parlance to describe the severity of an earthquake. However, the intensity of an earthquake is very different from its magnitude.

The *intensity* of an earthquake measures the strength of shaking produced by the earthquake at a specific location. It is assessed using a descriptive scale like the Modified Mercalli intensity scale and the Rossi-Forel scale. Quaking or shaking of the earth is a common phenomenon known from earliest times. The intensity of the earth-shaking was earlier based on the observed effects, as categorised on various seismic intensity scales.

Magnitude, on the other hand, measures the energy released at the source of the quake. It is determined from measurements

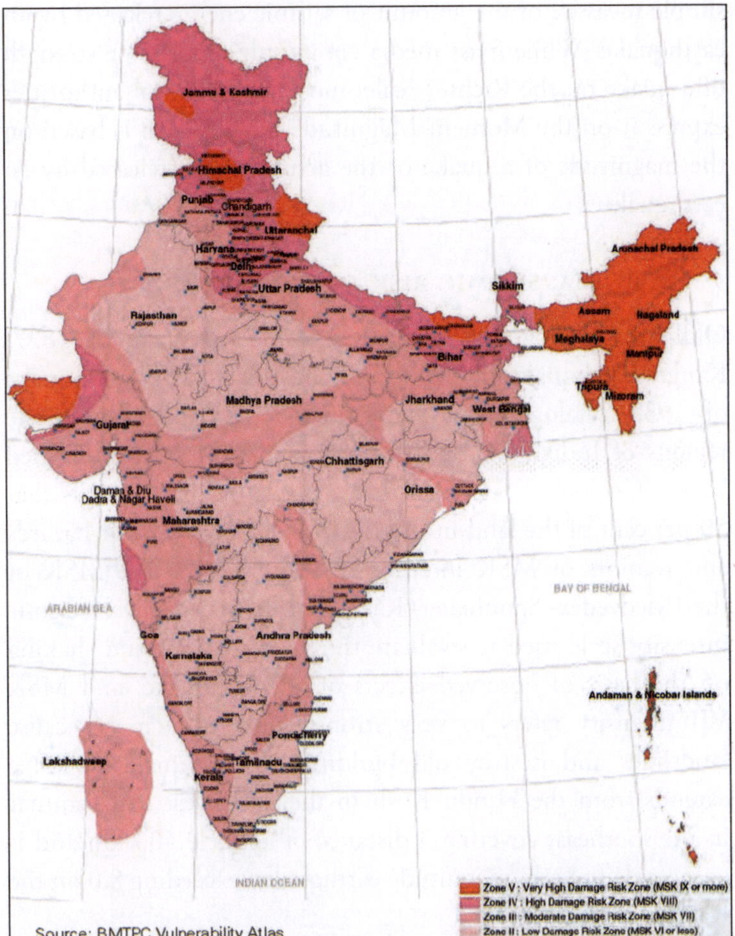

Figure 3.2 India: Earthquake-prone zones

on seismographs. It is a quantitative measure of the size of the quake at its source. Charles F. Richter in 1935 developed the first scale for measuring quake magnitudes. It is a relatively simple measure of the amount of seismic energy released by an earthquake. While mass media commonly reports the strength of a quake on the Richter scale, most seismological authorities express it on the Moment Magnitude Scale, which is based on the magnitude of a quake or the actual energy released by an earthquake.

INDIA: SEISMIC RISK AND VULNERABILITY

Oldham's monographs on the Assam earthquake of 1827, Kangra earthquake of 1905, and the Bihar-Nepal earthquake of 1934 catalogue the major faults and earthquake-prone regions of India. The *Seismic-tectonic Atlas of India* published by the Geological Survey of India (GSI) in 2000, reveals that 59 per cent of the land in India is vulnerable to seismic hazards and tremors of MSK intensity VII and above. The MSK or the Medvedev–Sponheuer–Karnik scale, is a macroseismic intensity scale used to evaluate the severity of ground shaking on the basis of observed effects of an earthquake, and MSK VII intensity refers to very strong quakes which van cause landslides and destroy old buildings. The Himalayan range extends from the Hindu Kush in the northwest to Myanmar in the southeast covering a distance of about 2,400 km and is vulnerable to high- magnitude earthquakes exceeding 8.0 on the Richter scale.

The Himalayas are young fold mountains composed mainly of uplifted sedimentary and metamorphic rocks. As a result, they are tectonically active, and the region is extremely vulnerable to earthquakes. They have distinct geomorphic features, and the effect of natural hazards in the Himalayas are more pronounced due to their topography, tectonic activity, lithological, structural, and ecological features. The Himalaya's geotectonic features are also shared by the alluvial plains of Indus, Ganga, and Brahmaputra and are similarly prone to seismic activity.

The regions that were at a distance from the Himalayas and other interplate boundaries were earlier considered safe from seismic events but the devastating earthquakes in Latur in 1993 and in Bhuj in 2001 dispelled the widely-held belief that only the Himalayas and surrounding areas were prone to seismic activity, while the rest of the country was safe. In 1967, a quake with a Mercalli magnitude of 8M struck Koynanagar town in Maharashtra near the site of the Koyna Dam. It caused a loss of 163 lives and raised questions about the risk of induced seismicity in India. Construction of the Tehri Dam in the Garhwal Himalayas, which eventually submerged the entire old town of Tehri, raised issues of seismicity in the fragile earthquake-prone region, besides raising concern in regards to community displacement and environmental degradation. The seismic risk and the vulnerability of the country cannot be more emphasised. India, not unlike Japan, needs to invest in earthquake risk reduction in a mission mode. Japan lies on a fault line and is inherently prone to hazards like earthquakes and tsunamis and has since then made a prudent investment in seismic risk reduction.

INDIA: SEISMICITY AND LOSS

In a span of about 50 years from 1897–1950, four significant earthquakes of magnitudes 8M and above have occurred in the Indian subcontinent. The 1897 Shillong quake was of magnitude 8.7M, and within eight years, it was followed by the 8.0M intensity quake in Kangra. There was immense loss of life and property in 1934 during the 8.3M Bihar-Nepal quake and in the 1950 Assam-Tiber quake, which struck with the intensity of 8.6M.

The United Nations observed the International Decade for Natural Disaster Reduction (IDNDR) in the 1990s. During this period, India witnessed four of the most tragic earthquakes—the 1991 Uttarkashi quake, the Latur quake of 1993, the Jabalpur earthquake of 1997, and the 1999 Chamoli quake in the Himalayas. A massive earthquake in Bhuj almost immediately followed these in 2001 and again in 2005 in Jammu & Kashmir. These six massive quakes left behind a death toll of more than 23,000 casualties.

Earthquakes have a lasting impact on the economy. The affected lose their homes, properties, assets, and livelihoods. Infrastructure is badly damaged, and means of communication is severely affected. Besides the economic loss caused by the quake and the concomitant slowdown of the economy, additional funds are required for reconstruction and rehabilitation. The 2001 Bhuj quake, for instance, caused widespread damage and destruction to buildings and public infrastructure in 7,900 villages in 21 districts of Gujarat. The severe economic loss restricted the local economy and influenced the savings, and adversely impacted investment patterns and the stock market behaviour. The economic impact of an earthquake in large metropolitan cities like Delhi and the NCR will have primary, secondary, and tertiary effects on the economy.

SEISMIC RISK AND BUILT-UP ENVIRONMENT

Earthquakes in the past have established that about 90 per cent of the deaths are caused by fatal accidents associated with the collapse of buildings. The built-up environment in India is exceptionally fragile. In the past, there have been severe injuries and an immense loss of lives when unsafe structures collapsed during earthquakes. Quakes of similar intensity and magnitude in countries such as Japan and the USA have not resulted in the enormous loss of lives as they did in India, because the former countries have invested in structural mitigation measures and earthquake resilient features in built-up structures.

There are about 12 million buildings in India that fall under seismic zones-III, IV, and V. Most of these buildings are not earthquake-resistant and are potentially vulnerable to collapsing in the event of a high-intensity earthquake. The seismic risk because of the fragile built-up environment, especially in moderate and high seismic risk zones, is multiplied manifold due to increasing urbanisation and demands of modernisation like flyovers, multi-storied buildings, super malls and technoparks in metropolitan cities. Flagrant violations of town planning bylaws and building codes exacerbate the risk. Builders and house owners ignore town planning bylaws since land is a scarce resource in urban areas. The building codes of a few local governments lack earthquake-resilient features; and where earthquake-resilient building codes do exist, the community blatantly violates them, putting themselves and their families at risk. This violation of codes is done either as an attempt to cut costs or to have a facade that is aesthetically pleasing to the builder or owner of the building. The all-glass

Figure 3.3 Fragile built-up environment causes 95 per cent mortality

facades of multi-storied buildings in cities, like Gurugram, add to the potential risk of the residents and the community at large.

SEISMIC RESILIENT INFRASTRUCTURE

The rapid expansion of the built-up environment in moderate or high-risk cities in India makes it imperative to incorporate seismic risk reduction strategies in various aspects of urban planning. It is in the interest of the community to ensure that there is minimal loss of life in the event of an earthquake through strict compliance of town planning bylaws and earthquake-resilient building codes and technical guidelines. All new structures need to be constructed to be earthquake resilient and resistant, while existing sructures need to be audited for earthquakes. The building materials and fixtures used during construction should be tested with the help of shock tests and shake tables. In India, the University of Roorkee built the first modern shock test facility and shake table capable of handling full-scale models to test seismic resistance of structures. The existing structures need to be audited and tested for earthquake resistance. Important and lifeline buildings like hospitals, bus depots, railway stations, airports, and schools need to be retrofitted, especially in high and medium seismic risk areas.

The Bureau of Indian Standards (BIS) prepares earthquake-resistant building codes and other safety codes. BMTPC, the Building Materials and Technology Promotion Council, in the Ministry of Housing, has also developed guidelines for improving earthquake-resistant housing. These guidelines are available on their website and provide technical and technological seismic risk mitigation measures that can be adopted for safer buildings. Native wisdom regarding area-specific earthquake-resilient techniques deserves recognition.

Indigenous houses in areas prone to seismic activity using quake-resilient techniques and technologies have proven to be earthquake-resistant over the years. The same seismic event has caused modern brick, mortar, and glass structures to collapse with tragic consequences. It is imprudent to disregard locally available construction materials and earthquake-resilient techniques that have proven to be effective over the years. Indigenous quake-resistant *bhongas*, wooden and *ekra* houses, and houses with *dhajji diwari,* and *dharia munia* walls have been mainly unaffected by earthquakes in the past. There are lessons to be learnt from the structural resilience of the techniques that are used in building such structures. It is judicious to incorporate indigenous earthquake-resilient features and promote those that have been effective in past seismic events.

200-year-old *Dharia munia* walls found in Mansiari and Dharchula areas of Uttarakhand in the Himalayas have withstood several seismic events. Highly intricate walls, requiring a specialised and laborious technique, made up of dressed stone masonry in mud or *urad dal* mortar called *Dharia munia* have been quake-resilient in earthquake-prone regions of the Himalayas for centuries. The stonemason walls are all 450 mm thick and are made up of laboriously cut stones, with each stone precisely 220 mm wide and 150 mm thick in size. This technique is still practised in the area but to a lesser extent.

The *dhajji diwari* and *taq* system of indigenous buildings in Jammu & Kashmir and the wood frame constructions with brick-nogs in Himachal Pradesh have quake-resilient features. *Dhajji diwari* is a construction technique that uses wooden tie beams with adobe infill and mud mortar. Houses made with *dhajji diwari* technique have withstood the two massive earthquakes that hit Kashmir in 1885 and 2005 with magnitudes of 6.3M and 7.6M respectively.

Assamese *ekra* bamboo buildings in the northeastern parts of India and the circular mud houses or *bhongas* of Kutchh in

Figure 3.4 *Dharia munia*-dressed stone masonry

Figure 3.5 Timber frame & *ekra* fill in Assam

Figure 3.6 *Bhongas* in Gujrat

Figure 3.7 *Phero*' in Himachal Pradesh

Indigenous Quake-resistant Houses in India

Gujarat in the West have been more relatively resilient to seismic activity than the brick and mortar houses that use cement and concrete. Assamese-type houses made up of timber frames with *ekra* filling, and thatched roofs and bamboo houses more prevalent in the more impoverished sections of the society remained safe for the inhabitants during the 8.7M magnitude Shillong earthquake that shook the area in 1897 and the 1950 Assam earthquake of magnitude 8.6M.

Houses that use the *taq* system with load-bearing masonry piers and adobe infill along with timber runners have also proved to be earthquake-resilient in the major seismic events that have occurred in the Himalayan state of Jammu and Kashmir over the years.

EARTHQUAKE MANAGEMENT

Earthquake management is a complex process, encompassing seismic risk reduction, preparedness and mitigation, monitoring and warning, immediate response and effective rescue and relief in the event of an earthquake, as well as post-disaster recovery and rehabilitation. Effective earthquake management entails investment in awareness generation about seismic risk, emphasis on structural mitigation measures, and enforcing quake-resistant building codes and town planning bylaws. It is appropriate to promote the use of licensed engineers and masons while constructing, as well as quake resilience in non-engineered construction practices. Preparedness, risk mitigation, and timely response are critical. Early warning systems are not yet been fully developed for seismic disasters, and there is a great deal of research being undertaken in this sphere globally.

In India, the Ministry of Earth Sciences is the nodal ministry responsible for developing the Earthquake Management Plan with six major components: quake-resistant design features for new structures, strengthening and seismic retrofitting of existing priority and lifeline structures in earthquake-prone areas, appropriate regulation and enforcement to improve compliance, stakeholder awareness and preparedness, and capacity building for emergency response. Response and immediate relief during major quake events are provided by the Ministry of Home Affairs. The NDRF is specially trained to undertake search and rescue efforts during earthquakes. Community participation is critical for ensuring the promotion of earthquake-resilient built-up structures to reduce risk; and for better preparedness and reduction of losses in the event of an earthquake.

EARTHQUAKE: PREDICTION FORECAST AND WARNING

Earthquake prediction is a scientific process, which specifies the time, location, and magnitude of future earthquakes. Despite considerable research and the global efforts of seismologists, scientifically reproducible predictions cannot yet pinpoint to a specific day or month. Probable forecasts of fault ruptures are precise, but specific occurrences of an earthquake cannot be forecast or forewarned with scientific precision. In the case of a well-understood fault, the probability that it may rupture during the next few decades can be forecast with a degree of certainty. However, the occurrence of a seismic event at a particular place, on a particular day, and at a particular time with exactitude and early warning systems have not yet attained precision. At present, scientific earthquake warning systems across the world do not allow for sufficient time to safely evacuate the affected community in the event of an earthquake.

Often the first tremor is a foreshock of a lesser magnitude and a precursor to subsequent tremors. It may sometimes act as the first warning of an impending earthquake and leaves little or no time to react. Earthquake forecasting has not yet evolved to the level of certainty that as it has been developed for hydro-meteorological hazards. Warning systems are concerned with the probabilistic assessment of the frequency and magnitude of earthquakes that occurred in a given area over years or decades.

The Indian Meteorological Department, in conjunction with the National Center for Seismology, is responsible for monitoring seismic activity and issuing warnings. The National Center for Seismology, under the Ministry of Earth Sciences, has a National Seismological Network for monitoring earthquakes. The Survey of India, at Dehradun monitors the tectonic movements across the plate boundaries with the support of national institutes specializing in geophysics, geology and earth sciences like the National Geophysical Research Institute in Hyderabad, the Wadia Institute of Himalayan Geology in Dehradun, the Mumbai-based Indian Institute of Geomagnetism, and the Centre for Earth Science Studies in Thiruvananthapuram. Hazard estimation, seismic ground movement measurements, seismic ground shaking measures, and seismic macrozonation is the Survey of India's mandate.

Earthquake warning systems today are developed to the extent that they can provide notification of an earthquake in progress before the ground surface begins to move. The warning potentially allows the affected population to seek shelter before the earthquake's impact is felt. Scientific systems for quake forecast will continue to evolve over the years. We have come a

Figure 3.8 Tracking animal behaviour portends earthquakes

Figure 3.9 Detecting seismicity—China 132 AD

long way from the time when seismic warnings were issued based on tracking animal behaviour, and there is still a long way to go.

Animal behaviour was observed and used to identify warning signals about impending earthquakes. In China, recorded evidence exists that shows that animal behaviour was tracked to use as an indication for an imminent earthquake, ever since 132 AD. Any strange or out of the ordinary animal behaviour, like a sudden deluge of frogs hopping away from their usual habitat was considered as a probable warning of an impending seismic event. This is neither a scientific method and nor can it be considered precise. Sometimes, the strange behaviour of a pet dog or other animals in the vicinity was taken as a warning signal portending a seismic activity in a quake-prone area. It was believed that the birds and squirrels outside the window and the monkeys on trees were able to sense the seismic activity before humans felt the tremors. However, subsequent experiences have not confirmed that animal behaviour is an indication of seismic activity and as such, cannot be used as a warning signal for an earthquake.

SEISMIC MITIGATION AND RESCUE

Appropriate risk transfer instruments are essential aspects of risk mitigation. Seismic risk mitigation requires vulnerability mapping of earthquake-prone areas and effective response including capacity building and preparedness of rescue teams and creating an inventory of resources. Promoting earthquake-resistant construction techniques goes a long way in reducing risk.

The Ministry of Home Affairs and its disaster management agencies have the mandate to ensure that adequate seismic risk mitigation measures are in place. Preparedness to cope with an earthquake is enhanced by conducting mock drills and earthquake safety education in schools, colleges, offices, and institutions that are located in a quake-prone region.

Figure 3.10 Locating survivors

Figure 3.11 Saving lives

Figure 3.12 Rescuing animals

A coordinated, prompt, and effective response system is crucial to rescue the affected and save lives during an earthquake. The Ministry of Home Affairs assists the concerned state governments in providing rescue and relief to the affected community in the event of an earthquake, which could be beyond the coping capacity of the local government.

Training, equipping and deploying the NDRF battalions and the SDRF in high seismic risk states goes a long way in sharpening the response operations. Rescue teams, along with pecialized equipment and sniffer dogs play a vital role in rescuing those trapped under the debris of collapsed built-up structures and in saving lives. An effective response requires the strengthening of medical preparedness. India has sent search and rescue teams to assist other countries after major earthquakes, such as in Nepal, Indonesia, and Japan.

PREPAREDNESS: SEISMIC RISK MITIGATION

The occurrence of an earthquake cannot be stopped. However, risk and impact can be reduced through effective risk reduction and mitigation. Survival and mitigating measures aid in enhancing preparedness in the event of an earthquake. Risk mitigation measures range from structural modifications, securing heavy objects and storing supplies, to investing in an insurance cover and putting together an emergency kit and evacuation plans.

Preparedness for a seismic event runs along a continuum from individual preparedness through family and community preparedness to governmental preparedness. All offices, schools, colleges, resident welfare associations, and other organisations need to have well-documented earthquake recovery plans stating actions that need to be taken before, during, and after a seismic event. Businesses and commercial ventures should also have a business recovery plan, which lays down a set of procedures to recover and protect the business in the event of an earthquake.

The challenge in improving seismic safety can be met through an earthquake-resilient built-up environment. Willful compliance of earthquake-resistant safety measures prescribed by the BIS, if in India, and similar standards elsewhere, will ensure personal safety and the safety of the family and community. While constructing a new building, it is necessary to comply with the town planning bylaws of the area and the earthquake-resilient building codes. The Building Materials and Technology Promotion Council (BMTPC) guidelines assist in siting of settlements and buildings, architectural design features, ductility in structural frames, and masonry strength. While constructing a built-up structure, it is prudent to engage trained and qualified civil and structural engineers, architects and masons proficient in earthquake-resistant design and construction. When one is purchasing a built-up accommodation, it is essential to check whether it has earthquake-resilient features and to verify if the building in which the property one intends to buy is earthquake resistant.

Structural safety audit of existing structures in earthquake-prone areas should be undertaken. It is important to repair cracks in ceilings and foundations. There is immense truth in the adage that a building is as secure as its foundation—go to the roots. In cases where the cracks are deep, and there are signs of structural defects, it is imperative to seek expert advice to ensure safety. Selective seismic strengthening and retrofitting of existing buildings must be carried out. Seismic risk reduction features should also be incorporated in non-engineered construction.

PREPAREDNESS: WHAT TO DO BEFORE AN EARTHQUAKE

Earthquake preparedness is a set of measures that can be taken by an individual, a family, an organisation, and by the community to minimise the effects of an earthquake. Standard survival measures include preparedness like storing food and water for an emergency and educating individuals about how to mitigate risk, as well as enhancing awareness regarding the procedure that must be followed when a quake warning is issued. In a high-risk seismic zone, mitigating measures that seek to minimise the effect of a seismic event need to be taken as a matter of course.

Survival measures and preparedness begin with a family discussion about the possibility of a seismic event if one lives in an earthquake-prone area. Educating members of the family about the possible effects of an earthquake and what needs to be done to ensure that tremors do not cause injury or worse can prove to be a boon. Adult members of a community residing in an earthquake-prone area, especially in zones-IV and V should learn first aid to help themselves and others in the event of an earthquake. First aid training should be given to children with the help of expert organisations like the International Red Cross and Red Crescent.

A family emergency plan should be prepared after discussions within the family to ensure safety in the event of an earthquake. The plan should include response processes, paths to a safe exit away from a built-up structure or towards an indoor quake-safe area, and the family emergency kit. Emergency telephone numbers of doctors, hospitals, the police, and local disaster management authorities should be stuck above the telephone in the house. All schools and colleges must also have detailed emergency and evacuation plans for a seismic event. The plan should incorporate the signal for evacuation, exit route details, indoor and outdoor quake-safe places, and a list of do's and don'ts. Children and young adults in the family need to undergo mock drills and also need to memorise emergency numbers by rote. A similar exercise to prepare emergency plans for offices, workplaces, and other organisations needs to be undertaken in-house or with expert advice.

A family emergency kit forms an essential part of the emergency plan of a household. An example of a basic family emergency kit is given in Appendix 1. The emergency kit needs to be put together after deliberating with the family listing the essential stocks and articles that need to go into it. The family kit must contain: battery-operated torch with extra batteries, battery-operated radio, first aid kit, emergency food with dry rations like biscuits and rusks, packed and sealed drinking water, can opener, thick ropes and cords, chlorine tablets or water purifiers to purify drinking water, essential medicines, and some cash and credit cards. A whistle for each member of the family should also be included to draw the attention of the others, and of first responders in case, someone gets trapped under the debris.

The family emergency kit should specifically cater to the needs of the elderly, children, and people with disabilities within the family who have special emergency needs. Prescription medicines for the sick, extra batteries for hearing aids for the elderly, sanitary napkins for women, and diapers for a baby are typical examples of other essential needs that are over and above the basic disaster emergency kit. A typical example of this kit can be seen in Appendix 2. The kit may also include items that have been deemed essential by members of the family after discussion. A child's special toy or book may be included to help lessen the post-disaster trauma. In case there is a pet in the family, a packet of pet food can also be included. The kit should then be wrapped in a waterproof packet and placed in a location, which all the members of the family know about and access.

A family communication plan should also be in place and known to all the members. It should, among other things contain phone numbers and addresses of a friend, relative or other people that can be contacted in the event of the family getting separated on the occurrence of an earthquake.

Children feel particularly vulnerable and frightened during an earthquake. A family discussion in a non-threatening manner around the possibility of an earthquake helps allay fears. A child's involvement in putting together the family emergency plan, the family communication plan, and in listing out and pasting the emergency telephone numbers along with deciding details of the family emergency kit, enhances their sense of security.

Quake-safe places within the house, as well as outdoors, should be identified together by the family. The identification of such indoor and outdoor quake-safe areas if done with the involvement of the entire family has the benefit of reducing fears and apprehensions and ensuring that each member of the family knows the exact places that they can go to in the event of an earthquake. This activity also enables a person to understand the kind of places that are considered as safe if the tremors occur while at school or in office or any other built-up structure.

An indoor quake-safe place would be one that has the least potential of damage in the event of an earthquake—away from a glass window, mirrors or a hanging chandelier that is liable to break or splinter. The indoor quake-safe place should also be at a distance from unsecured or heavy objects, like bookcases or furniture items that can topple over and cause accidents. The indoor quake-safe place should be at a considerable distance from pictures and chinaware, and sharp-edged or metallic furniture, or articles. A typical quake-safe place within a house can be against a wall with no paintings or fixtures, under a sturdy dining table or under a sturdy bed or any other piece of furniture which would not move easily.

Families should also identify outdoor quake-safe places well in advance that are closest to their homes and are away from other built-up structures, old, decaying trees, and also from electric poles. It is essential to ascertain the time it takes to reach the outdoor quake-safe place keeping in mind, the pace of the slowest member in the family. In case there is no time to go outdoors, it is best to use the predetermined indoor quake-safe places rather than getting caught unawares while rushing outdoors during a tremor and risk exposing oneself to the danger of accidents that could occur by falling objects and debris.

An exercise to identify indoor and outdoor quake-safe places in schools and colleges can be undertaken by a teacher with the children in her class. Indoor quake-safe places within offices, workplaces and commercial organisations need to be identified by an in-house seismic safety committee with expert advice. All employees need to be aware of the designated quake-safe places. In offices that deal with the public, like banks, hotels, malls, and other commercial organisations where a large number of people congregate, quake-safe places should be made known to the public at large through prominent signages.

Volunteering to assist one's neighbours and the community to enhance preparedness goes a long way in reducing risk to all. Information given in this book regarding the hazard of earthquakes and means to reduce risk can be published in local newspapers, or college and school magazines giving the information along with phone numbers of local emergency services and hospitals. Sharing knowledge and experience of making family emergency plans, going over the process of selecting appropriate quake-safe places, and in assembling the family emergency kit will enable others to do the same.

Accidents associated with earthquakes that occur on account of loose, heavy objects can cause damage far beyond the seismic event. To avoid accidents and injuries during quakes, it is essential to firmly secure large items of furniture, like bookcases and cabinets, televisions, and computer screens that may otherwise fall over due to tremors. It is also best to avoid storing items above beds or sofas to reduce the chance of the objects falling on individuals. Other measures can also help minimise the effect of an earthquake, like anchoring overhead light fixtures to the ceiling, bracing overhead light and fan fixtures, securely fastening shelves to the walls, placing large or heavy objects on lower shelves, storing breakable items like bottles, glasses and china in low, closed cabinets with latches, and hanging heavy items such as pictures and mirrors away from beds and sofas.

Fires often occur during or after an earthquake. They can be avoided by adopting safety measures related to electricity and flammable products. The risk of a fire after an earthquake can be reduced by repairing defective electrical wiring and leaky gas connections. Strapping water heaters and LPG cylinders to the walls or bolting them to the floor is also a risk-mitigating measure. Flammable products, like kerosene oil, alcohol, and spirit, should be stored securely on bottom shelves inside closed cabinets with latches.

WHAT TO DO DURING AN EARTHQUAKE

Earthquake warning is probabilistic and not precise, but it needs to be taken with immense seriousness to ensure survival. It is prudent to react immediately once a warning is issued. If time permits move to an outdoor quake-safe place away from any built-up structure if not then move to a pre-identified indoor quake-safe place after the first tremor. On reaching the quake-safe place, one should drop to the ground, cover the head to save it from any falling object or debris and hold, i.e. follow the DCH mantra for quake protection—drop, cover, and hold.

After receiving the warning, the affected community in an earthquake zone should ideally rush outdoors at the earliest along with their family emergency kits. In an ideal situation, if time permits, moving outdoors is essential—away from tall buildings, trees, telephones and electrical lines, flyovers, and bridges. It is important not to panic. Power fails during a quake are normal as electric poles are pulled down and torn apart because of the tremors. It is prudent not to use elevators if one is in the upper storey of a building and to exit through the stairs.

All movements after the foreshock should be minimised to a few steps. The first tremor is likely to be a foreshock and a precursor to a stronger earthquake. It is imprudent to attempt to rush out during a tremor. It is safer to move to the closest predetermined indoor quake-safe place until the shaking stops, and one is certain that exiting the house is safe.

When the first tremor of an earthquake is felt, while indoors, one should never try to exit while the ground is shaking. The first thing to do is to drop to the ground, take cover under a durable, sturdy table or a heavy, four-poster bed and hold on until the tremors stop. When indoors, remembering the mantra 'DCH—drop, cover, and hold' is vital. Drop under firm and heavy piece of furniture like a four-poster bed or a sturdy dining table and cover as much of the head and upper body as possible.

Hold onto a heavy piece of furniture like the legs of the bed or table under which one is sitting or lying down.

In case a person is in bed when the earthquake strikes and the tremors are too strong to go under the bed, it is best to stay there and hold on to the sides of the bed after protecting the head with a pillow. If the bed is under a light fixture that could fall, it is better to take a chance and move to the nearest quake-safe place. 95 per cent of quake-related casualties is due to accidents related to collapsing walls, flying glass, and falling objects.

In cases where there may not be a sturdy table or bed to take shelter under, crouching against a corner of an inside wall of the building is a safe way to wait for the tremors to pass. A person should sit with the back to the wall, bring the knees to the chest and cover the face and head with their arms. It is crucial to ensure that there are no windows nearby. The wall near which the person is crouching should not have any hanging painting or loose fixtures. Another indoor quake-safe place is the lintel of an inner door. If nearby, sitting under the lintel of a doorway for shelter helps to keep a person safe until the shaking stops, especially if the doorway is load-bearing and strongly supported.

Casualty research of earlier seismic events has shown that most injuries occur when people attempt to exit the buildings they are inside of during the earthquake. It is wise to stay indoors until the shaking stops, and it is safe to go outside. The greatest danger exists directly outside the building exit. A large number of casualties have occurred alongside exterior walls. It is best to stay in an open space if one is already there, until the shaking stops. It is essential not to move unless one is close to buildings, trees, streetlights, and utility wires. It is better to move away from the structure or utility wires as fast as possible if standing close to them.

A moving vehicle is at high risk. If one is in a moving car or bus when an earthquake occurs, it is necessary to stop as quickly as safety permits. Attempts should be made to stop the vehicle as far away as possible from buildings, trees, overpasses, and utility wires.

WHAT TO DO AFTER AN EARTHQUAKE

It is imperative to proceed cautiously once the tremors stop. Roads, bridges, or over-bridges that might have been damaged by the earthquake should be avoided. In cases where a person is inside a building or is standing near collapses, and is trapped under debris, it is important not to light a match as that can cause a fire hazard. For these reasons, a small battery-operated torch or a whistle is an essential part of the emergency kit. When trapped under debris, it is crucial to not move about or kick up dust. The mouth must be covered with a handkerchief or a piece of cloth to avoid suffocating.

If a situation arises where a person gets trapped under the debris of a building collapse, they should not panic or shout as shouting will cause the person to inhale dangerous quantities of dust, which can cause asphyxiation and death. In order to draw the attention of rescue teams, try to tap on a pipe or a wall, or use a whistle if one is available to draw the rescuers' attention. Shouting should be considered as a last resort.

The rescue operations begin with minimal reaction time, so one should not panic and wait for the rescue team if trapped. Teams of the NDRF are stationed specifically around hazard-prone areas to reduce the reaction time. In the event of a disaster, additional rescue teams along with canine squads and equipment are airlifted to reach the site of the earthquake to rescue those trapped under the debris.

After an earthquake, the affected should check themselves first for injuries. Then check others in the family, office, and the neighbourhood and provide first aid to anyone who needs it. After that, the injured should be taken to the nearest medical camp or an undamaged hospital with the help of the rescuers.

Damaged buildings should be exited immediately. The inhabitants can go to the temporary shelters provided by the local administration. Aftershocks are common after an earthquake. It is crucial not to risk one's life by staying in a damaged building.

Even when a building is unaffected by the quake, it is still essential to check water, gas, and electrical lines for any damage. If damaged, shut off the valves. It is essential to the family's safety to be careful around broken glass and debris. Wear boots or sturdy shoes and stay away from damaged areas. If the odour of cooking gas is present, then all the windows and doors should be opened, and one must leave the premises immediately and report the gas leak to the authorities.

In case a family lives near the seashore, all the members should stay as far away from the beach as possible because there could be a chance that a tsunami could hit soon after the ground has stopped shaking.

The psychosocial needs of the affected and the rescuers must be addressed. The latter often gets ignored as it is assumed that they are hardened after having witnessed so many hazards. They are expected to handle their traumas, if any, by themselves as rescuing lives is their job. However, we must remember that beyond their jobs, they too have psychosocial needs. After a complex rescue operation, a team can suffer trauma that prevents them from being able to sleep or conduct other rescue operations unless the issue is addressed. I recall an incident where an NDRF rescuer tried to save a child that was trapped under some debris. After five hours of continuous efforts, the rescuer managed to cut through the concrete to rescue the child, but despite best efforts, he reached the child a few minutes after the child had breathed her last. The rescuer suffered from depression that stemmed out of a nebulous feeling of guilt.

Lonesome homeless
Vacant eyes:
– Distraught.

Bustling villages
Swept asunder:
– Devastated.

Trees and homes
Alive and dead:
– Ravaged.

Screaming infants
Silent carcasses:
– Lifeless.
Unlived lives:
Man and beast
– Conquered.

Watery graves
Unlit pyres:
– Extinguished.

And then
There is an eerie silence:
As the Tsunami ebbs away....
– The Author

Nagapattinam

December 28, 2004

FOUR

Tsunamis

Tsunami is a Japanese word—*tsu* meaning harbour and *nami* meaning wave—used for a series of long-period waves that are produced by the sudden or abrupt vertical displacement of a large body of water, usually an ocean. Tsunamis are long-wavelength sea waves caused by the movement of large volumes of water mostly because of seismic activity at sea. A tsunami can also be caused by non-seismic events like landslides or meteor impact. Earthquakes of magnitude 7.5M or more at sea cause tsunamis. Subduction earthquakes of a lesser magnitude usually do not cause a tsunami. Tsunamis caused by seismic activity can travel thousands of kilometres across the ocean and wreak destruction on faraway shores, sometimes several hours after the occurrence of the earthquake that generated them.

The first time I heard the name tsunami, it was in conjunction with a story my grandmother used to tell me during thunderstorms of how a savage monster called *Tsunami* would rise out of the sea in Japan and gobble up the whole village. As a child, I would listen in horror until I grew older and learnt to discredit my grandmother's tales as just fables and myths. However, I witnessed the destruction caused by the 2004 Indian Ocean tsunami. To my consternation, I found that my grandmother's Japanese sea monster could indeed gobble up entire villages and leave behind a tragic ravaged shore.

NATURE AND GENESIS

Seismic-generated tsunamis are caused by earthquakes that occur below the ocean or seafloor, which leads to a vertical displacement of the water above. A tsunami occurs after a build-up of energy below the earth, over centuries. The release of this energy produces tsunami waves of small amplitude, of up to 1 km, but with incredibly long wavelengths—often up to hundreds of kilometres long. A tsunami deep in the ocean can travel with a speed of 800 kmph, and the distance between wave crests can surpass 100 km. A tsunami can remain undetected by a ship at sea. However, when it approaches the coast, the wavelength of a tsunami diminishes and its amplitude increases. Large waves produced by earthquakes or submarine landslides can overrun nearby coastal areas in a matter of minutes. They can strip the beaches of sand, coastal vegetation, and destroy buildings along with anything else that comes in its way.

TSUNAMI: INCIDENCE

Though tsunamis are frequent in the Pacific Ocean, they occur to a lesser extent in the Indian Ocean. In the past, a few devastating tsunamis have also occurred in the Mediterranean Sea and the Indian Ocean too. Even though tsunamis rarely occur in the Indian Ocean, they pose a significant threat to all the countries of the region. One of the largest tsunamis in the Indian Ocean was the one associated with an explosion of the volcanic island of Krakatoa in August 1883. The explosion reportedly triggered a 30m high tsunami wave that killed 36,500 people in Java and Sumatra in Indonesia. In recent times, the Indian Ocean Tsunami that occurred on 26 December 2004 was one of the most destructive tsunamis known to have hit India and 13 other countries in the Indian Ocean region. It left behind a death toll of 238,000, including 51,500 people who were reported as missing and are now presumed to be dead. More than 1.5 million people from 14 countries lost their homes and were displaced.

TSUNAMIS IN INDIA

The tsunami risk assessment of India reveals that the east and west coasts of India and the island territories of India are most likely to be affected by tsunamis. The possible zones for such an occurrence are the Andaman-Nicobar-Sumatra Island arc and the Makran subduction zone north of the Arabian Sea in Pakistan. In the last three centuries, four tsunamis have occurred in the Andaman and Nicobar region. The details of the location of the epicentre, death toll, and economic losses are not known. The tsunamis that affected the Andaman and Nicobar Islands and were recorded, occurred on 19 August 1868, 31 December 1881, 26 June 1941, and on 26December 2004. The last tsunami also affected coastal communities on the mainland, particularly in particularly Tamil Nadu and Puducherry.

INDIA: VULNERABILITY

The 2004 Indian Ocean tsunami exposed the inherent vulnerabilities of the coastal communities along India's long coastline of 8,118 km. During the 2004 tsunami,10,749 people lost their lives, and 5,640 people were reported missing in the tsunami-affected areas of India. The tsunami also resulted in damage and destruction of property, assets, and infrastructure along the coast. Innumerable were left homeless. The loss occurred mostly because there were no means of detecting impending tsunamis in India then, and the affected coastal community was caught entirely unawares. This vulnerability has since been significantly reduced with the setting up of the Indian Tsunami Early Warning Centre (ITWEC) with state-of-the-art scientific technology in 2007. The Centre is the most advanced at the Regianal level – it provides early warning to 12 other countries in the Indian Ocean region. The Indian National Centre for Ocean Information Services, INCOIS, studies oceanographic data, provides information and advisories to help mitigate risk and reduce losses during oceanographic disasters, including tsunamis. Emergency plans and Standard Operating Procedures that have been developed, and which are to be followed by all after a tsunami warning has been issued, along with other risk mitigation methods, go a long way in reducing vulnerability.

Lessons from the past and risk mitigation

A post-disaster analysis of the 2004 Indian Ocean tsunami highlighted that the maximum damage occurred in low-lying areas near the coast; thickly populated areas reported higher casualties and substantial destruction occurred in areas like Nagapattinam where sand dunes had been mined. The analysis also revealed that mangroves, sand dunes, and cliffs had proved to be the best natural barrier against the tsunami. It also became evident that the agencies responsible for managing tsunami-related rescue and relief efforts should not be concentrated in only one region that is close to the seashore, as was the case in Chennai, where all the authorities and the control room were within the State Secretariat. They should be dispersed and at different distances from the shore so that in case of a tsunami, one agency can function even if the other is affected.

The coastal population has been increasing steadily due to increased exploitation of marine resources as well as economic activities propelled by urbanisation in the coastal areas and enhanced employment opportunities due to the unprecedented expansion in tourism-related activities. One of the most challenging tasks in improving the preparedness is the sensitisation of stakeholders to the prevalent risk and the need for tsunami preparedness. State governments and State disaster management authorities in collaboration with nodal agencies and key stakeholders, make efforts to mobilise communities to carry out tsunami mitigation efforts. Electronic and print media can also help in creating greater public awareness of tsunami vulnerability and structural and non-structural risk reduction measures that need to be taken in coastal regions.

The tremendous loss of life and property can be avoided if coastal communities recognise the importance of incorporating tsunami safety measures in the siting and construction of residential buildings. Risk mitigation would be further enhanced by the insistence of tourists to visit and reside only in tsunami-resilient resorts or hotels, which have their emergency plans in place and synced with the local authorities and their Standard Operating Procedures (SOPs) and also have access to tsunami-cum-cyclone shelters in the event of a tsunami.

PREPAREDNESS: WHAT TO DO BEFORE A TSUNAMI

Lessons from the past fundamentally form the basis of a roadmap concerning preparedness and risk mitigation. In coastal areas, it is vital to have a buffer zone of grass, coastal forests, mangroves, and sand dunes as a natural barrier against tsunamis. Communities and all stakeholders should actively protect existing plantations and also make efforts to assist in reforestation of the coast.

An active role on the part of the community in protecting the ecosystem will, in turn, shield and protect them in the event of a disaster. It is imperative to safeguard geomorphologic features like beaches, cliffs, and sand dunes. Mangrove wetlands also need to be regenerated. The local community should report any illegal mining of sand dunes to the authorities as sand mining can be a potential threat to the community.

Coastal plantations of casuarinas, palms, bamboos and salicornia trees act as a natural shield to protect coastal communities. It is a good idea to plant a strip of casuarinas outside houses that are located close to the sea; especially on the sea-facing front. Besides adding to the beauty, a row of casuarinas can protect against a tsunami by acting as a buffer.

People living along the coast should find out if their home falls under the danger zone. It is necessary to secure one's home by buying a homeowner's policy that covers a tsunami. All residents should know how much higher than the sea level their residence is located, as well as the distance from the coast. Living too close to the coastline should be avoided. It is essential to live at least 200m away from the high tide coastline. It is also prudent to live in elevated coastal homes. While visiting coastal regions, it is wise to select a hotel that has been built more than 3m above sea level as most tsunami waves are less than 3m in height.

Tsunamis and their impact should be discussed with members of the family, including children. Evacuation plans and a safe route for evacuation from home, school, hotel, and office, in the event of a disaster, must be established well in advance.

Residents along the coastline should maintain contact with the sub-divisional magistrate and the local revenue and relief officers as well as with officials like the tehsildar, revenue officers like the *Kanungo Talathi* or *Patwari*; the panchayat in the rural areas, and the municipal corporation or any official of the municipal corporation to know about the location of the closest tsunami shelters and the emergency and evacuation plan in the event of a disaster. A visit to the nearest multipurpose cyclone-cum-tsunami shelter to become conversant with the route well in advance is also an exercise in prudence.

Tourists and visitors to a coastline region should find out if the hotel they intend to stay in is in the tsunami danger zone. General awareness and demand from stakeholders will increase the availability of tsunami-resilient resorts and hotels along the shoreline. While deciding upon a seaside hotel, a tourist should find out about its proximity to the sea and the height at which the hotel has been built. They should also ask for the hotel or resort's cyclone-cum-tsunami emergency and evacuation plan and should check the hotel's distance from the nearest multipurpose cyclone-cum-tsunami shelter.

Local emergency management officials can give information about the best route to safety and likely shelter locations, in case the hotel staff is not able to, although residents should insist that a hotel should be able to provide the necessary information. On arrival, a walk down to the shelter can ensure that the disaster risk is reduced.

WHAT TO DO DURING THE EVENT

It is essential to listen to local or weather radio channels and local television stations to get the latest information. All official warnings must be heeded, and you should be ready to evacuate when asked to do so. Early warnings from the meteorological department and by the local government must be taken seriously.

A shaking of the ground or of objects and furniture in a room or an intense rumbling of the ground near the coast that lasts for 20 seconds or more is a warning signal that a tsunami is probably imminent.

At the beach, one of the early warning signals of a tsunami is that the seawater begins to recede several metres, exposing fish in shallow water or on the beach. If one sees the seawater receding in this manner, it is imperative to leave the beach and reach a designated shelter or go to higher ground away from the beach as soon as possible. Thereafter, at the safe place, the tsunami mantra is similar to the one during earthquakes DCP—drop, cover and protect oneself.

On receiving a warning, it is best to stay away from the beach. It is not wise to go towards the beach to see the tsunami or capture a photograph of the event. It is essential to go as far away from the coastline as one can. Areas that are 30 m above sea level and about 3 km inland are relatively safer.

Every metre inland or upward makes a difference. It should be possible to reach a safe location on foot. In case one is a visitor and is not aware of the layout, evacuation by foot is a preferred mode to driving. Footpaths typically lead uphill and inland, while many motorable roads run parallel to coastlines and are at the same elevation and vulnerable.

After the tremors stop, a person should gather members of their family and quickly move to an evacuation site or a cyclone-cum-tsunami shelter. The pre-tried tsunami evacuation routes should be followed to reach safety. It is of utmost importance to move quickly but in an orderly fashion and without panic. In case it is difficult to reach the tsunami shelter in the short time available, one can climb to higher ground away from the coastline. Climbing up to a raised platform or going to the terrace or the highest floor of any house, office, hotel or other building reduces risk.

WHAT TO DO AFTER A TSUNAMI

One should always first check for injuries and get first aid before assisting other injured and trapped people. In case someone needs to be rescued, notify the trained and well-equipped rescue personnel of the NDRF, the Army, Coastguards and the Navy present in the vicinity. It is imperative to stay away from damaged and flooded areas.

Use of telephones should only be for emergency calls as telephone lines are often overwhelmed in disaster situations. In order to get an update on the situation, stay tuned to a battery-operated radio for the latest emergency information and updates.

Aftershocks often accompany a seismically-induced tsunami, especially if it was a high magnitude earthquake, registering more than eight or nine on the Richter scale. Some of the aftershocks can be large enough to generate another tsunami. One should return home, or to the hotel, only after the authorities advise that it is safe to do so. While re-entering one's home, caution needs to be taken. It is essential to check for electrical short circuits and live wires. Tsunami flood water can flush out snakes from their homes, so it is essential to keep a lookout for wild animals, especially snakes and scorpions.

Damage to the house must be assessed, and foundations should be checked for any damage or cracks for all the houses that have been flooded or impacted by a tsunami. While entering the house, battery-powered flashlights should be used instead of candles or lanterns to avoid a fire. It is necessary to check for fire hazards, impairment of electric systems, sewage, and water lines as well as leaking gas lines. Food supplies need to be checked and drinking water tested before using.

Rebuilding better is at the core of post-tsunami rehabilitation. Building a house or living in a new apartment that is within 200m of the high tide coastline should be avoided. Constructing a disaster-resilient building designed for tsunami safety at an elevation of over 3m above the sea level is an exercise in prudence. In case it is essential to rebuild closer to the coast, the building should be built with deeper foundations that are protected against scour and erosion. A natural shield of coconut, palm, and casuarina trees should also be planted as a buffer between the coastline and one's home or school.

Disposal of cattle carcasses and other dead animals poses a significant problem and must be done swiftly. Decaying and rotting carcasses, besides the stench associated with them and other sensibilities, can cause potential epidemics. It is a task that only a few people volunteer to perform. After the 2004 tsunami, several municipal workers needed to take the help of alcohol to deaden their senses to be able to pick up the ravaged carcasses.

Post-tsunami, the responsibility of picking up the dead, cremation, and burial of the unidentified and unclaimed dead bodies is left to the local authorities. Dead bodies provide closure. However, missing family members, especially those missing at sea during a tsunami, are the most difficult to give up on and leave behind a traumatic psychosocial impact—especially on children and the elderly. It is crucial to understand and treat any change in behaviour, which could take the form of depression, anxiety or aggression if not addressed through proper care.

A SPARK IS ALL IT TAKES

FIVE

Fire

Fire typically represents the efficacy of the philosophy of balance in life. A controlled fire has been of immense use to humankind since humans learnt to spark a fire by rubbing stones. However, an uncontrolled fire is a man-made hazard that can have disastrous effects. man-made hazards like fire have a high order of incidence and wreak havoc.

Fire is the chemical reaction of combustion between oxygen in the atmosphere and combustible materials, like wood or gasoline, heated to its ignition temperature. Combustion is an exothermic reaction, which can be slow or rapid depending upon the amount of oxygen available. When combustion is rapid and associated with a flame, it is called a burning fire and generates enough heat to kill a person without being engulfed in flames.

During a fire hazard, the temperature in a room varies from 100°C at floor level to 600°C degrees at eye level. Inhaling super-hot air can scorch the lungs and prove fatal. The heat can melt clothes, especially those made of synthetic fibres, such that they coalesce with the skin. In about 5 minutes a room can get so hot that everything in it can go up in flames all at once. Fires also produce thick dark smoke, which reduces visibility. The smoke and toxic gases produced by a fire travel faster than heat and hence cause more casualties than scorching flames. Breathing even a small amount of smoke and toxic gas can make a person drowsy, disoriented, and short of breath. The odourless and colourless fumes can lull a person into deep sleep, which could be fatal even before the flames reach the person's door.

FIRE: HAZARD AND SAFETY

A fire hazard can be of two main types: a situation that increases the likelihood of occurrence of a fire or one that may impede escape in the event of a fire. Fire hazards that belong to the former category are those that encourage a fire to start or increase the severity of a fire. Fuel hazards like flammable and combustible gases, liquids, chemicals, dusts and combustible metals are a type of fire hazard that have to be attended for safety. Heat source hazards may be chemical, electrical, mechanical or nuclear.

Hazards vary by different occupancies. Both commercial buildings and private residences have several fire hazards. Heating, lighting or power equipment if not maintained, repaired or replaced as required, can pose significant fire hazards within a residential building, a school, office or factory. A spark or a stray match can cause immeasurable destruction. Common reasons behind fires stem from poor housekeeping, unsafe habits and practices, as well as improper storage of hazardous items. Threats to fire safety are commonly referred to as fire hazards.

Fire safety is a set of practices that is intended to reduce the destruction caused by fire. Fire safety measures include those that are intended to prevent ignition of an uncontrolled fire and those that are used to limit the development and effects of a fire after it starts. Fire safety is often a component of building safety. Concerning built-up structures, fire safety measures include those that are planned during the construction of a building or implemented in structures that are already standing, and those that are taught to occupants of the building. In the event of a fire, pre-planning and preventive measures help to reduce the potential of loss of life and property.

FIRE SAFETY: SCIENCE AND THE RATIONALE

The rationale behind fire safety measures, including prevention, control, evacuation, and rescue, are based upon the scientific verities associated with fire. Essentially a fire is the visible effect of the process of combustion, which continues as long as there is enough heat, fuel, and oxygen. A burning fire is rapid exothermic combustion associated with a flame.

The Fire Triangle of fuel, oxygen, and heat, represents the critical core for fire safety. In order to prevent a fire from starting and to control a fire hazard, at least one of these three elements should be brought under control. Fuel can be in all three states of matter—solid, liquid, and gas. During the exothermic chemical reaction, that produces fire, the flame heats the solid and liquid fuels so that they release vapours from the surface. A fire spreads when a flame ignites the gases.

Heat, from the perspective of the Fire Triangle, is the energy required to increase the temperature of the fuel to a point where sufficient vapours are produced for ignition to occur. A fire requires three elements to start or spread, which form the edges of the fire prevention triangle—heat, oxygen, and fuel. A key strategy to prevent fire is to remove one or more of these three elements—safety measures to prevent and control a fire stem from the disruption of the Fire Triangle.

Fire needs an atmosphere with 16 per cent oxygen while the air we breathe in contains 21 per cent oxygen. Fires are dangerous because they are self-perpetuating as the oxygen content in the atmosphere is sufficient to burn until infinity until the fuel is available or until the interface with the atmosphere is proactively blocked. The heat of the flame itself keeps the fuel at its ignition temperature so that it continues to burn as long as there is fuel and oxygen. Safety measures related with controlling the spread of a fire work on ensuring that the availability of fuel is curtailed, the heat generated is not enough to ignite the fuel or by cutting off the oxygen supply through the use of fire extinguishers or wet sand for instance.

On Earth, gravity determines how the flame burns. Since the hot gases in the flame are hotter and less dense than the surrounding air, they move upwards. This is the reason why a flame is pointed at the top and why fire typically spreads upwards. This also forms the rationale behind the fire safety measure of crouching on the ground below the fire line in case one cannot escape from the site of the fire.

Figure 5.1

FIRE SAFETY RISK ASSESSMENT

A fire safety risk assessment assists in the prevention of fire even in complex institutional structures. At work, the employer, at home, the head of the family and in schools and other institutions, the head of the organisation should identify sources of fire hazards and assess risks. The risk assessment should also include details about the risk associated with all the three elements needed to start or spread a fire, viz., oxygen, heat and fuel. Safety risk assessment concerning fire, among other things includes details regarding three fundamentals—prevention of fire, detection and warning, and emergency response in the form of escape and rescue.

Comprehensive fire safety statements based on the safety risk assessment need to be made for all built-up structures. At the micro-level, for every residential building, a family fire safety statement comprising of the fire safety risks that were identified after an assessment along with the safety measures that can be taken to reduce those risks can be drawn up. The fire safety statement should state the fire hazards, risks, and safety measures that have to be taken with regard to prevention and detection, mode of warning, details of emergency escape routes, Standard Operating Procedures, and manner of escape in an office, factory, and institution, including a school. The possibility of arson should also be considered while doing a risk assessment and should form an integral part of the fire safety statement. Arson can be controlled if detailed thought goes into its prevention. Appropriate security measures like good exterior and interior lighting, intrusion alarms, guard service, well-secured access openings as well as protection of stored materials, and prompt removal of rubbish can alleviate the problem.

INDIA: FIRE HAZARD—HIGH INCIDENCE

On an average, about 600,000 man-made disasters and accidents, including uncontrolled fires, occur in India. These man-made disasters leave behind about 350,000 dead and 400,000–500,000 injured every year.

India has a long history of fire accidents. Every year about 20,000 large and small accidental fires occur on an average. The fires result in immense casualties, and about 17,000 people die every year in the country in fire-related accidents. Loss of life in accidental fire events is higher than the loss of life in terrorist attacks.

Most of the fire-related incidents where major causalities happen—70 per cent of all fires—occur in residential areas. Kitchen-related accidents are the most common. In India, on an average 3,500 lives have been lost every year due to bursting of cooking gas cylinders and stoves. Hence home fire prevention is a top priority for fire safety. Improving safety conditions will reduce risk.

Figure 5.2 Kumbakonam: A school on fire

Figure 5.3 Kolkata: Fire in a hospital

Figure 5.4 Burnt train: T N Express

Figure 5.5 Oil and gas installation on fire

Figure 5.6 A high-rise building on fire

Figure 5.7 A chemical plant burnt to cinders

Fire Related Incidents

Fires that occur in crowded places like a mall or a movie theatre are less frequent but are associated with an even more significant number of lives lost per accident. In the past, raging fires with tragic consequences have broken out in factories, oil installations, hospitals, schools and even on trains. Details of some severe fire accidents that have occurred in crowded places over the last two decades in India, including the recent 2019 blaze that occurred in Surat, which claimed the lives of 21 students at a coaching centre, are presented in the form of case studies in Appendix 5. These case studies will assist in highlighting the lessons that can be learnt regarding fire hazards and safety issues.

FOREST FIRES

Forest fires are as old as the forests themselves. A fire in the forest poses a threat not only to forest wealth like timber, resin and other commercially exploitable forest resources but also to the fauna and flora. Besides the loss of timber and a deleterious effect on catchment areas, a forest fire has wide-ranging ecological, economic, and social impact. A massive fire can reduce forest cover and potentially lead to the extinction of some species of plants and animals. Fires can also cause an imbalance of the forest ecosystem and harm the bio-diversity of the affected region. A forest fire can also adversely impact natural regeneration. Forest fires play a significant role in the loss of carbon sink resources. Fires enhance the percentage of carbon dioxide in the atmosphere, contribute to the depletion of the ozone layer, and aid in global warming.

A forest fire may be a 'surface fire' or a 'crown fire'. A surface fire spreads along the ground burning the surface litter on the forest floor. A crown fire burns the crown of trees and shrubs and is more dangerous in a coniferous forest because the resinous material given off by the burning logs enflames the ferocity of the fire. A crown fire is often accompanied and sustained by a surface fire. Forest fires occur because of natural and man-made causes. During summer, when there is no rain for months, the ground of a forest is littered with dry incendiary leaves and twigs. These get ignited by the slightest spark and burst into flames. High temperatures and dry winds aggravate their spread.

Summers have conducive climatic conditions like dry, hot weather for a fire to start. Natural causes like a lightning strike can also spark trees and set a forest on fire. However, the rain that follows a thunderstorm or a lightning event often extinguishes such fires without causing much damage. In hot, dry weather, the friction of bamboos swaying with strong winds can also spark a fire. Rolling stones that result in sparks can often set the highly inflammable leaf litter on the forest floor aflame.

Figure 5.8 Forest ablaze in Uttarakhand, 2018

Forest fires are more often sparked by human intervention through a carelessly thrown matchstick or a cigarette that has not been stamped out. A smouldering campfire, an electric spark, or any other source of ignition can also cause a forest fire. Grazers and gatherers of minor forest products can also accidentally start fires. The practice of shifting cultivation and lighting fires to ward off wild animals by the villagers living at the edge of forests are also potential causes of fires.

Once a forest fire is sparked, it can spread quickly under conducive dry weather conditions and high atmospheric temperatures. After a prolonged dry spell, especially when the moisture levels of the soil and the atmosphere are low, the likelihood of forest fires increases. Wind speed and direction of the wind also determine the extent and direction of the spread of fire.

The rate of growth and spread of a forest fire is extremely rapid. If a forest fire starts on a hilltop, it is unlikely to spread to the lower slopes. On the other hand, a fire that is sparked off at a lower altitude rapidly spreads uphill as the heated air tends to flow up the slope, spreading the flames along with it. In such an eventuality, evacuation of the community living in the upper reaches becomes imperative. The Fort McMurray wildfire in Alberta, Canada required a massive evacuation of the affected community to reduce risk.

In India, it is estimated that 90 per cent of forest fires are man-made. They cause immense economic loss and loss of livelihoods for members of tribes and the rural poor. The livelihood of around 300 million Indians revolves around the collection of non-timber minor forest produce in the forests of Madhya Pradesh, Odisha, Chhattisgarh, and Maharashtra—where most of the major fire accidents occur. Traditional methods of fire prevention are not effective in arresting forest fires. According to the Forest Survey of India (FSI), 6.17 per cent of the forests in the country is prone to severe fires. Out of the 63 million hectares of forests in the country, more than 3.5 million hectares are affected by 35,000 small and large forest fires that occur annually. The Ministry of Environment and Forests, has prepared a National Master Plan for Forest Fire Control.

FIRE SAFETY SERVICES

Fire safety services comprise of qualified and capable fire officers and firefighters who are the first responders in the event of a fire. Often, they are also the first responders to all other natural and man-made disasters around the world and rescue the affected community on the occurrence of a calamitous event. Fire prevention officers ensure that there are no violations of the fire code. They also conduct mock drills to aid in capacity building of the community.

In India, regular fire services originated in Bombay (Mumbai) and Calcutta (Kolkata). The great fire of Bombay occurred in 1803, and the first nucleus of fire services in Calcutta was organised under the Calcutta Police. Delhi is believed to have had a fire brigade in 1867. Organised fire services in India started in 1896 under the municipal corporations when the first fire station was set up in Delhi. The Madras City Fire Brigade was established in 1908 by the municipal corporation after a devastating fire in the city.

Under the Constitution of India, it is the primary responsibility of the state governments to protect life and property from fire hazards. Fire services are subject to state governments as per Article 243 (IV) of the Constitution. Fire services in Gujarat, Chhattisgarh, Punjab, Maharashtra, Himachal Pradesh, Haryana, and Madhya Pradesh are under the concerned municipal corporations and municipal committees, while in the rest of the country the fire services are the State

Home Department's responsibility. There are no uniform bylaws or standard regulations for firefighting installations across states. Fire prevention officers inspect buildings for violations of the respective fire code of the concerned state government. They are also responsible for generating awareness and enhancing capacity in the sphere of fire safety, including through the conduct of mock drills. On the national level, the Ministry of Home Affairs is the nodal ministry for policymaking and standardisation of fire services including training of firefighters. In 1956, the government set up the Standing Fire Advisory Committee under the MHA with the mandate to examine technical problems related to fire services. Over the years the Committee has been instrumental in suggesting solutions and policy measures to the states.

PREPAREDNESS: FIRE PREVENTION AT HOME

The safest way to deal with a fire is to prevent it. The Fire Prevention Triangle is a rational scientific set of Standard Operating Procedures (SOP)s and measures that aim at preventing fires and controlling their spread. The best way to prevent a fire is to practice safe behaviour within the home.

Over 70 per cent of all fires break out in residential areas, and a majority of the causalities occur at home. It is essential to teach children and adolescents that fire is not a toy, and home fire prevention is a top priority for fire safety. Improving fire safety conditions, inculcating fire-safe habits and utilising fire systems help mitigate risk.

The heat generated as a by-product of activities like cooking must be controlled and supervised at all times. It is essential for the person cooking the food to be in the kitchen, and the stove should not be left unattended. While cooking, it is important not to wear loose clothes with veils and sleeves that can dangle near burners. There should be no curtains near a cooking range. The burner must be cleaned after use to avoid grease build-up on the cooking stove or oven.

Gas safety devices in the kitchen help to protect against cooking gas leakage and blasts. In the case of any leakage, the device detects it and shuts the gas supply either from the cylinder or from the pipelines and can send an SMS to the owner. It is essential to check that the gas has been turned off before leaving the kitchen.

About 60 per cent fires are of electric origin on account of an electric short circuit, overheating, overloading, use of non-standard appliances, illegal tapping of electric wires, improper electrical wiring, carelessness, and ignorance. Severe fires and fatal accidents can occur if proper fire precautions are not followed.

Electrical equipment and electronics in the house require careful preventive measures to avert a fire. All electrical equipment and installations must be installed, maintained, and used after checking that they are designed and manufactured to prevent danger. In the interest of persona and family's safety, one should hire a qualified electrical contractor to carry out the installation of new electrical equipment and fittings while building a house and even while getting old electric equipment repaired.

Electronics with frayed wires need to be disposed of as they could lead to a fire. Electrical equipment should be checked, and all defective equipment should be repaired or replaced from time to time. Electrical cords should always be in good condition. Proper pest control needs to be done to avoid rodent damage to electric wiring and equipment. Electrical outlets should not be overloaded with multiple appliances. In case an extra electrical outlet is required in an area where there is none, it is better to have it installed by a qualified electrician. Extension cords should be avoided and not put under carpets or around walking areas. It is prudent to use only one device per outlet. Appliances and lights should be plugged into separate electrical outlets.

Portable heaters should be used sparingly. In conditions of extreme cold, portable heaters and electric blankets may be used to warm up a room or a bed, but they should be switched off before one goes to sleep. The same goes for *bukharis* used in Kashmir and or small *angithis* that are used by the hill folk in the hilly states of Himachal Pradesh and Uttarakhand to warm their rooms during winter. Portable heaters should not be used to dry clothes or hair. Electrical heaters should have emergency tip-over switches and thermostatic limiting controls. While using a portable heater, it should be placed at least a metre away from anything that can burn.

Fuel consists of materials that burn readily in the atmosphere and include flammable liquids like petrol, flammable gases, and flammable solids like wood and paper. It is necessary to identify all flammable materials that are present in homes and workplaces and put proper controls in place. The authority's advice on LPG must be meticulously followed. All flammable material must be stored away correctly.

All buildings should have emergency exits with wide, uncluttered paths leading towards the exit. Apartments in taller buildings may need fire escapes, which are special kind of emergency exits, that are usually mounted on the outside of a building and occasionally inside but are separate from the main areas of the building. A fire escape provides a method of escape in the event of a fire or other emergency that could make the stairwells inside a building inaccessible. It is possible to retrofit fire escapes in older buildings with alarms and warning systems. A modern type of evacuation slide with a vertical spiral escape chute is a common and efficient means of evacuation.

The building management and resident welfare association of building complexes should prominently display the evacuation plan of the building where everyone can see it.

Improved building codes have gone beyond the requirement of emergency exits and fire escapes. They necessitate the presence of fire detectors, technologically advanced communication and firefighting equipment. The access and reach of firefighting ladder trucks should also be ensured while constructing a building. As per India's National Building Code, high rise buildings are mandated to have smoke detectors, sprinklers, firefighting systems, public address systems for issuing warnings, fire pumps, adequate water supply to control a fire before the fire brigade arrives, fire escape routes, firemen's lift, service shaft enclosures, and sufficient compartmentation as well as first aid kits. Outside of a high-rise building, it is essential to have access roads, and surrounding areas must be designed to allow emergency vehicles, including fire trucks, to get close to the building. International building codes and other authoritative agencies have mandated fire sprinklers not just for skyscrapers but also for multi-story buildings below 15 storeys.

A home is considered prepared for safety against a house fire when the smoke detectors are functioning and have fresh batteries when windows can be easily opened, and window screens can be easily removed. If the windows have security bars, they must also have quick release devices to allow them to be opened quickly. There should also be a standardised collapsible ladder in case one needs to use it to get down from the roof or balcony. As much as possible, bed sheets, curtains, and linen in the house should not be made of synthetic fibres.

Installing smoke detectors helps to detect both smouldering and burning fires to ensure early control and sufficient time to escape. Smoke detectors sense abnormal amounts of smoke or invisible combustion of gases in the air. Smoke detectors come in two basic types—photoelectric and ionisation. Upkeep and inspection of smoke detectors should be done once a month, and the batteries should be changed at least once a year. Automatic sprinkler systems used to distribute water directly on the fire are highly efficient and have an effectiveness of about 96 per cent in controlling or extinguishing fires.

Fire-safe habits must be cultivated within the family. These include an ingrained habit of switching off all appliances after use and removal of plugs from sockets, especially portable heaters. Electrical wires should always be kept away from hot and wet surfaces. Use of good quality fuses of correct rating, miniature circuit breakers, and earth leakage circuit breakers is vital. Fuses and switches should always be mounted on metallic cubicles for better safety against fire. Broken plugs and switches must be replaced immediately. Electric switches should not be turned on or off if there is a gas leakage as it could create a spark and cause a fire. During an electric fire, an appropriate extinguisher should be used. Wires should not be placed under carpets or mats as they can get crushed, resulting in short-circuiting. Fire exits and stairways should be kept clear. When leaving for a vacation or a long duration, it is imperative to switch off the gas and the main electrical switch.

Smoking within the house is not a good practice for both parents and youngsters. Separate smoking areas, like rooftops, balconies or a particular smoking room with no flammable material, should be identified and agreed upon by the family. It is safer to use a lighter instead of matchsticks if one smokes. Smoking in bed is a sure way of inviting trouble. Cigarettes and matches need to be disposed of safely, and away from other combustible waste. A stray spark or a lit match can cause havoc.

Every home should have a family fire safety plan as well as a fire safety kit consisting of specialised fire blankets, fire extinguishers, and masks among other things, so that in the event of a fire, the affected can escape wrapping the blanket on their bodies and putting on a mask on their faces for protection against smoke.

During festivals and occasions like Deepawali and Guy Fawkes Day when firecrackers are burst, special care should be taken to avoid wearing long and loose clothes as they can catch fire quickly. Clothes made of synthetic fibres should also be avoided as they melt and stick to the skin, causing severe burns if they catch fire. Avoid lighting candles unless they are directly in one's line of vision. There should be no lit candles in empty rooms. Firecrackers should not be burnt inside the house, in crowded, narrow lanes or congested places. Covering crackers with tin containers or glass bottles to amplify the sound is asking for trouble.

PREPAREDNESS: FIRE PREVENTION—SCHOOLS, COLLEGES, OFFICES, FACTORIES, AND INDUSTRIAL PLANTS

Fire safety risk assessments should be conducted in schools, offices, factories, and plants as well as in commercial places. A Fire Safety Statement that records the risk so assessed and the safety measures that should be taken should also be included. The Fire Safety Statement should spell out the manner of detection of a fire and the mode of warning in the office, factory, institution or school. Exits should be prominently marked.

Mock drills for safe evacuation in the event of a fire should be conducted periodically. At least 10 per cent of a building's occupants should be trained in safe modes of a fire evacuation. The nearest fire station can provide information and training. Children should be taught to trust firefighters and not to hide from a firefighter in the event of a fire.

A separate Fire escape and evacuation plan should also be in place, which encompasses details of warning systems, emergency escape routes, and manner of escape. The plan should integrally incorporate the individual needs of people who may have less mobility because of old age, different types of disabilities including mobility-impaired people, wheelchair users, people who are hard of hearing, blind or partially sighted, and people with cognitive disabilities. The fire escape plan should also address the needs of children.

All schools, colleges, offices, factories, plants, and other commercial buildings like hotels, restaurants, malls, theatres, and cinema halls must have clearly identified means of escape in the event of a fire. Ideally, there should be two escape routes from each room. Escape routes must be kept clear at all times to ensure that everyone can exit the place in the event of a fire or any other emergency. It is not a good idea to escape into an enclosed yard or courtyard.

Premises which are small and have an uncomplicated layout can have a simple escape and evacuation plan. The regular entrances and exits are sufficient escape routes. There should be no possibility of anyone being cut off by smoke or flames. In large multi-story buildings with more complex layouts, escape routes need to be more sophisticated. The general rule is that people should be able to turn their back on a fire, wherever it may start in a building, and move away from the fire to a safe place outside the building at a safe distance in case the fire grows. Escape routes should be at least 1 metre wide to prevent a stampede. The escape route should lead to a place of safety, which is usually outside and away from the building.

Egress without the use of a key to doors on escape routes should be available. Security cannot take precedence over safety. Locked emergency exits can be fatal and can prove to be an immense hindrance in evacuation and escape during a fire or any other calamity. Technologically it is now possible to have a solution that takes care of both safety and security concerns. In the case of the 2019 Delhi hotel fire, a locked emergency exit was the cause of two persons panicking and jumping out of the upper floors of a hotel in an attempt to reach safety.

Fire precaution can be ensured conveniently and cost-effectively by installing a reliable automatic fire detection system that is linked to an active fire warning system. Fire warning systems can prove to be a boon and lifesaver. All fire alarms should be sufficiently loud for the warning to be heard clearly throughout the building. The sound used as a fire warning should be distinct from all other sounds. It is necessary to install a visual alarm such as a distinctive flashing or rotating light to warn hearing-impaired people and where background noise levels are high.

Proper housekeeping of an office, plant, factory, and other establishment goes a long way in preventing fires. Potential sources of ignition should be closely watched and attended to within the premises. Chemistry laboratories in schools, colleges, and plants, for instance, need special SOPs placed on the door and the wall for all users.

Electrical and electronic equipment, and frazzled cables, which are not adequately maintained, are often the cause of fires. All work equipment needs to be protected against overheating and catching fire. Heat-producing equipment like burners, heat exchangers, boilers, ovens, and stoves need proper cleaning and maintenance. Electrical equipment requires to be serviced regularly by a competent person to prevent sparks and fires.

Plants, factories and other workplaces need to have a planned maintenance program to maintain plant and equipment, which needs to be reviewed intermittently. The maintenance program should deal with frictional heat, electrical malfunction, flammable materials used in contact with hot surfaces, leaking valves or flanges, and static sparks due to inadequate electrical earthing. Ventilation points on machinery and in vehicles need to be kept clean to prevent clogging with dust as it can lead to overheating. Workplaces where large amounts of flammable materials are stored or used, present a more significant hazard, which needs to be addressed with efficient safety measures.

Every floor of a built-up structure should be equipped with at least two lightweight aluminium fire extinguishers to ensure that women are also able to operate the extinguisher. Restaurants need to be equipped with water mist systems and fire safety kits. Every hotel room should be provided with a fire safety kit that consists of a specialised fire blanket and masks so that guests can exit safely without inhaling smoke in the event of a fire. While selecting a hotel, a potential guest should ask if the hotel has fire safety and escape plan in place as well as a fire safety kit in the hotel room.

Hospitals need to be protected with specialised fire safety products like auto fire detection with mist-based water suppression systems. The duvets and blankets used in a hospital should be fireproof so that a patient can be rushed out in case of fire by wrapping the blanket and putting on a mask on the face to protect from smoke. All hospitals should be connected to and monitored 24/7 by the control room of the nearest fire station.

Trains and railway stations should take special preventive measures to avoid hazardous fire incidents. Auto heat detection-cum-suppression systems should be installed in air-conditioned coaches and pantry cars. Other suitable systems installed to protect power coaches, control rooms and signal telecommunication rooms go a long way in preventing fires in trains. In developed countries, artificial intelligence and analytics are used to forge efficient and constant connections between fire services and vital strategic locations like hospitals, airports, schools, and railway stations to keep fire safety facilities in readiness at all times and reduce risk.

In educational institutes and at workplaces, it is essential to ensure that all employees and students are aware of their specific personal responsibilities to report dangers and to take charge of a fire extinguisher to douse a spark if they are close by. Smoking within the college or workplace premises should be banned except for in specially designated smoking areas, which are at a distance from flammable materials. No-smoking signs should be in place at appropriate locations. Cigarettes must be wholly stamped out after smoking.

Arson or deliberately started fires pose significant risks to all types of workplaces and educational institutions. The majority of deliberately started fires occur where there is a known history of vandalism or fire-setting. Employers, the management of an institution, students, and employees need to be aware of the potential threat of arson and should remain alert for early signs of one like a series of small unexplained fires.

Typically, local youths commit arson outside a building as an act of vandalism and use locally available materials. By adopting adequate security measures, it must be ensured that unauthorised persons do not have access to premises. Occasionally, a disgruntled employee or an ex-employee has committed a deliberate attack of arson in a factory or office. On one occasion, an ill-informed unhappy teenager in a boarding school attempted arson and tried to set fire to a dormitory so that he could be sent home by the school authorities. However, the fire was contained well in time and without any loss of life or property.

PREPAREDNESS: WHAT TO DO BEFORE A FIRE BREAKS OUT

Emergency procedures must be in place to ensure safe evacuation in the event of a fire. A family fire safety plan and a family fire evacuation and escape plan help to reduce risk. Offices, schools, colleges, factories, and other commercial and community buildings like malls, hotels, airports, hospitals, and railway stations can also reduce risk through similar safety and escape plans after conducting a detailed risk assessment of their premises.

The fire safety plan identifies the action that residents and occupants should take in the event of a fire. This plan may include the duties of family members, employees, and students to check that areas within the building are clear, and there are no flammable substances lying around. Escape routes to a place of safety, including areas outside the premises are to be kept clear. As per the safety plan, an employer or the head of an institute can also nominate a team of teachers or employees to carry out checks and routine maintenance work of all fire safety equipment, including warning systems. It is crucial to ensure the reliability of fire-fighting equipment and installed systems such as fire alarms and emergency lighting.

Most homes have family members with special needs who require assistance to make their escape in the event of a fire. They must have means of summoning help by their bedsides like a buzzer, an intercom, a telephone or a whistle. Systems are now available which can automatically dial on the telephone to summon help or send a signal to a staffed control room, thereby ensuring timely rescue.

The escape and evacuation plan needs to lay down an evacuation strategy and define essential roles and responsibilities in the event of a fire. Roles should be made clear and should include giving the warning and activating the fire alarm if it is a manual system, calling the fire department and assisting children and people with special needs in the event of a fire. Children, students, and employees need to be aware of all the possible escape routes.

Emergency mock drills should be practised regularly utilising the escape routes. The plan of escape and evacuation in the event of a fire should be practised twice a year to get comfortable with the routine and the escape route as well as to know each person's role. Practising the plan and conducting a mock drill ensures that everyone is clear-headed enough to carry it out if a fire breaks out. Escaping by crawling in the dark with eyes shut or blindfolded should be practised to simulate a situation where a fire in one part of the building leaves the rest of it in smoke. More so since fire is generally accompanied by a power failure.

Infirmities in the fire safety plan and the fire evacuation and escape plan are brought out by mock drills, which help to plug holes in the plans. A mock drill also helps in testing the functioning of the alarm systems and the fire safety equipment, thereby ensuring their proper maintenance. The necessity to ensure that the escape route is clear of flammable matter and that the fire exit is not locked is brought out in the course of fire preparedness mock drills.

All homes, institutions and workplaces should have arrangements for detecting a fire. The nature and extent of the fire detection and warning arrangements need to satisfy the requirements indicated in the risk assessment statement. All places should have arrangements for issuing a warning once a fire is detected to help people escape safely.

In premises where a fire could develop before being discovered, it is essential to protect vital escape routes like staircases with fire-resistant doors. There should be a second mode of exiting the room in case the main door is blocked. Where there are two or more escape routes, it is prudent to ensure that the smoke and flames do not affect more than one escape route at the same time in the event of a fire. If any door is blocked, it is essential to find a way out through a window or a different door.

Fire safety equipment and measures, including fixtures and fittings such as fire doors, staircases, corridors, fire detection and alarm systems, fire-fighting equipment, and emergency lighting, must be maintained in an effective working order. Fire equipment like fire hydrant systems, fire hoses, fire extinguishers, and sprinkler systems must be in working order. Regular checks and periodic servicing should be carried out towards this end.

Fire equipment, including fire extinguishers, must be of the requisite quality and sufficient in number. There are four classes of fire extinguishers—A, B, C, and D. Each class of extinguisher can put out a different type of fire. Class A extinguishers are used to put out fires of ordinary combustibles such as wood and paper. Class B extinguishers are used to put out fires where flammable liquids like gasoline and oil are involved. Class C extinguishers are suitable only for putting out electrically energised fires, while Class D extinguishers are designed for fires related to flammable metals. Multipurpose extinguishers can also be used on different types of fires like A–B, B–C or A–B–C extinguishers. At home and in offices, class A and sometimes class C extinguishers are more suitable, while the other types are used in factories and industrial plants. In homes, fires are most likely to start in the kitchen and the garage. There should be a fire extinguisher in both these places and also there should be at least one fire extinguisher on each level of the house.

In a recent capacity-building session of doctors and surgeons in a multi-disciplinary hospital, I found that none knew how to use a fire extinguisher. There was an esoteric element associated with their usage. The shared view was that it was too technical and so maintenance officials who were responsible for the upkeep of the extinguishers would use them when a fire broke out. Often those who happen to be closest to a fire extinguisher at the time of the ignition of a fire, and can help extinguish it timely, do not do so due to lack of knowledge regarding how to use one. All members of a family, office, and other organisations should be conversant with the method to use fire extinguishers. Most are easy to operate using the P.A.S.S. technique:

- P. Pull the pin on the fire extinguisher in order to break the tamper seal.
- A. Aim the fire extinguisher low, with the nozzle pointed at the base of the fire.
- S. Squeeze the handle of the fire extinguisher to release the extinguishing agent.
- S. Sweep the nozzle from side to side while pointing at the base of the fire until the fire is extinguished. In case the fire re-ignites, the last three steps may be repeated until it is extinguished.

Buckets of damp sand kept at crucial intervals have also been effectively used as fire extinguishers in rural schools and panchayat buildings. Until recently such buckets were a common sight in cinema halls and other larger buildings in small towns. It should be ensured that the sand buckets, wherever in use, must be replenished from time to time.

The property—home, school, office, or factory—should be secured by buying insurance that covers an accidental fire as well as arson.

WHAT TO DO IN THE EVENT OF A FIRE

Early discovery and warning provides more time for escape and enables safe and timely evacuation before the fire blocks all escape routes or makes escape difficult. As soon as a smoke or fire alarm is heard, the inhabitants of a building should try to establish the source. In case the source is close to a person, they should try to extinguish the fire by aiming the fire extinguisher at the base of the fire. Water should never be used to douse an electrical fire. It is better to use an appropriate extinguisher.

Exiting the premises as soon as possible is the best recourse in case the fire is not extinguished, or if the source of the fire is not visible. Sometimes there are only a few seconds available to escape and to get the family out into the open safely. While escaping, it is not wise to try to locate and grab valuables or any other important possessions. The only concern should be assisting family members and colleagues who may need assistance, and to exit into the open without panicking. After one has escaped from a fire, it is best to stay out and not go back for any documents or valuables that may have remained inside.

A large number of casualties occur when a fire breaks out at night. Smoke from a fire can often put a sleeping person into a deeper slumber and lead to death through smoke inhalation. Of the 17 people who died in the Delhi hotel fire of 2019, a majority died in their sleep due to smoke inhalation and asphyxiation. In case a fire breaks out at night, it is essential to shout as loudly as possible to wake up the entire family. Members of the family who have a hearing disability need to be shaken awake.

Generally, in order to escape in the event of a fire, one tends to run and rush out of the building to escape. It is not a good idea to run out. It is best to bend low—well below the fire line and stay closer to the floor. Crouching or crawling on hands and knees to evade smoke can keep a person safe as they make their way to the exit that leads out of the building and into the open, and not into an enclosed space or courtyard.

Smoke inhalation causes disorientation and can render a person unconscious. If one has to walk through a smoke-filled room while exiting, it is best to cover the nose and mouth with a shirt or a wet cloth to filter the smoke, which is noxious and poisonous. Cleaner air is available up to 1–2 ft above the floor. While escaping through the smoke, it is best to crawl as the heat and smoke rise above. A cardinal principle is to always breathe through the nose and not the mouth during a fire to filter the smoke that could be inhaled. A wet towel over one's nose can help in additionally filtering the inhaled air. Zen Sadavarte, a 10-year-old girl, ensured that her family members and neighbours remained safe when a fire broke out in 2018 on the twelfth floor of Crystal Towers—a building in Mumbai where she lived with her parents on the sixteenth floor. When asked how she had achieved the feat, she informed the news reporters that she had applied what she had learnt in school to the real-life situation, '*There was a lot of smoke, and we could have suffocated but I remembered that we should be sitting down to avoid the smoke line. We also draped ourselves with wet cloth. That kept us protected till the fire brigade could come and rescue us.*'

It is generally considered safe to exit through doors except when there is smoke coming from under a door. If there is no smoke under a door, the temperature of the door should be checked with the back of the hand to make sure that it does not feel hot. One can exit through a door that feels cool after opening it slowly to ensure that there is no fire on the way out. In case of fire, the door of the room should remain firmly closed. Compartmentalising the fire by closing all doors after leaving a room while exiting helps to delay the spread of fire and smoke. In case there is smoke coming from under one of the doors of the exit route, it cannot be used as an exit as deadly smoke and fire are sure to follow. In such an eventuality, it is best to put a wet towel in the space under the door and look for alternative exit routes from the room.

If it is unfeasible to exit a room through the door—when the door is hot, when there is a fire outside the door that obstructs the exit or when there is smoke under the door— and there are no other doors, it is necessary to escape through the window. One can carefully go out into the balcony or the ledge and climb outside the building if the room is on the ground or first floor.

On the upper floors, if there is a fire escape, it should be used to move to the ground after exiting through the window.

Under no circumstances should an elevator be used in the event of a fire. It is better to use a fire escape or a chute if there is one. The first option, if feasible, should be to escape safely from a second or upper storey window. While using a collapsible ladder when exiting a window on an upper floor, it is best to always face the building structure.

In the event of being trapped in a room on the second or upper storeys without a fire escape, it is best to go to a window where a person can be seen or heard and call for help. It is necessary to be visible at the window or balcony even as one makes a telephone call to the emergency number. It is prudent to hang a white sheet or any other cloth out of the window to signal the rescuers where help is needed. It is essential to shut the window, as leaving it open draws the fire into the room towards fresh oxygen. After that, it is best to wait for the first responder to assist in exiting the building rather than trying to jump out in panic. Of the 20 students who died in the 2019 Surat fire in a coaching centre, mostly between the ages of 15–19 years, four were those who jumped out of a fourth storey window to their deaths in sheer panic. While waiting for assistance, it is crucial to stay calm until help arrives and to take measures to delay the spread of fire and keep the room as safe as possible. All electrical appliances in the room should be unplugged. If available, buckets of water and blankets should be kept ready to snuff out any stray sparks.

A person is probably safer staying put and waiting for fire responders to arrive in the event of a fire if immediately exiting a building is not possible. Compartmentalisation by closing doors between the fire and the space where a person is trapped helps to delay the spread of smoke and fire. The most important thing to do is to ward off the smoke and stay safe. The doors and windows must be closed, and all vents and cracks under or around the doors and windows should be covered with a wet towel or cloth to keep the smoke out for as long possible. A person should stay crouched close to the ground, below the smoke line and put, a wet towel or cloth over the nose and mouth to filter the air until the first responder arrives. In a fire in Mumbai, a large number of casualties occurred due to inhalation of smoke and asphyxiation as well as the stampede to exit because of panic. The fire department after dousing the fire found a group of Japanese tourists trudging out safely from the restaurant they had been dining in before the fire broke out in a different part of the complex. They had dropped to the ground when the fire alarm rang and had sat crouched on the ground with their noses covered with damp table napkins, saving themselves from smoke inhalation.

In case one's clothes or the clothes of a family member or colleague catches fire, the mantra is SDR—Stop, Drop, and Roll. Stop and stay calm rather than running around in panic. Drop flat on the ground and cover the face with hands for protection. Roll until the fire is stamped out as rolling around smothers the fire quickly.

WHAT TO DO AFTER THE FIRE

After exiting from the burnt structure, it is essential to move as far away as possible. While keeping at a safe distance from the fire, necessary safety measures need to be taken. As per the family communication plan, in the event of a calamity, the family should reach the pre-fixed safe area outside the building, a headcount must be done to ensure no one is missing. If a person is missing, rather than going back into the building to search for the missing person, one should inform the firefighters as they are equipped to perform rescues safely.

The local emergency services number must be called. In India, the affected can call 101 or the particular number for fire services in the area. The emergency numbers to be called in the event of a calamity in some of the other countries are: 911 in North America, 000 in Australia, 111 in New Zealand, 999 or 112 in the UK from mobile. This number has priority on the mobile phone network in the UK as too many unintentional 999 calls are made. In Europe, the emergency number in the event of a fire is 112. It gets redirected to the local emergency number of the area by the network if necessary.

Checking for injuries to oneself, family members, colleagues, and other affected persons is the next step. It is advisable not to remove burnt clothing unless it comes off easily. An injury assessment must be done, and first aid should be provided to the injured before being taken to the nearest hospital. Any burn injury should be washed in cold running water for about five minutes until the burning sensation subsides. Then a thin layer of ointments such as petroleum jelly or Aloe vera can be put on the burn. The ointment applied as first aid does not need to have an antibiotic in it. To protect the burn, it should be covered with a sterile, non-adhesive bandage or clean cloth. No adhesive dressing should be applied on the burnt area. Care should be taken not to pop any blister. Since burns are excruciating, a mild painkiller like ibuprofen that is available over the counter can be administered until the ambulance arrives and takes the injured to the hospital.

After attending to medical needs, it is crucial to protect the site of the fire from further damage by weather, theft or vandalism. The site is to be secured and cordoned off. The fire brigade and the police help in cordoning off and securing the premises. All openings should be protected and covered against rain and entry by unauthorised people. An attempt should be made to lock and secure the main doors of the property.

It is imprudent to try to re-enter the building until after the fire is completely doused. Only when the fire service officers declare that it is safe to re-enter a burnt building should one try to save any of the valuables that may have remained in the building after the fire. Once it is safe to do so, identification details, vital medicines of the family members, eyeglasses, hearing aids, prosthetic devices or personal aids and valuables like credit cards, chequebooks, insurance policies, money, jewellery, and valuables can be located and secured.

The burnt building should be checked for damage with the help of experts. If the fire has left the building unsafe, the occupants may have to leave their homes or offices temporarily until the building can be rebuilt and restored. The local police can be contacted in such an eventuality so that they can keep an eye on the property until it is safe to return. Gas, fuel, and electricity supplies should be disconnected before leaving the site. It is essential to notify one's new address to the police, insurance company, employer, family, friends, children's schools, and the post office. The telecom department and the suppliers of gas, electricity, and water should also be informed about any new contact address and phone number.

Experts need to be employed to assess if the building can be repaired and to evaluate the repairs that may be required to make the place livable. Structural damages caused by the fire need to be checked and attended as roofs and floors may have been weakened. Before the power is turned on, a licensed electrician should check the household wiring which may have become damaged by water while dousing the fire. Food, drink, and medicines exposed to heat, smoke or soot should be discarded appropriately.

Insurance claims in the event of a fire need to be lodged as early as possible. An inventory of all the property that has been burnt and lost during the fire, along with its value needs to be drawn up. It is crucial to get the burnt building photographed, and the insurance agent contacted as early as possible to report the occurrence of the fire and the resultant loss incurred. In case arson is suspected, the matter must be reported to the police for investigation.

Victims of fire incidents and burn injuries require behaviour therapy and support post-disaster besides immediate medical attention.

SIX

Hydro-meteorological Hazards I: Floods, Tropical Storms, Lightning, Dust & Hail Storms, and Urban Flooding

Hydro-meteorological hazards are cataclysmic events that are related to atmospheric, hydrological, and oceanographic phenomena. They cause loss of life, property and livelihoods. They also impact the environment adversely. Hydro-meteorological hazards include tropical cyclones, floods, flash floods, tornados, hailstorms, thunderstorms, blizzards, heavy snowfall, avalanches, coastal storm surges, drought, heatwaves, and cold spells. This section deals with heavy rains, floods and other hydro-meteorological hazards like tropical storms, lightning, dust storms, hailstorms, and urban flooding. Hazards relating to droughts, cyclones, avalanches, and the concomitant disaster risk reduction are discussed later in the book.

FLOODS

A flood is a hydro-meteorological hazard wherein there is an overflow of water over land, which is usually dry. A water resource like a river, lake or pond gets flushed with excess water beyond its holding capacity and inundates the surrounding areas. Excess water collects either due to high rate of snow meltdown in the case of snow-fed rivers or incessant heavy rainfall over a short period. Floods cause immense loss of life, property and livelihoods. They also damage infrastructure and public utilities.

Climatic conditions, natural topography, and ecological systems of an area affect the occurrence of floods. Floods are often accompanied by unusually heavy rains, which can be the precipitating factor for flooding a water body—landslides or ice jams that block streams, typhoons and cyclones also cause floods. Sometimes flash floods can occur due to a cyclone or a cloudburst upstream, especially in a river or stream which has high sedimentation and inadequate holding capacity. Urban floods are a recent phenomenon associated with poor drainage and unregulated irregular construction of built-up structures. Floods are also associated with atmospheric depressions, which can deepen and magnify into cyclones—a hazard that is discussed in detail in a separate chapter.

INDIA: FLOOD MAPPING

India is one of the most flood-prone countries in the world. Floods have recurred in India, year after year, mainly during the monsoons when the rainfall is about 70–90 per cent of the total annual rainfall in the country. Consequently, rivers and water bodies silted with heavy sedimentation are in a spate. One-eighth of India, comprising of 23 of the 35 states and union territories, is flood-prone. Floods occur in and around the major river basins of the country, including the Himalayan river basin—particularly the Kosi and Damodar Rivers, the northwestern river basin—mainly Jhelum, Ravi, Sutlej, and Beas rivers, and the central and peninsular river basin—Narmada, Chambal, Godavari, Krishna, and Cauvery rivers. In the northeast, the Brahmaputra basin is also prone to recurrent floods. Floods cause havoc, and besides

Figure 6.1 India: Flood vulnerability mapping

ecological and economic losses, floods are also associated with loss of lives and livelihoods. On an average 1,600 human lives are lost across the country due to floods each year. The highest number of lives lost was during the 1977 floods when 11,316 people died.

FLOODS IN INDIA: CAUSE

Flooding of rivers in India is a recurrent weather-related phenomenon which occurs due to heavy rainfall in the monsoons—mainly during the southwest monsoons between May and September. Sometimes floods can also occur during the northeast monsoons which occur between October and January. Frequent flooding of rivers is due to the high intensity of rainfall in a short period. India receives 80 per cent of the year's precipitation during the southwest monsoons. The average rainfall during the monsoons is 1,150 mm. In the Western Ghats, in the Khasi Hills and the Brahmaputra valley, rainfall can sometimes be as high as 2,500 mm. The wettest places on Earth, Mawsynram and neighbouring Cherrapunji in the Khasi Hills in Meghalaya, experience the highest rainfall of about 11,871 mm on an average. The Himalayas and some other mountains in India are prone to soil and water erosion. Most rivers carry excessive silt and sediments from their catchment areas, and their carrying capacity declines. Heavy siltation, coupled with the reduced carrying capacity of rivers makes them flood-prone. The combination of heavy rainfall and reduced capacity of rivers to carry the flood discharge is further aggravated by inadequate drainage. Areas with hardpan just below the surface of the soil are more prone to floods as water fails to seep into the deeper layers.

VULNERABILITY

Over 40 million hectares of land in India is prone to floods and river erosion. Every year about 7.5 million hectares of land is flooded. Lately, floods have occurred in areas, which were earlier considered flood-safe. Demographic factors like population density and the resultant pressures on land exacerbate India's vulnerability to floods. There is often a risk of losing human lives along with the lives of cattle, other domestic animals, and birds are also affected by floods. There is large-scale damage to crops, houses, infrastructure, and public utilities. The economic loss associated with floods is immense. The poor are the most vulnerable during floods.

THUNDERSTORMS, LIGHTNING, HAILSTORMS, AND DUST STORMS

Thunderstorms, lightning, dust storms, hailstorms, squalls, and strong winds have emerged as major hazards in recent years. Floods are usually associated with tropical storms. All storms harm life and property, standing crops, power lines, infrastructure, communication, and the aviation sector. Thunderstorms are frequent across India, from Kashmir to Kerala. On the other hand, hailstorms and dust storms are only frequent in the northern, western, eastern, central and northeastern parts of India. The southernmost part of the country is free from both dust storms and hailstorms. India is likely to witness an increase in the severity and frequency of thunderstorms and dust storms in the future.

Dust Storms

Dust storms are meteorological phenomena that is common in arid and semi-arid regions. Dust storms arise when a gust of

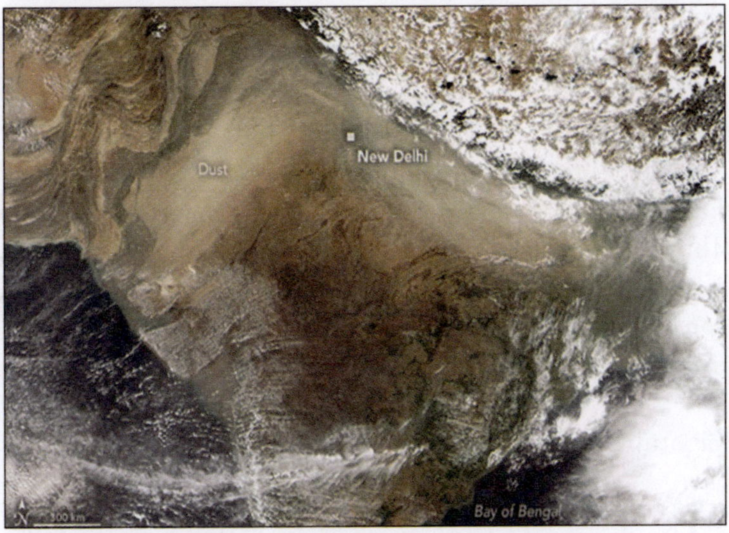

Figure 6.2 Dust storm-prone arid and semi-arid areas of India

strong wind picks up and blows loose sand. The storms typically occur in the summer, when winds pick up dust and sand as they pass over arid and semi-arid areas.

Dust storms are a feature of India's seasonal weather patterns. The death toll in a dust storm rarely exceeds 10. However, 108 people died in May 2018 when a high-velocity dust storm swept across North India. The death toll was higher than usual because the dust storm occurred at night and took the sleeping community unawares. 43 people died in Agra alone while 35 lives were lost in Rajasthan. The storm also uprooted more than 8,000 electric poles and hundreds of trees.

Thunderstorms

Thunderstorms are accompanied by thunder and lightning and are typically followed by heavy rain or hail. As winter transforms into spring, the temperature rises initially in the southern parts of India and gives rise to thunderstorms and squally weather. Thunderstorms often lead to the formation of a squall, which is hazardous. The distinctive characteristics of a thunderstorm include strong updraft and downdraft, towering cumulonimbus clouds associated with turbulence, in-cloud electrification associated with lightning and localised heavy rain and hail. Historical data reveals that in three decades, more than 80 thunderstorms and lightning occur each year over North East India and some parts of Kerala and Jammu & Kashmir. Thunderstorms have a devastating impact on socio-economic sectors like agriculture, aviation, surface transport, power, and communications. Severe thunderstorms lead to loss of human lives, property, and livelihoods.

Lightning

Lightning typically occurs during a thunderstorm. Lightning is a sudden electrostatic discharge, which occurs between electrically charged regions of a cloud, between two clouds (C–C) or between a cloud and the ground (C–G). The charged regions in the atmosphere temporarily equalise themselves through this discharge, which is referred to as a lightning flash. Lightning creates a light in the form of black body radiation from the hot plasma created by electron flow and sound in the form of thunder. A lightning flash can also become a lightning strike if it involves an object on the ground in a cloud to ground or C–G lightning strike. Every year about 2,500 people die in India during thunderstorms due to a lightning strike.

Hailstorms

Hailstorms are thunderstorms that produce ice as precipitation. Hailstorms can cause severe damage to crops and property. Unlike snow, hailstones are hard as they are made up of packed ice and as they fall, their impact is strong enough to crack open glass windows and shatter the windscreen of a car. In the hills, hailstorms can be life-threatening. While trekking in the Himalayas, I have seen hailstones the size of table tennis balls pelting down and forcing people to take shelter under a rock or in a cave to avoid injury. The 1888 Moradabad hailstorm was one of the most severe hailstorms in the North Indian state of Uttar Pradesh. The hailstones were, reportedly, as big as oranges and accumulated up to 2 ft in height in some places. 246 people died, along with 1600 cattle and sheep.

FLASH FLOODS

Flash floods occur when a high rate of water flows into streams, drainage channels, canyons, and other areas known to flood suddenly. They can occur unexpectedly with or without the typical warnings of clouds, thunder or heavy rain. Flash floods are further aggravated by reduced permeability of the soil in a riverbed. They are more hazardous as they occur suddenly without warning. Lack of warning and the sudden onslaught of flash floods, particularly those caused by cloudbursts, are associated with disproportionately high mortality rate. Flash floods cause loss of life as a calm shallow stream, without warning, suddenly enters a forceful spate and washes away all that lies in its path. A busload of schoolchildren out on a picnic in the Himalayas have been swept away within minutes and lost forever. They had been playing in knee-deep water in a shallow mountain rivulet when a flash flood caused by a cloudburst upstream flooded it and swept them away within minutes.

URBAN FLOODS

Urban floods typically occur due to heavy rainfall in a short span caused by flash floods, coastal or river floods or due to flooding caused by lack of drainage in urban areas. Urban flooding is a more recent and universal hazard that poses a significant challenge to urban planners globally. The impact of urban floods can be widespread, requiring temporary relocation of people. Civic amenities get damaged, and there is deterioration of water quality, which also poses a risk of epidemics. Flooding of Hull in England and Mestre in Italy in 2007 are instances of urban floods in Europe. The 2007 urban floods were relatively localised events of inundation, which lasted for several days.

Urban floods in India have started to become a regular phenomenon. In Mumbai, urban flooding is almost an annual feature. Recent events of urban floods include the 2013 Uttarakhand floods which occurred due to cloudbursts and the Srinagar deluge a year later due to torrential rainfall. Chennai saw its first-ever urban flood in 2015 mainly because of unrestrained construction of houses and tall buildings across low-lying marshlands, erstwhile ponds, and over the natural drains. Srinagar was flooded for the first time in human history in 2014 when floodwater of Jhelum River, which passes through Srinagar flooded the entire city.

Figure 6.3 Urban flooding is a recent phenomenon

Illegal and indiscriminate encroachment of land, particularly along the natural drainage features and encroachment of waterways in an attempt to construct housing projects is one of the leading causes of urban flooding. Inadequate capacity of existing drains and poor maintenance of the drainage infrastructure enhances the risk. High-intensity rainfall causes floods when the city sewage system and drainage canals do not have the necessary capacity to drain the excess rainwater they have received in the short span. The economic damage during urban flooding is high, but the number of casualties is usually limited because the water rises slowly on the streets, giving enough opportunity to the affected community to respond. Furthermore, during urban floods, the water level rarely reaches life-endangering heights.

FLOOD FORECASTING

Flood forecasting and warning systems used for issuing alerts before a hazardous event have a well-established protocol. The early warning of the arrival of floods enables the evacuation of the affected population to safer places and flood shelters. The CWC, in 1958, made a beginning in scientific flood forecasting. The flood forecasting network of the CWC covers all the major flood-prone inter-state basins in the country. The CWC works closely with the IMD in forecasting floods. Flood forecasting is done through observation and collection of hydrological and hydro-meteorological data, its transmission to forecasting centres for data analysis and the formulation and dissemination of the forecast along with an advisory. The accuracy of flood forecasts has now increased to 98 per cent. The accuracy of the forecast is a boon as it allows for effective preparedness and timely evacuation of the area that is expected to be flooded, thereby reducing casualties.

EVACUATION PLAN

Evacuation is carried out as a precautionary measure based on warning indicators before the occurrence of a flood. Timely evacuation of vulnerable communities and livestock is a crucial means to save the affected from the fury of floods. The process of evacuation is one of the most challenging operations when a large population is involved.

Figure 6.4 Preparing for floods: evacuation of vulnerable communities

A comprehensive evacuation plan is prepared at the district and sub-district levels. Among other things, it includes identifying flood-prone areas, building flood shelters, identifying high grounds for temporary shelters, laying out route maps, devising the most appropriate methods of communication, and stocking up of food and essential commodities including medicines.

Community involvement in the preparation and dissemination of an evacuation plan is critical. Furthermore, progressive companies, hotels, schools, colleges, resident welfare associations, panchayats, and families should prepare their emergency evacuation plan in sync with the evacuation plan of the area. They should also conduct mock drills to ensure that all the stakeholders are familiar with the evacuation process.

PREPAREDNESS: WHAT TO DO BEFORE THE HAZARD

It is prudent to avoid building a home in a flood-prone area unless the building is elevated and reinforced. The foundations and the walls in the basement should be built to ensure that they are sealed with waterproofing compounds to avoid any seepage in the event of a flood. While constructing a house in an area susceptible to floods, it is necessary to ensure that 'check valves' are installed in sewer traps to prevent the floodwater from entering the drains in the event of a flood. The furnace, water heaters, and electric panels must be fixed in elevated areas.

In order to minimise risk in flood-prone areas, it is imperative not to encroach on and build over a dry riverbed or across the natural flood drainage channels in the area. If others do so, it is a part of one's civic duty to report the matter to the authorities. The construction can endanger the lives of not only the families who live in the disaster-prone dwellings but will also put the entire community at risk, as the habitation will block the natural flow of excess water during heavy rains.

Every member of the community should learn to swim to reduce risk to life in a flood-prone area. They should be able to swim enough that they can stay afloat until they are rescued during a sudden cataclysmic event. Schools and employers in flood-prone areas can help to reduce risk by building capacities in this regard. The capacity of a family, employees of an organisation, and the community to cope with floods, can be enhanced by attending mock drills and capacity-building programs organised by the local government and by resident welfare associations with the help of disaster management authorities.

In a flood-prone area, it is essential to discuss within the family, and amongst the community the impending dangers of floods and the response to a flood situation. Children and the elderly should be an intrinsic part of the family discussion. A list of essential items that the family may need in the event of evacuation should be prepared. Essential articles like rescue equipment and stores including rations as well as means of communication like a radio, a torch with extra batteries, and a cell phone with power pack and charger are an intrinsic part of the list. This list can also include a favourite doll, a toy or a book that a child might need to help in reducing the trauma of the disaster.

The family emergency kit, based on the list prepared, should be packed in a waterproof covering. Ready-to-eat food, baby food, essential medicines for members of the family, and some money should form an integral part of the kit. It should be kept ready in a safe, dry place known to all the members of the family, along with spare keys to the house. The family emergency kit should cater to the individual needs of the children, the elderly, and the sick and differently-abled members of the family. All offices, schools, colleges, workplaces, and other commercial places like hotels in flood-prone areas should have their emergency and evacuation plans, as well as emergency kits, put together on the lines of the family emergency kit.

Flood preparedness also needs to include plans to evacuate and rescue pets, livestock and, other animals. I have a fond memory of an elderly lady who lived alone with her goat in a small, secluded dwelling in Kerala. During the 2018 Kerala floods, she refused to be rescued even as the floodwaters entered her house and continued rising unless the rescue team first rowed her goat to safety. 'Rescue my *Aadu* before me. I will stay here with my goat and will not go until you first help her…' True to her word, she did not budge until her goat—her Aadu—was first rescued and put on the boat by the NDRF rescue team.

Communities in Assam that live on small islands and along the Brahmaputra River build the crafts made with traditional knowledge by fishermen for instance-like rafts of bamboos before the rains set in. These country rafts are constructed from locally available materials like empty drums and bamboo tree trunks tied with rope. They are used as a means of evacuation for the family and the small domestic animals before the mighty river is in a spate and inundates their homes and fields. In one village, the community builds an enclosure of bamboo on the

Figure 6.5 'Rescue my *Aadu* before you rescue me...'

highest ground in the area. This is used as a safe animal shelter, and all animals of the region are herded into the enclosure before and for the duration of the floods.

In areas prone to tropical storms, thunderstorms, and lightning, a lightning conductor built outside the house, especially if it is a tall building with spires, helps to conduct and earth the electric charge, thereby reducing risk. It is wise to unplug all electronic equipment well before the storm arrives as a means of protection against a lightning strike. Television sets, computers and air conditioners should be turned off.

Rubber-soled shoes and rubber tires do not protect from lightning. It is only a myth that they do. During a thunderstorm, there should be no contact with electrical equipment or cables. Sitting on wooden chairs and beds is less risky than sitting on a concrete floor or leaning against concrete walls.

Preventive measures, including a flood rescue and evacuation plan are put in place by the local authorities each year by the beginning of May. The flood-cum-cyclone shelters are duly identified and notified. The authorities in a flood-prone area also start to stock essential commodities including medical stores and potable water by the end of May.

If a person stays in or is visiting a flood-prone area, they should be proactive and should try to ascertain whether the flood evacuation and rescue plan is in place and available with the *Sarpanch*, the village headman, the *Patwari*, who is the block development officer, *Tehsildar*, the sub-divisional magistrate, the Collector or Deputy Commissioner, revenue officers, and municipal officers.

The rescue and evacuation plan should be checked, and the cyclone-cum-flood shelter that is closest to the house, hotel, office, school or college should be visited before the floods are expected to occur. While tracing the evacuation route to the flood shelter notified by the authorities, one should calculate the amount of time it takes to reach the shelter on foot after

Figure 6.6 High grounds serve as good temporary shelters till rescue arrives

factoring in the speeds of the elderly, the differently-abled, and the young children in the family.

In case the plan is not in place in a flood-prone area, concerned citizens can inform to the local authorities. In the meantime, it is prudent to not remain vulnerable during monsoons and to ensure that personal and family's safety is not compromised. It is wise to identify well in advance a temporary safe family shelter at a high place.

One can check with neighbours and the local community as to which of the high grounds that are closest to the house, office, school, college or the hotel, that was not affected by floods and was used as a shelter in the past. Locate a similar place on a high ground that could be used as a temporarily-safe family shelter.

High ground is an excellent temporary shelter in the event of a flood. It is best to go to the roof or the upper floors of the house, or an elevated ground like a hillock near the house and wait for help. Rescue teams have even found people precariously perched on treetops or clinging to tree branches that they had managed to climb to save themselves from the floodwater.

A situation of heavy or prolonged rainfall is usually observed along with hydro-meteorological reports and warnings. It is essential to be vigilant of reports in the local media and to listen to the radio as well as announcements made by local authorities by the beat of drum or over a megaphone. Once an early warning is given, it must be heeded, and all instructions must be followed meticulously.

WHAT TO DO DURING THE FLOOD

A constant watch must be kept on the floodwater levels. It is imperative to evacuate as soon as the authorities announce that the area must be immediately evacuated.

After the initial warning of the likelihood of floods and before the evacuation, if time permits, one should try to secure the house, office, and other property against potential damage by the anticipated floods. The outdoor furniture needs to be brought indoors along with any other loose articles. All essential items should be moved to a higher location or the upper floor. Utilities like cooking gas and electricity must be turned off at the main switches or valves, and all electrical appliances should be disconnected.

Before water enters the home, office, school, or any other building, it is essential to shut all windows and secure the doors. If possible, all the windows and doors could be boarded. It is imperative not to touch electrical equipment or the main switch if one is wet or standing in the water.

The family emergency kit—the prepacked package of essential items and stores that were identified by the family and kept packed in waterproof materiel—should be taken along and kept safe and dry.

In case there is no time to get to the pre-identified shelter, it is better to proceed to the nearest highest place. If there is no time to evacuate with the family, it is best to go to the upper floors of the building, to the highest level possible or the roof. The staircase should be used to climb up instead of the elevator.

Evacuation should be carried out as soon as an announcement is made by the local authorities. Any delay in the evacuation process puts the affected person, family, and community at risk.

Figure 6.7 Delayed evacuation during the floods is beset with risk

The evacuation route, as planned earlier, should be followed without panic. It is crucial to assist the elderly and the young first and to remain at a safe distance from riverbanks in a flooded area.

When boats are used for evacuation, it is best to wait for the next rescue boat rather than overloading it and putting everyone on board at risk and endangering lives. The elderly, the sick, and the children should be the first ones to be rescued. The rest should wait for their turn to be rescued by the next boat or the second round of the same boat. Fisherfolk often help in the rescue operations with their country boats and sometimes ply without life jackets and hence it is imperative to not overload these country boats.

Without sufficient information about the depth and current, it is better not to use vehicles on flooded roads. Often the floodwaters can quickly sweep the vehicle away along with its occupants.If trapped inside a vehicle on a flooded road, it is best to exit the vehicle and take shelter on a raised ground and wait for the rescue teams.

WHAT TO DO AFTER THE FLOOD

After the floodwaters recede, the affected can return to their houses when the local administration declares that it is safe to do so. Able members of the family should make a reconnaissance visit before the family decides to return to their village or home. Children should not be permitted to enter the house until the house has been checked and found safe. Until the flood-affected house is completely dry, electrical connections should not be switched on.

Walking through the debris left behind by the floods is beset with dangers of being bitten by poisonous insects or snakes which may have taken shelter in the debris. There is also the imminent danger of being cut and injured by sharp-edged pieces of glass and metallic wires. The latter is accompanied by the potential danger of being infected with tetanus.

Lime and bleaching powder should be used to disinfect the areas in and around the house. It is also vital to ensure that dead animals or birds in the vicinity are appropriately buried to avoid the spread of an epidemic.

Cremating and burying the dead is an issue. During the 2018 Kerala floods, a village in Ernakulum district could not give the dead a decent burial for several days until the floodwaters receded, which besides being traumatic for the community posed a significant health hazard.

Floods tend to bring the human population in greater proximity with scorpions, poisonous insects, and snakes, as the floodwater disrupts their natural habitat. It is important to be alert and vigilant in this regard. It is also essential to stay away from stagnant water, as it is a breeding ground for mosquitoes.

Mosquito repellants and nets must be used while sleeping, during and for several months after the floods.

Until potable water is available or supplied by the rescue and relief teams, it is best to drink rainwater after boiling it for a minute. After a flood, until it is declared to be safe after assessment by the public health authorities, water from wells or ponds should not be drunk. Food contaminated by floodwater must not be consumed. It is prudent to avoid eating raw, uncooked food. Hot and cooked meals are the safest.

The whole family should be inoculated against post-flood infectious diseases by the medical team in the flood shelters. Residents who live in safer homes or are visiting the area and staying in hotels built at an elevation and were not required to be evacuated to a flood shelter should ensure that they are inoculated to avoid the risk of post-flood infections.

After the initial shock, children recover early and may want to swim or play in the floodwater. They should be discouraged from entering the floodwaters or from swimming in them to prevent infections and snake bites.

The ennui and despondency linked to the vulnerability associated with the loss of a dear one or the loss of one's livelihood and property in the flash of a moment must be addressed. The psychosocial trauma associated with a flood situation when the community has to leave their homes and live in a temporary flood shelter should not be underestimated.

SEVEN

Hydro-meteorological Hazards II: Cyclones

A cyclone is a natural hydro-meteorological phenomenon, which is comprised of a large-scale air mass that rotates around a strong centre of low atmospheric pressure. Cyclones are devastating hazards that occur in the earth's atmosphere and are characterised by inward spiralling winds. Globally, there are different types of cyclones depending on their location, the cyclogenesis, and the storm system. A cyclone may be a tropical cyclone, typhoon or hurricane, an extratropical cyclone, a subtropical cyclone, a mesocyclone, a polar vortex or a polar low depending on where it occurs in the earth's atmosphere. Astronomers have also observed cyclones on planets like Mars and Neptune.

TYPES AND CYCLOGENESIS

Tropical Cyclones, Typhoons or Hurricanes

These are rapidly rotating storm systems which are characterised by a low-pressure centre or zone—the eye—encircled by strong winds and a spiral arrangement of thunderstorms that produce heavy rain. Depending on its location and strength, a tropical cyclone is known by different names in different parts of the

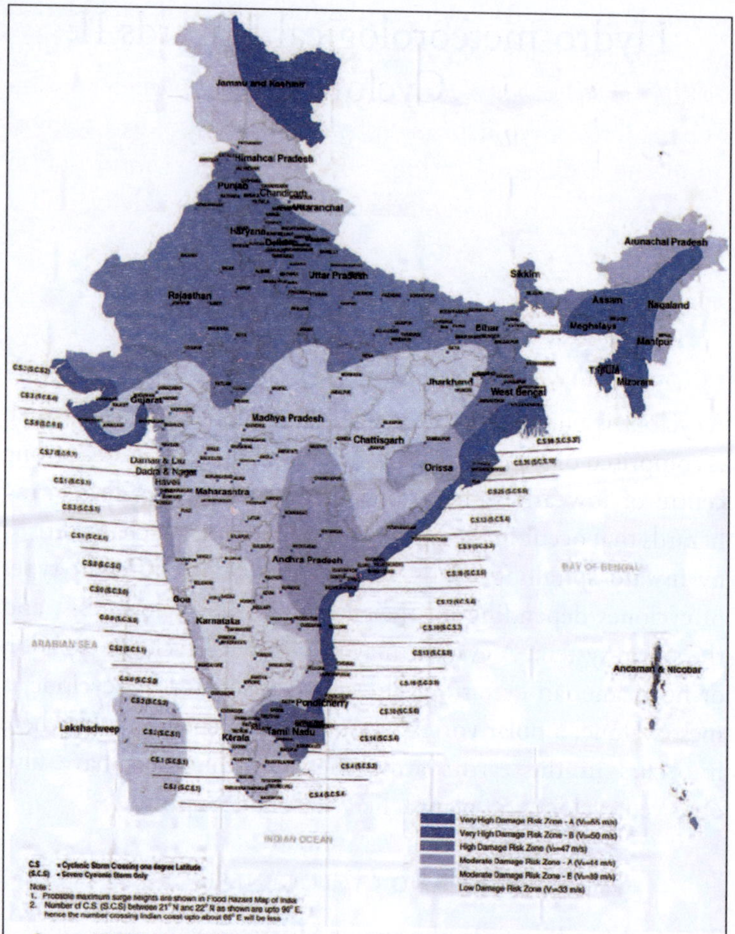

Source: BMTPC Vulnerability Atlas

Figure 7.1 Cyclone risk zones of India

world. It is referred to as a 'hurricane' when it occurs in the Atlantic Ocean and the northeastern Pacific Ocean. In the northwestern Pacific Ocean, it is called a 'typhoon'. Comparable storms in the South Pacific or the Indian Ocean, are referred to as tropical cyclones or severe cyclonic storms. In the Indian Ocean and the Bay of Bengal, a low-pressure tropical depression worsens into a deep depression before it evolves into a tropical storm and a full-scale cyclone. Tropical cyclones form due to latent heat driven by significant thunderstorm activity, and a warm core.

Extratropical cyclones

These cyclones are low-pressure areas, which along with the anticyclones of high-pressure areas drive the weather over a greater part of the Earth. Extratropical cyclones are also known as mid-latitude cyclones, as they are large-scale or synoptic low-pressure weather systems that occur in the middle latitudes of the Earth. They begin as waves in large regions in mid-latitude temperature contrasts called baroclinic zones. The baroclinic zones contract and form weather fronts as the cyclonic circulation intensifies. Later in their life cycle, extratropical cyclones occlude as cold air masses and undercut the warmer air to become cold core systems. Extratropical cyclones are capable of producing strong and heavy gales, thunderstorms, blizzards, and tornadoes.

Subtropical Cyclones

These are weather systems that occur between the equator and the 50th parallel. They share characteristics of tropical and extratropical cyclones and hence were earlier known as quasi-tropical and semi-tropical cyclone hybrids. Subtropical cyclones have broad wind patterns with sustained winds located farther from the centre than typical tropical cyclones. They form from extratropical cyclones and have colder temperatures.

The temperature of the sea surface should be around 23°C–3 degrees lower than tropical cyclones—for a subtropical cyclone to form. Subtropical storms rarely have hurricane-force winds, but they may become tropical as their cores get warm. The National Hurricane Center of the United States of America officially recognised subtropical cyclones as a different category of cyclones in 1972.

Mesocyclones

Mesocyclones are vortices of air within a convective storm. The air rises and rotates around a vertical axis, usually in the same direction as the low-pressure systems. They are most often cyclonic and associated with a localised low-pressure region within a severe thunderstorm. The Doppler radar is used to identify mesocyclones. Thunderstorms containing persistent mesocyclones are supercell thunderstorms. Mesocyclones are localised within a strong thunderstorm with a diameter ranging from 2–10 km. Mesocyclones often occur together with updrafts in supercells, within which tornadoes may form at the interchange with downdrafts.

Polar Vortices or Polar Lows

These are small-scale, short-lived atmospheric low-pressure depressions found over the ocean areas of the polar region in both Northern and Southern Hemispheres. Polar lows were first identified in the 1960s on the meteorological satellite imagery as many small-scale cloud vortices at high latitudes. Polar lows dissipate rapidly when they make landfall. The most active polar lows are found over the Norwegian Sea, the Labrador Sea, Gulf of Alaska, and other ice-free maritime areas in the Arctic during winter. Antarctic systems tend to be weaker than their northern counterparts.

INCIDENCE: INDIA

India has a long coastline of about 7516.6 km along the Arabian Sea, the Indian Ocean and the Bay of Bengal. About two-thirds of the Indian coastline, 5,700 km is prone to cyclones. On an average five or six tropical cyclones form in the Bay of Bengal and the Arabian Sea and hit the coast every year. Of these, two or three are severe. The impact of the super cyclone of Odisha in 1999 has been the most tragic in recent times. It left behind a death toll of almost 10,000.

The number of cyclonic disturbances per year from 1984–1987 range from 7 to 23. Cyclonic storms with wind speeds between 65–117 Kmph and severe cyclonic storms with wind speeds between 119–164 Kmph hit the coasts of Tamil Nadu, Odisha, and Andhra Pradesh during the northeast monsoon season. The coastline along the Bay of Bengal is impacted by the

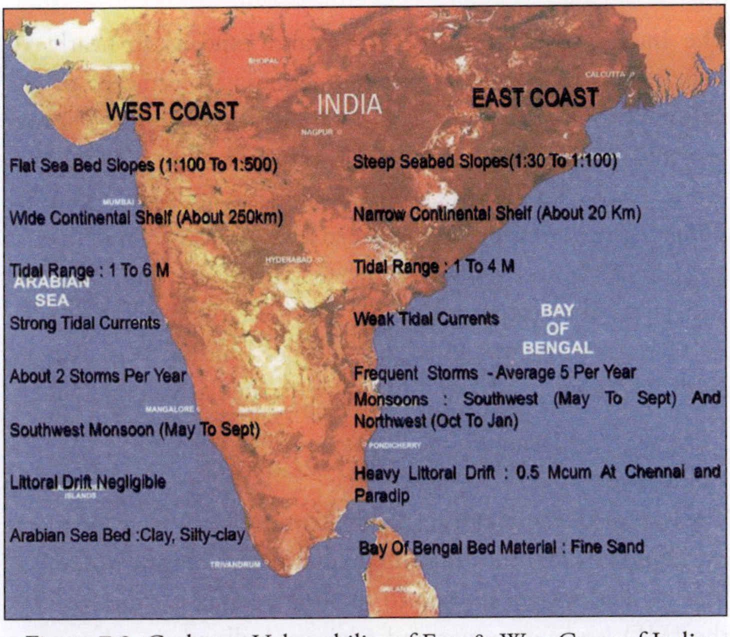

Figure 7.2 Cyclones: Vulnerability of East & West Coast of India

southwest (May to September) and the northeast (October to January) monsoons.

The incidence of cyclones is widespread in the Bay of Bengal, followed by those in the Arabian Sea. The ratio between the two is approximately 4:1. The nature of the coast and the sea bed is different along these two coasts. The Arabian Sea has a flat sea bed with a wide continental shelf, and the seabed is mainly comprised of clay and silty clay. In the Bay of Bengal, the seabed has steep slopes and a narrow continental shelf, which is comprised mainly of sand. The Arabian Sea has stronger tidal currents but has fewer storms per annum as compared to the Bay of Bengal. In terms of frequency, the incidence of severe cyclonic storms is very high in Odisha, Andhra Pradesh, Tamil Nadu and West Bengal during the Southwest monsoons.

VULNERABILITY

The Indian coastline is vulnerable and exposed to nearly 10 per cent of the world's tropical cyclones. 70 per cent of the cyclone-prone area of the country lies in 10 states and union territory, namely Gujarat, Maharashtra, Goa, Karnataka, Kerala, Tamil Nadu, Puducherry, Andhra Pradesh, Odisha, and West Bengal. The islands of Lakshadweep and Andaman and Nicobar are vulnerable too. Most cyclones occur during the monsoons and affect the regions along the coast of the Bay of Bengal. The coastal communities in the states of Odisha, West Bengal, Andhra Pradesh, and Tamil Nadu are particularly vulnerable.

FORECAST AND WARNING

The Indian Meteorological Department, IMD, in New Delhi has the mandate of monitoring and predicting cyclonic disturbances. The predictions are specific to the hour. Based on the forecast, the IMD issues warnings and advisory bulletins in advance to all stakeholders through state agencies. The IMD also functions as the Tropical Cyclone Advisory Centre for International Civil Aviation. The Indian Meteorological Department has prepared a roadmap for cyclogenesis and further intensification, monitoring, and prediction of cyclones. Warnings concerning cyclones are issued to state governments in four stages: the 'Pre-Cyclone Watch', which is issued 72 hours in advance, the 'Cyclone Alert' that is issued at least 48 hours in advance, the 'Cyclone Warning' that is issued at least 24 hours in advance,

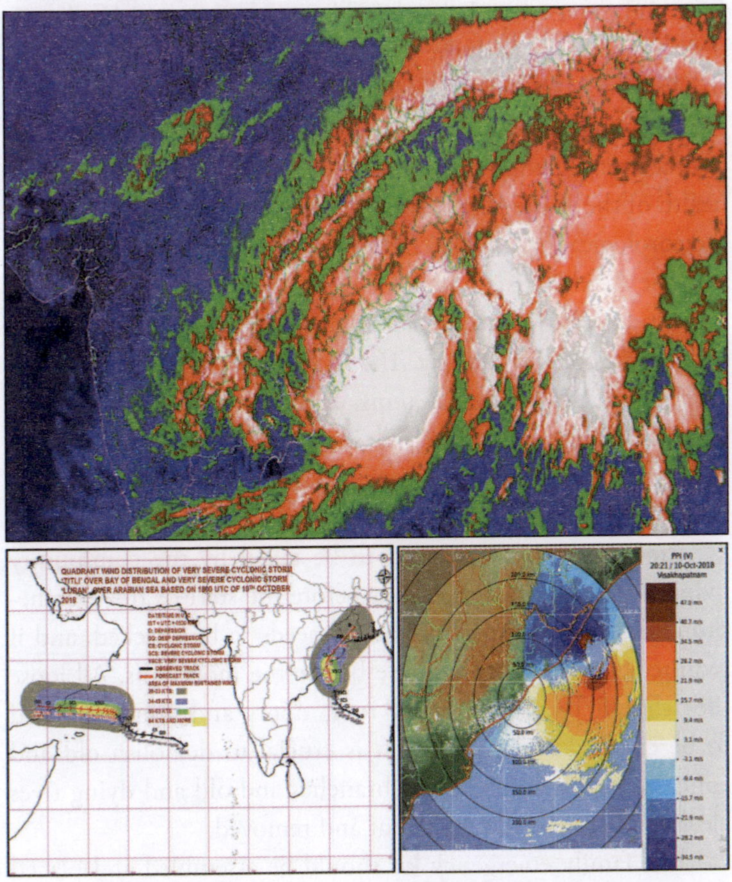

[Nil – 0 per cent, Low – Up to 25 per cent, Fair – 26–50 per cent, Moderate – 51–75 per cent, High – 76–100 per cent]

Figure 7.3 Probability of cyclogenesis

and a 'Post Landfall Outlook', which is issued at least 12 hours in advance of the expected time of landfall.

PREPAREDNESS: WHAT TO DO BEFORE THE CYCLONE

A tourist or a casual visitor to a cyclone-prone coastal area, especially along the Bay of Bengal, should avoid going during the period when cyclones are anticipated. Tropical cyclones usually occur during the southwest Monsoon season between June and September. It is advisable to schedule a visit when it does not coincide with the monsoon season.

Financial prudence requires that residents in a cyclone-prone area should get the insurance that covers risk and insures their assets, valuables and property against cyclones. The life and health of the entire family should also be insured against hydro-meteorological hazards, including cyclones.

The NDMA is implementing a Cyclone Risk Mitigation Project (NCRMP) to enhance preparedness in 10 cyclone-prone states of the country. The Project will help in improving forecasting and warning systems, enhance the coping capacities of stakeholders, and also aid in large-scale construction of multipurpose cyclone shelters and embankments along the cyclone-prone coastline.

Preventive measures need to be taken by the community living along the coast each year before the start of the cyclone-prone monsoon season. The house needs to be checked, and if required, repairs must be done before the monsoons. All loose tiles should be secured, and roof, doors and windows need to be checked and repaired. It is crucial to demolish old and condemned structures. Dead branches and old and dying trees close to the house should be cut and removed.

The family emergency kit should be assembled and placed in a waterproof package based on the list of essentials prepared after a family discussion. The stock that is packed should be sufficient to last the family for a few days. It should include medicines, special food for babies, children, and elders. A few dry ready-to-eat non-perishable food items like biscuits should also be included for use in an emergency. The family emergency kit should be kept ready in a safe, dry place along with spare keys to the house. Battery-operated torches and sufficient dry batteries for torches and transistors should also form an intrinsic part of the kit.

When residing or visiting a coastal area, which is cyclone-prone, it is wise to continually monitor the pre-cyclone warnings and listen to the radio as cyclone related warnings, and weather updates are broadcast over All India Radio channel.

As part of one's civic duty, it is essential to share authentic information regarding the Pre-Cyclone Watch, Cyclone Alert and the Cyclone Warning issued 72 hours, 48 hours and 24 hours before the cyclone respectively. Rumours must be checked, and only information from official sources should be passed on to as many people as possible. The spread of rumours can cause a situation of panic.

Once the warning for Pre-Cyclone Watch is issued, there are 72 hours available for taking preventive measures before the cyclone makes landfall. The garden furniture and other objects kept outdoors should be brought indoors. Potential threats to safety, which can be swept away by strong cyclonic winds, should be anchored and secured. Loose objects that can cause injuries, like lumber piles, tin sheets, loose bricks, garbage cans, and sign-boards should be anchored or moved into the house, office, or other establishments. During the Pre-Cyclone Watch period, it is prudent to shift all valuable objects and articles including furniture, paintings, carpets and electronics to upper floors of the house to minimise damage caused by floods that may follow the tropical cyclone.

In case the property a family resides in is securely built in an elevated area, they can take shelter in the safer parts of the house. As soon as the Cyclone Alert is issued two days before the cyclone is expected to arrive, sufficient food, medicines, and potable water that could last a few days should be stocked in the safer portions of the house. There should be sufficient torches and extra dry batteries in the house. Provisions for children and adults that require a special diet should be made.

A Cyclone Alert means that the danger is expected sometime within the next 48 hours. During this time, it is crucial to secure the house, board up all the glass windows and doors or put storm shutters in place, anchor any loose furniture and objects, and keep essential articles like the family emergency kit ready. If there are no wooden boards, pasting paper strips on the glass will do well to prevent splinters. However, paper strips may not be as effective as wooden boards. It is essential to switch off the electric mains and to shut off the cooking gas valves.

After the Cyclone Warning is issued one day before the calamitous event, it is vital to do a headcount and keep track of the whereabouts of all the members of the family. It is imperative to ensure that everyone stays away from beaches. The Fishermen need to avoid going into the sea to fish.

The affected community must prepare to evacuate if asked by the authorities. It is essential to leave early for the cyclone shelter. Any delay in the evacuation process can be life-threatening.

Figure 7.4 Evacuation: A step towards safety

WHAT TO DO DURING THE CYCLONE

The eye of the cyclone is a relatively calm area. If the centre of the cyclone is directly overhead, it imbues a false sense of safety. It is important not to become unduly lax and to remember that once the eye shifts, which it will momentarily, the calm will be followed by storms and winds of exceptionally high speed.

A family or community that does not follow the evacuation plan meticulously or delays their departure runs the risk of being marooned and adversely affected by the cyclone. Even when one's house or the hotel seems secure, it is imperative to evacuate if asked by the authorities. It is essential to remain calm and to evacuate calmly as soon as asked to do so by the authorities. The predetermined route should be taken to reach the closest shelters or evacuation points as indicated by the local authorities.

It is essential to be careful around trees and electric poles, which often get uprooted due to the strong winds associated with a tropical cyclonic storm. Signboards and tin roofs can fly off and cause accidents. Houses and other fragile built-up structures like *kutcha* houses and structures with weak foundations tend to collapse in the event of a severe cyclone.

At the shelter, each person should follow instructions of the person in charge and be willing to share and help others. Until the authorities declare that it is safe to leave, it is essential to remain in the shelter and not try to go back home, or to the hotel.

POST-CYCLONE: WHAT TO DO

After the cyclone blows over, it is better to avoid driving a vehicle. However, if it is imperative to drive, then it is vital to stay at a distance from loose, dangling wires and from lamp posts to avoid getting an electric shock.

Even after local authorities declare that it is safe to leave the shelter and return home, it is essential to conduct a thorough

Figure 7.5 Cyclones: be careful near trees and electric poles

inspection of the house first. Children and the elderly should only be allowed to enter the house after damage caused by the cyclone has been repaired. Loose bricks and boards can be a potential source of severe accidents.

The debris in and around the house should be cleared. It is also essential to be vigilant about glass fragments, sharp objects, snakes, scorpions, and poisonous insects post-cyclone.

It is essential to wait for the roof and the walls to dry completely before electrical fixtures and connections can be checked. Loose wires need to be taken care of quickly. To avoid falling sick and to reduce exposure to any post-disaster epidemic, immediate inoculation against diseases is imperative. It will provide immunity against air and water-borne diseases, and from an outbreak of any post-cyclone epidemic.

The post-cyclonic psychosocial needs, especially of children and adolescents, must be addressed. The trauma of being vulnerable to a severe cyclone, of having to leave one's home and live in a shelter is enormous and should not be ignored or swept under the rug.

A judicious assessment of losses attributable to the disaster should be made, and an insurance claim must be filed at the earliest. The loss suffered can also be reported to the appropriate authorities to seek compensation if any is available. Most state governments provide due compensation for losses.

Both cities and towns are vulnerable to landslides

EIGHT

Landslides and Avalanches

Landslides are downward and out of place movements of a body of rock, earth, debris, and other slope forming materials under their weight. A landslide or landslip is a geological phenomenon which includes a wide range of ground movements such as rock falls, failure of slopes, and shallow debris flows. Landslides often cause trees, built-up structures, and roads to collapse and rifts to occur on roads. Gravity is the primary driving force for landslides to occur. Pre-conditional factors adversely affect slope stability and build up a sub-surface condition that makes the slope prone to failure. Landslides can be triggered by various factors like heavy rainfall, earthquakes, floods, and sometimes volcanic activity.

An avalanche or snow slide is a specific type of snow and snowpack that slides along a slope. Avalanches are not rare or random events. They are endemic to a mountain range which accumulates a standing snowpack. Although an avalanche typically occurs during winter or spring, glacier movements may also cause ice and snow avalanches at any time of year in the upper reaches of a mountain.

AVALANCHE

In mountainous terrain, avalanches are the most severe natural hazards to life and property. When snow or a snowpack slides along a steep mountainside, it is called an avalanche. Avalanche formation requires a specific gradient of the slope of a mountain. The slope should be shallow enough to allow the snow to accumulate and at the same time steep enough for the snow to accelerate once it is set in motion by the combination of gravity and mechanical failure of the snowpack. The slope angle or the angle of repose that can allow moving snow to accelerate depends on a variety of factors. These factors include the configuration of the layers of snow and inter-layer interfaces as well as the sheer strength of the snow, which in turn depends upon its crystal form and moisture content. Some forms of drier and colder snow stick to shallower slopes, while wet and warmer snow can bond to very steep surfaces. In coastal mountains like the Cordillera del Paine region of Patagonia, deep snowpacks collect on vertical and even overhanging rock faces.

Avalanches can be spontaneous if caused due to gravitational force. Most avalanches occur spontaneously during storms under increased load due to snowfall. They can also be triggered by other conditions such as seismic activity or human activities. Once initiated or triggered, an avalanche accelerates rapidly and grows in mass and volume, collecting more snow on its way down the slope.

Most natural avalanches are caused by metamorphic changes in the snowpack, like melting due to solar radiation. Other natural causes of avalanches include rain, earthquakes, rockfall, and icefall. Artificial triggers of avalanches can be skiers, snowmobiles, and controlled explosive work. Contrary to popular belief, avalanches do not get triggered by a loud sound. The pressure from any sound is too small to trigger an avalanche.

Avalanches are triggered when a cohesive slab of snow lying upon a weaker layer of snow gets fractured and slides down a steep slope. An avalanche is typically a slab avalanche, but it can also be a loose snow avalanche. A slab avalanche gets triggered by a mechanical failure in the snowpack. Sometimes a loose snow avalanche is also triggered when the avalanche is made up of loose snow with air pockets that give it a misty appearance. It is as dangerous as a slab avalanche as it accelerates rapidly after its initiation. Avalanches are primarily composed of flowing snow and air. However, more massive avalanches entrain ice, rocks, trees, and other material. If an avalanche is very rapid, some snow may mix with the air and form a powder snow avalanche.

LANDSLIDE: NATURE AND TYPES

Landslides may be active, suspended, inactive, stabilised or relict depending upon their state of activity. Active landslides continue to move in the range of 1–4 cm a day. Suspended landslides are those that occurred last year but are not moving anymore, while inactive landslides are those that occurred more than a year ago. Inactive landslides may be 'dormant' if the cause of the movement remains, or it could be 'abandoned', where the cause of movement no longer exists. Dormant landslides are likely to move and are potential hazards. A typical instance of an active landslide becoming an abandoned one is when a river which previously eroded the toe of the slope changes its course. Relict landslides are those that were once dormant but have now redeveloped under changing geological or climatic conditions.

A landslide is categorised either as a landfall, a rotational slide, a topple, a lateral spread, a land flow, a land creep or a complex landslide based on the nature of the movement of the slide or fall. A landfall has a rapid slope movement. Rolling landfalls on a 76 degree or steeper slope are perilous. Depending on whether the type of material affected in the landslide is fine soil, coarse soil or bedrock, landslides are further sub-categorised. Landfall may be an earthfall, debris or a rockfall. Falls, slides, topples, and lateral spreads can occur in all types of material. Flow can only occur in a slope made up of debris and rock. Debris and rock flows comprise of the movement of a viscous fluid consisting of soil and rock particles suspended in the water down a slope. Creep can occur only in fine or coarse soil. Complex falls are a combination of two or more types of movements, which can be a fall, slide, topple, lateral spread, flow or creep.

LANDSLIDES: CAUSES

A landslide occurs when the force of gravity exceeds the resistance due to the sheer strength of the material, making up a slope, its cohesion, and internal friction. This leads to instability and loosening of materials, thus triggering a landslide. Gravity is the primary driving force for a landslide to occur as the gravitational force drives materials that make up a slope—rocks, earth, and debris. Steep and mountainous slopes of more than 30-degree gradient are generally prone to landslides. The gradient of a slope is a measure of the steepness and direction of a slope. The gradient is the ratio of the vertical distance of a slope over its horizontal distance. Depending on its gradient, a slope is termed as 'steep' if it has a gradient of 60 degrees or more, 'mountainous' if it has a gradient of 25–60 degrees, a 'rolling slope' if it is a 10–25 degree gradient or a 'plain slope' with up to 10-degree gradient. Indiscriminate construction of built-up structures, especially on steep hillsides, puts excessive pressure on soil beyond its load-bearing capacity. The strength of the soil also decreases over time due to fatigue and can lead to landslides.

Pre-conditional factors adversely affect slope stability and build up a sub-surface condition that makes the slope prone to failure. Landslides are also triggered by various factors

Figure 8.1 *Podu* cultivation

Figure 8.2 Coal mining

Figure 8.3 Dynamite blast

Landslides Triggered by Human Intervention

like earthquakes and floods. Intense rainfall in the form of a cloudburst or an incessant monsoon and volcanic activity are also some of the natural factors that can trigger a landslide. Landslides can also occur due to the human intervention, which can weaken a slope and make it more susceptible to a land, rock or debris slide.

Man-made factors that can trigger a landslide include the construction of large dams, coal mining, and blasting of rocks with dynamite for road construction. Unregulated construction of buildings on steep slopes that are prone to landslide, deforestation, and other native slash and burn cultivation practices, like *Jhoom* and *Podu* cultivation that speed up soil erosion, can also trigger a landslide.

LANDSLIDES: EFFECTS

Landslides are natural hazards that cause immense damage to life and property in the affected regions. No one can outrun an approaching landslide or mudflow. They are fast and devastating and can wipe out trees and rocks in their way. They also disrupt life along the entire region beyond the landslide site, affecting communication as they damage infrastructures like roads, water pipes, power lines, and telephone lines. The spillover effects of landslides due to road blockades subsequently lead to short supply of essential goods as well as the loss of productivity of agriculture and forest.

Landslides can cause seismic disturbances and can also result from seismic disturbances. Earthquake-induced slides have often caused loss of life. Landslides can cause disastrous flooding, particularly when dams built across streams are breached. On the other hand, flooding may also trigger landslides. The adverse economic effects of landslides include the cost of repairing structures, loss of property value, disruption of transportation routes, medical costs in the event of injury, and indirect costs such as lost timber and fish stock. Water availability, quantity, and quality are also affected by landslides.

In India, landslides are more pronounced during the monsoons and cause enormous losses. They also adversely affect the socio-economic fabric of the country and the environment. On an average, more than 500 human lives are lost in the country every year due to landslides.

INCIDENT: INDIA

Landslides affect at least 15 per cent of the land area in India—about 0.49 million km. Landslides of different types are frequent

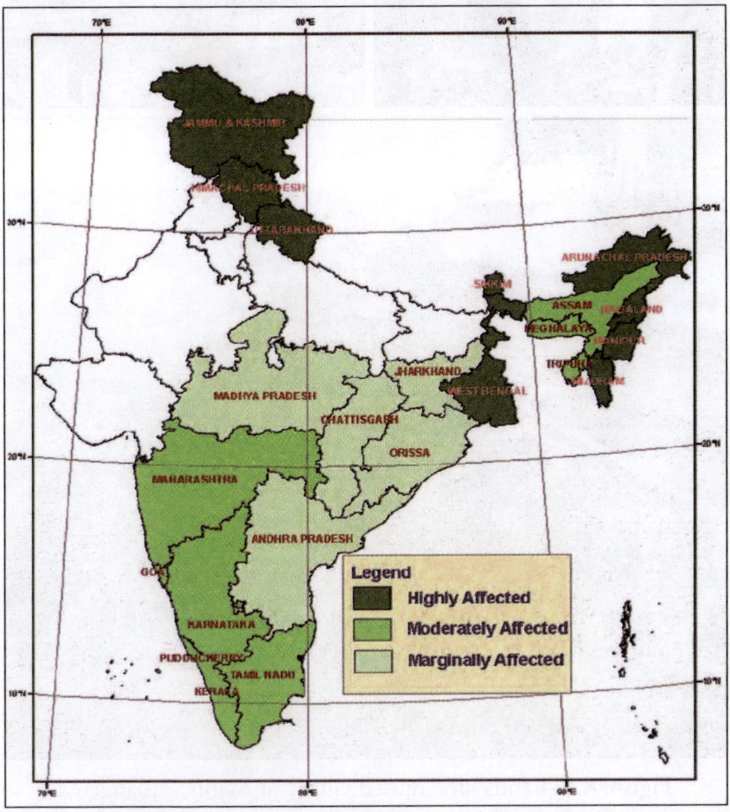

Figure 8.4 India: landslide hazard zonation map

in the geo-dynamic regions of the Himalayas and along the Arakan-Yoma belt in the Northeast. Even the relatively stable hilly regions of India like the Meghalaya Plateau, Western Ghats and Nilgiri Hills are landslide-prone. Landslides affect 22 states of the country and parts of the union territories of Puducherry and Andaman & Nicobar Islands.

Figure 8.5 Landslides: buried village of Malin, endangered Darjeeling Heritage Rail, plummeting buildings

Over the years, India has had a record of devastating landslides precipitated by various factors. Major landslides occur in the Himalayas due to their geomorphological features triggered by heavy rain in the monsoons, flash floods, and seismic activity. The Darjeeling floods of 1968 destroyed vast areas of Sikkim and West Bengal unleashing a spate of landslides causing immense loss of life and property. In 2005, a landslide triggered by a cloudburst killed 52 people in Bhavi village of Himachal Pradesh. Landslides along National Highways, NH-1A and NH-1B in Jammu and Kashmir, the Rishikesh-Badrinath pilgrimage route in Uttarakhand, highways and roads in Darjeeling and Sikkim, and the Dimapur-Imphal and Shillong-Silchar National Highways are prominent and recurrent.

Several tragic landslides have occurred over the years in the Himalayan state of Uttarakhand due to the natural topography and man-made factors. The Malpa, rock avalanche tragedy, killed 220 and wiped out the entire village of Malpa on the right bank of Kali River in 1998. The Varunavat landslide of 2013 lasted for fifteen days and endangered the entire town of Uttarkashi. The Goregaon landslide which killed 136 and washed away the entire village of Malin, and the Konkan landslide of 2005, which killed 190 people in Maharashtra, are instances of major landslides in the Western Ghats.

Landslides also occurred in the Nilgiri hills in 1978 with a loss of 23 human lives and in Amboori, Kerala in 2001, killing 90 people. Entire hillsides and thousands of acres of tea plantations were lost during the 2018 monsoon landslides in Kodagu district in Karnataka.

PREPAREDNESS: LANDSLIDE RISK MITIGATION

Landslides can be averted by undertaking remedial and risk mitigation measures. Regulatory mechanisms and codes for mining, excavation, and construction activities in a landslide-prone area go a long way in mitigating risk. Illegal mining, excavation, and haphazard construction in slide-prone areas can destabilise slopes and enhance the vulnerability of the community as well as the environment. Mitigating landslide risk can be done through the treatment of vulnerable slide-prone slopes and restricting development in such areas.

Prevention of soil erosion with bioengineering is an efficient and cost-effective risk mitigation technique. Enhancing vegetation cover through seeding and sodding grasses and legumes reduces surface erosion. Seeding techniques like dry seeding done with the help of rotary disks and air-blown seeders, which shoot seeds and fertilisers into the ground, or hydraulic-seeding, which involves the application of seeds in a water slurry that contains fertilisers, soil binders and mulch can also help reduce landslide risk. Vetiver is the most promising grass for stabilising slopes against erosion. Sodding or the direct application of mature grass with developed roots onto the slope surface is a quicker method of biotic risk mitigation.

Slope stabilisation, is an important risk mitigation measure, which involves landslide control and restraint works, slope protection works and mass improvement techniques. A landslide-prone slope is considered stable when the toe of the slope is protected against erosion. Slope stabilisation can be done through several methods including prevention of soil erosion through various methods including bioengineering, construction of embankments and retaining walls, and through special techniques like rock-bolting and scaling.

Scaling is a means to stabilise slopes by removing unstable and loose rocks. Benching of a slope stabilises it by reducing its height. Benching is a process of excavating horizontal slopes by reducing the gradient of the slope—much like terraced agricultural fields to protect steep slope failures. Benching of slopes has been carried out effectively for steep slope stabilisation in Sikkim.

Construction of embankments on high gradient slopes, building walls to divert debris flow and re-forestation and plantation of trees in landslide-prone areas are a few measures that go a long way in enhancing landslide risk mitigation.

Rock-bolting is another landslide risk mitigation method whereby jointed, or highly fissured rocks are secured by anchoring a steel bar in pre-drilled holes. Construction of a retaining wall gives support to slope material by restraining the lateral movement of the material. A retaining wall can be of various types: a gravity wall that resists lateral pressure through its weight; a counterfort retaining wall which stabilises slopes through tie backs that tie the stem and the base slab; reinforced cement concrete walls and cantilever retaining walls.

Figure 8.6 Landslide risk mitigation: Stabilizing slopes

Control and prevention of wildfires and forest fires is a critical risk mitigation measure—both to prevent loss of life and environmental degradation as well as to mitigate landslide risk. Forest fires lead to loss of soil nutrients and also reduce the cohesive forces within the soil. The latter makes it vulnerable to erosion and increases the risk of a landslide.

Monitoring and early warning systems help to mitigate risk in a landslide-prone area. The coordinated response of the disaster management authorities during landslides involves emergency search and rescue through an operational incident command system. The state maintains a community-level disaster response mechanism. Specialised paramilitary rescue teams in a state of readiness along with emergency logistics, go a long way in mitigating landslide risk.

PREPAREDNESS: WHAT TO DO BEFORE LANDSLIDES

The landslide history of an area should be studied before deciding to visit or settle in the area. Slopes prone to debris flows and landslides are likely to experience them in the future also. In case debris flows have occurred in the past in that area, it is prudent to avoid building a home or a commercial venture there. Bulging ground at the base of a slope is one of the signs of a landslide-prone slope.

Landslides can be averted by following proper land-use. Indiscriminate construction in the mountains, as in the case of Shimla and Mussoorie in the Himalayas, is asking for trouble. Construction on very steep slopes should be avoided as it increases the risk of landslides. No building should be constructed near the edge of a mountain, across natural drains, and along natural erosion valleys. Before constructing a new house, it is prudent to adopt a planned outlay involving geologists and engineers to ensure that the area is not prone to landslides.

A house in the hills should always be built along the contour lines and not perpendicular to them. Many of the houses that were destroyed in the Kodagu landslide following incessant rains in the 2018 monsoon were constructed perpendicular to the contour of the hill. Houses that were built parallel to the contour and designed at different split levels bore minimal damage.

Designing a house at split levels minimises the disturbance to the hill slope, thereby controlling erosion and earth slip. While building a house in the hills, it is wise to protect the property by planting trees and bushes on slopes, and also building engineered retaining walls.

Standard building norms need to be followed meticulously, and no chances should be taken while constructing a house in the mountains as any digression impacts safety. Filling material in the foundation should be well-compacted and supported. At least two evacuation routes are required in case one of them gets blocked by debris in the event of a landslide. A structural ring beam constructed around the top of doors, windows and walls, and connected to columns will ensure structural integrity so that the structure can act as one unit. Flexible pipe fittings should be used as they resist breakage.

In older buildings on landslide-prone slopes, it is prudent to adopt retrofitting measures. Proper risk-mitigating measures need to be taken to protect buildings from falling debris or a sliding slope. Sandbags or timber deflectors can be used to direct debris away from the house. Removable windows and door protections of plywood or steel shutters can also be installed towards this end.

A family emergency kit with food supply, sufficient water, relevant documents, medicines, and a few personalised items, identified as essential for the family, should be prepared and stored in a waterproof container. The kit should be placed in a safe and dry place along with a set of spare keys to the house and important emergency numbers. The family communication plan should be known to all the members along with the phone number and address of the friend or relative to contact in the event of the family getting separated.

Preparedness before the rainy season in a landslide-prone area involves maintenance of the built-up structure. All tension cracks in the building should be sealed. The drains must be cleaned up to ensure that there is no water clogging.

Landslide warning signs must be heeded. When a landslide is imminent, a faint rumbling sound that increases in volume is audible. Tilting of walls, telephone poles, power lines, trees or fences also indicates an impending landslide. Unusual sounds like cracking of trees or boulders knocking together indicate moving debris. Other signs of a threatening landslide include rapid water or mudflow, which did not exist before, and irregular or sudden cessation of the flow of a stream.

The tightening of electrical wires attached to poles near the edge of a hill or mountain indicates that a landslide has begun as the poles arch and shift underground. Often scars occur on the side of hills in conjunction with a landslide due to the movement of the earth or water runoff. On hill roads, it is far-sighted to be watchful and to try to note features like cracks on roads and slopes. Warning signs of a landslide include cracking sounds and falling of material, cracking or slumping of embankments, walls, retaining structures, concrete floors or movement of soil away from the foundation of a building. Broken or fractured water pipes and underground facilities also indicate that the slope is unstable. In case signs of the imminent danger of a landslide are noticed, it is a person's civic duty to dial the police control room number, 100 or even 121 if in India, to inform the authorities and also to inform neighbours and other people about the potential threat.

When one resides in a landslide-prone area, it is advisable to ensure financial security. Insurance coverage should be bought for one's life and property. It is also vital to obtain a cover for medical and accidents for the entire family, school, or office.

WHAT TO DO DURING A LANDSLIDE

Landslides are generally triggered during intense and short bursts of rain. More so, if the intense burst of rainfall occurs after long periods of incessant and heavy rains, during monsoons in India and damp weather. It is essential to be careful during the intense short burst of rain and a sudden cloudburst. Listening to local news stations on a battery-powered radio for warnings of heavy rainfall can provide the requisite opportunity to reduce the losses caused because of the landslide. It is necessary to stay awake during a severe storm in a landslide-prone area. Many deaths from landslides occur while people are sleeping.

During heavy rainfall, it is best to avoid going near river valleys and low-lying areas. Any sudden increase or decrease in water flow in the vicinity and a change in colour of the water from clear to muddy, especially near rivers running along the road that are susceptible to landslides is a reason to become alert. Such changes signify that there is debris flow activity upstream. In such an event, it is best to go as far as possible in a downstream direction.

While crossing a bridge, it is crucial to look upstream and not to cross it if a mudflow is visible. Move away as fast as possible if there are signs of a potential mudflow. Mudflows can move very fast—faster than most people can walk or run.

Damaged pavements and fallen stones, mud and debris indicate that a landslide is imminent. Any unusual sounds that might indicate moving debris, like trees creaking or boulders knocking together, are clear signals of a landslide.

Evacuation from the affected site is the best protection. It is vital to stay out of the path of a landslide and move in the opposite direction, protecting one's head all the time. If escape is not possible and one cannot exit a building, it is best to curl into a tight ball under a piece of sturdy furniture and protect the head during a landslide.

Usually, local authorities send expert rescuers to conduct rescue operations at the earliest. Once the rescuers arrive, it is essential to allow the experts to conduct the search and rescue and not to venture into the landslide-affected area.

WHAT TO DO AFTER A LANDSLIDE

Landslides can make a person feel particularly vulnerable. It is rather alarming to feel the ground move and give way under one's feet. All that once seemed stable and rock-solid flows down the mountain in the form of a debris flow. After a landslide, it is crucial not to panic and to calm the distressed members of the family and make them feel secure.

Rescue on an unstable slope, post-disaster, is a tricky affair requiring specific expertise. In the event of an avalanche, it is imperative that the rescuers are from the local area, as they would already be acclimatised. Flying in a rescue team from the plains does not work. At high altitudes of 2,000 meters or above or about 6,500 feet above the sea level, even expert rescuers need a few days of acclimatisation before they can operate

In case the rescue team does not arrive timely, it is a person's civic duty to try to save others after ensuring one's safety. One has to be safe first to be able to save others. It is imprudent to be reckless while helping others who may require special assistance—infants, elderly, and disabled. The debris needs to be checked for injured or trapped victims near the slide. Those who can be rescued quickly need to be evacuated from the affected area and provided with first aid in case one is trained to do so. First aid by an untrained person is likely to cause more harm than help.

Even after a landslide or avalanche seems to be over, it is crucial to continue to listen to the local radio for updates in the affected area as there is often a danger of recurrence. Besides, other potential hazards like flooding are likely to follow a landslide or debris flow, and one should be prepared for the same.

Broken utility lines and damaged roads or rail tracks because of the landslide should be immediately reported to the appropriate authorities in order to avert any subsequent calamity. The utilities need to be turned off as quickly as possible to prevent other potential hazards.

The erosion caused by loss of ground cover can lead to flash floods and additional landslides in the near future. The damaged ground should be replanted with grasses like vetiver, derived from the Tamil word used for *Chrysopogon zizanioides* of the Poaceae family, which is native to India. In other parts of the world, sorghum and related species of perennial bunchgrasses can be planted to stabilise slopes and prevent soil erosion. Quick-growing trees and bushes should be planted to stabilise the slope as soon as possible.

Landslides often recur in the same place repeatedly. Seeking advice from a geotechnical expert for evaluating landslide hazards and adopting corrective techniques will aid in mitigating future landslide risks. After a landslide, even if the house or other built-up structure appears to be undamaged, it is vital to check the building foundations and the chimney as well as the surrounding land for damage. Any damage to the foundations and chimneys should be assessed. It is also prudent to check the surrounding area for land deformations if any to ensure the safety of the area post-disaster.

After the occurrence of a landslide or an avalanche, the loss and damage to property should be documented and reported immediately for an insurance claim if it is covered and for any compensation that may be available from local authorities.

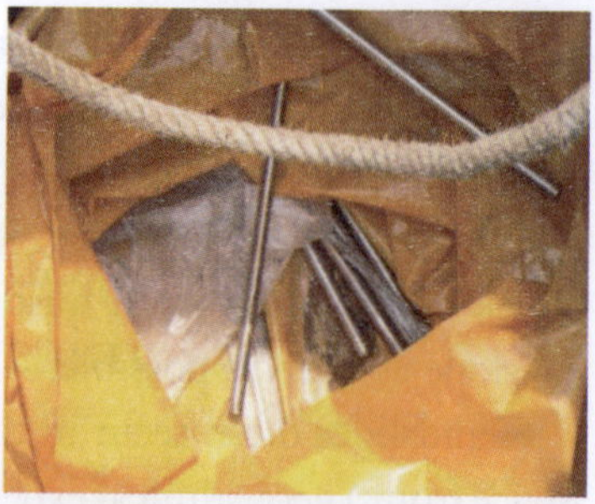

NINE

CBRN I: Nuclear, Radiological, and Chemical Disasters

Chemical, biological, nuclear, and radiation-related disasters or CBRN hazards are more recent than the other natural and man-made disasters. CBRN hazards can cause mass causalities. Although the incidence of CBRN disasters is less in terms of frequency as compared to other climatic and hydro-meteorological disasters, their impact is just as devastating. This is compounded by the fact that the subject is somewhat esoteric and there is little familiarity of it in the public domain. Lack of knowledge about CBRN hazards is often the reason behind a community's inability to take adequate precautions or to deal with a CBRN disaster. The nature of nuclear and radiation-related hazards as well as chemical hazards, their potential sources and effects are discussed here along with risk mitigation measures and preparedness to reduce risks and losses. Biological disasters and epidemics are detailed later in the next chapter, CBRN II.

NUCLEAR AND RADIOLOGICAL DISASTERS

There is natural radioactivity in the Earth and its atmosphere. Cosmic radiation and radiations emanating from bedrock are forms of natural radiation to which human beings and other living organisms on Earth are exposed continuously. Ionising radiations can result from either the natural radioactivity, i.e. decay of a radioactive element or from nuclear facilities and radiation generating machine. Over time, nuclear energy has been harnessed for generating electricity. Radioisotopes are used in various sectors, including industry, agriculture, medicine, and research. The level of exposure to radiation above the natural background radiation has increased over time but is kept within permissible regulatory limits by enforcing strict regulations. Nevertheless, the potential exposure to ionising radiation has increased, particularly in the case of professionals like physicians, nurses, medical technicians, scientists, and researchers.

A nuclear or radiological hazard is one that involves exposure of a community to ionising radiation energy resulting from either the decay of the radionuclides, products of a chain reaction, or from radionuclides produced by a nuclear reaction in radiation generators. Ionising radiation comprises of particles like alpha (α) and beta (β) and electromagnetic radiations like X-rays and gamma rays (γ) that have sufficient energy to cause ionisation as they interact with matter or human tissues. Radiation associated with nuclear and radiological events has led to a few tragic hazards. The nuclear weapons that were dropped on Hiroshima and Nagasaki in the Second World War resulted in a cataclysmic disaster leading to immense loss of life and inheritable health issues spread over subsequent generations of the affected population. Nuclear reactor accidents at the Three Mile Island in the USA and Chernobyl in the then USSR as well as in Fukushima in Japan are some of the other major nuclear and radiological emergencies of the recent past.

Ionising radiations

Ionising radiations are particles (α and β) and electromagnetic radiations (X-rays and γ) that have sufficient energy to cause ionisation of matter as they interact with it. The process of ionisation of matter, including of human tissues, on which ionising radiations impinge, involves the removal of electrons from atoms of that matter, or sometimes the addition of electrons to the atoms. The resulting atom after removal of the electron(s) or with an extra electron(s) is called a positive or a negative ion respectively. An ion is unstable, and the process of ionisation can lead to damage of cells and tissues in living organisms. Ionising radiations (α, β or γ) are also generated by decaying radioactive material. All species on the earth are continually exposed to bedrock and cosmic radiations. International Atomic Energy Agency (IAEA) and World Health Organization (WHO) and several other international bodies like the International Commission on Radiation Protection (ICRP) have defined limits of radiation dose as well as radio exposure as related to its effects, including the effect of radiation on living tissues. Based on this, the IAEA has developed codes of conduct for safety and security.

TYPES OF RADIATIONS

Ionising radiation may be of various types, including alpha and beta particles as well as X-rays and gamma rays. The latter are electromagnetic rays. Neutrons are non-ionising particles but generate radiation emitting radionuclides as a result of their interactions with the medium in which they travel or the medium on which they impinge. It is relevant to know about the types of radiations a person is exposed to both naturally from the radioactive material in the atmosphere and the bedrock as well as from devices like X-ray machines, subatomic particle accelerators and more. These are also the type of radiations that communities could get exposed to in the event of an accident in a nuclear facility or a potential radiological and nuclear emergency/ disaster, like a possible terrorist attack using a dirty bomb or in the event of radiological warfare. A pictographic representation of the different types of radiations and their penetrating powers is shown in Appendix 17.

Alpha radiations consist of positively charged particles comprising of two protons and two neutrons, which are emitted by radionuclides of heavy elements like uranium, radium, radon, and plutonium. Alpha radiations are highly ionising and can be blocked by a sheet of paper and make them unable to penetrate the skin. Alpha-emitters can be harmful to humans only if they are inhaled, swallowed or absorbed through open wounds.

Beta radiations consist of electrons, which are much smaller than alpha particles and can penetrate little deeper. They can pass through paper but can be blocked by a sheet of metal or glass. Beta radiations can penetrate bare human skin up to the germinal layer, where new skin cells are produced. If beta emitters remain on the skin for a long time, they can cause skin injuries.

It should be noted that alpha and beta radiations are not treated as external hazards because of their inability to penetrate deeper into the skin, but they are considered as internal hazard, especially if they enter into the body.

Gamma radiations comprise of electromagnetic waves. They have a high penetrating power. Dense materials such as lead and concrete are suitable barriers/shields against gamma rays.

X-ray radiations are similar to gamma radiations but are usually produced artificially by bombarding a metal target with electrons in vacuum, for instance, in an X-ray tube. They can pass through human skin, but dense materials such as bones, metals and lead can attenuate X-rays to a large extent.

Neutron radiations consist of a stream of neutrons, which are uncharged particles and are not ionising radiations by themselves. However, when a neutron hits a nucleus, it may activate it or cause the emission of a gamma ray or charged particle, indirectly giving rise to ionising radiation. Neutrons are more penetrating like gamma rays, and its intensity can be reduced only by a thick barrier like concrete, water or paraffin.

There is evidence that X-rays, gamma rays, and neutrons cannot be blocked entirely, and that their beam intensities can only be attenuated or reduced.

THE SCIENCE OF RADIATIONS AND RADIOACTIVITY

Ionising radiation comprises of electromagnetic radiations and particles that have sufficient energy to cause ionisation as they interact with matter they pass through or impinge on. Radiation is generated by spontaneous decay of unstable isotopes and naturally occurring radioactive material in the earth's bedrock and atmosphere as well as by particular apparatuses devised by humankind like X-ray machines. In nature, radiation is generated by unstable nuclides of isotopes, which spontaneously disintegrate at random by emitting radiation. The process of spontaneous disintegration and emission of excess energy in the form of ionising radiation is called radioactive decay. Radioactivity is the rate at which the radioactive decay of a radioactive material takes place and is measured in becquerel (Bq), where 1 Bq is defined as one disintegration per second.

The nucleus of atoms of all elements comprises of positively charged protons and neutrons, around which the negatively charged electrons orbit. Some elements have more than one isotope, where the nucleus is comprised of the same number of protons but with a different number of neutrons. For instance, the three isotopes of hydrogen are hydrogen-1 (proton), deuterium (H-2) and Tritium (H-3). Most nuclides with a given number of neutrons are stable. If this configuration gets disturbed, the nuclide becomes unstable and spontaneously disintegrates at random. As it disintegrates, the unstable nuclide emits radiations in the form of either electromagnetic waves like gamma radiations or streams of high energy particles like alpha

Figure 9.1 Damaged Chernobyl Reactor-1986

Figure 9.2 Damaged Nuclears Reactor at Fukushima Daiichi-2011

and beta particles. The half-life of the unstable radionuclides of an element is the time it takes for it to decay into half of its value, i.e. half of the number of nuclides to disintegrate. Half-lives range from fractions of a second to millions of years, depending upon the nuclide concerned. Radioactivity is, in fact, this spontaneous disintegration of unstable nuclei.

EFFECTS OF RADIATION

Ionisation in biological materials like living cells and tissues can cause cellular damage, which may lead to the death of a cell or damage it in such a way that it cannot perform its original function. The ionisation of atoms in tissues, when radiation passes through them, occurs when the tissue absorbs the energy from the radiation. This is accompanied by chemical changes that cause harmful biological effects. Radiations have two types of detrimental effects on living tissues: deterministic and stochastic effects. Deterministic effects of radiation occur when radiation ionises DNA molecules directly and lead to cell death as well as abnormal cell development. Tissue reactions or deterministic effects occur above a threshold dose of radiation expressed in Grays (Gy). They occur only if the dose is higher than the threshold value for that biological effect. Below the absorbed dose, no clinical effect is observed, as most organs and tissues of the body have natural biological mechanisms to address the same. Deterministic effects are more severe for higher doses as well as for higher dose rates, i.e. dose per unit time. Skin burn, sterility, and acute radiation syndrome are examples of deterministic effects of radiation. Stochastic effects, on the other hand, are indeterminate. It is not certain if and when they would occur. The likelihood of stochastic effects increases with higher doses of radiation, but their severity does not depend on it.

Appendix 16 gives details about the ICRP recommended radiation dose exposures for practitioners and the public at large.

These have been adopted by the Atomic Energy Regulatory Board, AERB, in India since 1991. The psychosocial effects of radiation, like acute organic brain syndrome, anxiety, and post-traumatic stress disorder, are also explained. The physical, deterministic, and hereditary effects of exposure to radiation are tabulated, depending on different dosages of exposure, in Appendix 18.

NUCLEAR AND RADIATION-RELATED EMERGENCIES

A nuclear or radiological emergency occurs when a community is exposed to ionising radiations and when the contamination with radionuclides exceeds the permissible limits. Nuclear and radiological emergencies are mainly man-made. Sometimes they are associated with natural disasters like earthquakes and floods in an area where nuclear facilities like a nuclear power plant exist. Facilities using radioactive sources have the potential of triggering a radiological emergency as they may release ionising radiations into the environment or increase radiation exposure in their surroundings due to an accident, faulty systems or loss of radioactive source.

The possibility of an accident taking place in a facility of the nuclear fuel cycle and a nuclear reactor is rare due to the stringent safety measures adopted in such facilities. However, a 'critical' accident sometimes occurs in a nuclear fuel cycle facility, leading to bursts of neutrons and gamma radiation. When an accident occurs in a nuclear reactor, it is a major nuclear emergency or a nuclear disaster, as was the case of the Chernobyl nuclear reactor.

India has embarked on the use of nuclear energy for the generation of electricity, and has 22 nuclear reactors currently in operation at different nuclear power plant sites, apart from the research reactors at Bhabha Atomic Research Center (BARC) and Indira Gandhi Centre for Atomic Research (IGCAR). Best safety practices and standards followed in the reactors, and various applications of radiation and effective regulations by the Atomic Energy Regulatory Board (AERB) minimise the possibility of a potential accident and the risk of exposure to radiation of workers and the common public to absolute nought. Despite the strict controls, the stringent regulations and SOPs, there may still be a potential danger of a nuclear emergency due to factors beyond human control. Failures like human error, system failure or sabotage of nuclear facilities may lead to an on-site or off-site emergency anywhere in the world.

Transportation of radioactive material also poses the threat of a potential accident occurring en route. However, the probability of accidents during the transportation of radioactive materials is low due to the unique design features of the containers in which the material is transported and the exceptional safety and security measures that are taken. The United Nations has recommended procedures and codes for transporting dangerous goods like chemicals and radioactive material. Codes for transporting such goods by various modes are mentioned in Appendix 15. The International Maritime Organization, for instance, has formulated an International Maritime Dangerous Goods Code for the transport of such goods by ship. Similar codes for the transport of dangerous goods by road, rail, and air have been formulated by the United Nations Economic Committee for Europe (UNECE) at Geneva, the Office of International Rail Transport, Berne and by ICAO, the International Civil Aviation Organization in Montreal respectively.

Pilferage is another potential source of a radioactive or nuclear hazard in the virtually impossible eventuality of an unauthorised person gaining access to radioactive sources. Although it has not yet occurred, the malevolent use of radioactive material as a radiological dispersal device or a 'dirty bomb' by terrorists to cause panic is a potential threat. A radiological dispersal device is a conventional explosive device in which radioactive material has been added so that, on its explosion, there would be dispersal of radioactive material in the environment.

Occasionally, nuclear accidents may occur in conjunction with other natural calamities like landslides, earthquakes, and floods which impact nuclear installations. The impact of natural hazards is a matter of concern, as nuclear facilities can be damaged or affected adversely on the occurrence of such natural disasters. However, all nuclear facilities, including nuclear power plants, are designed and built to take care of such extreme events. They have robust emergency preparedness and response procedures to meet any exigency.

NUCLEAR AND RADIOLOGICAL WARFARE: RADIOLOGICAL WEAPONS

The atomic bomb explosion in Hiroshima and Nagasaki in Japan by America in the Second World War is an instance of radiological warfare through the use of nuclear weapons involving a fission reaction which resulted in extreme heat, blast, pressure waves, and ionising radiations that caused severe destruction and death of hundreds of thousands of people. The bomb also resulted in contamination of large areas and left its impact on several generations of the affected community. Radiological warfare may involve deliberate radiation poisoning or contamination of an area with radiological sources. Most radiological weapons, except nuclear bombs, are weapons of mass disruption and not mass destruction as they do not possess enough energy to cause mass destruction. Some radiological weapons can also be target-specific. The case of radiation poisoning of Alexander Litvinenko, a Russian spy, by the Russian FSB is a typical instance. The radiation poisoning of the specific target was done using radioactive Polonium-210, one of the isotopes of the element Polonium with a half-life of 138 days.

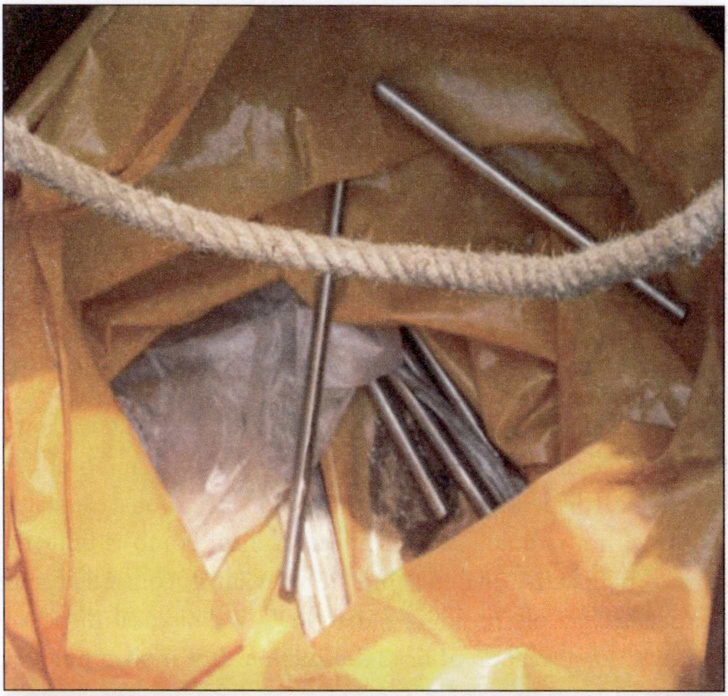

Figure 9.3 and 9.4 Co-60 Pencils Recoved from Scrap and the Response at Mayapuri 2010

The thermonuclear weapon also called a hydrogen bomb in common parlance is also a weapon of radiological warfare and can be more powerful compared to a nuclear fission bomb. However, the explosion of a cobalt bomb, which is a nuclear fission bomb, is due to fission of Co-60 and can thus contaminate large areas around ground zero with a strong gamma emitter (Co-60) for a long time. Both hydrogen and cobalt bombs have continued to be conceptual ideas, and no such bomb has been tested yet.

RADIOLOGICAL DISPERSION DEVICE

A 'dirty bomb' or a radiological dispersal device, RDD, is a low-tech radiological weapon as compared to a nuclear bomb. A radiological dispersal device is effectively a conventional explosive bomb with a radiological side effect. A dirty bomb is built by mixing radioactive material into it. It is an uncontrolled and inefficient way of spreading radiation. A radiological dispersal device is not a weapon of mass destruction. It is more a weapon of mass disruption.

There is a growing concern about the possibility of terrorist attacks involving radioactive materials through the use of a dirty bomb. It is hypothetical and has not been used by terrorists before, but the possibility exists of terrorist groups threatening a large number of people with exposure to radioactive materials. The use of a radiological dispersal device by itself would not result in fatalities due to radiation. The fatalities would primarily be due to the explosion. A dirty bomb does not cause an atomic explosion, and its effect is less widespread and tragic than a nuclear bomb's. It can only contaminate a relatively small area with radioactive material. International treaties have made the possibility of radioactive material falling into the hands of terrorists extremely low, thereby reducing the threat. However, if not contained, terrorists supported by rogue states may still have access to such material to threaten the world community in the future.

Human senses cannot detect radiation. People present at the site of an explosion will not know whether or not radioactive materials were used in the bomb. It is also difficult to assess how much effect radiation will have on human health, especially when the source type and activity are not known. However, if we consider the most probable source of radiation, a dirty bomb would not be radioactive enough to cause significant illness. Well-trained medical health physicians and radiobiological experts can assess risks after the exposure level has been determined. Cancer risk from a dirty bomb is estimated to be very low because the radiation dose may not be high.

INDIA: RISK MITIGATION AND RESPONSE MECHANISM

In India, the Atomic Energy Regulatory Board, AERB, has powers to license the operation of a nuclear facility. The AERB prepares guidelines and SOPs for nuclear facilities. The Board also has the power to order either partial or full shutdown of any facility that violates the AERB guidelines. The Crisis Management Group of the Department of Atomic Energy activates the emergency response and also manages nuclear and radiological emergencies that may occur in the public domain, such as transport accidents, handling of orphan sources, and the explosion of radiological dispersal devices. There are 22 emergency response centres established by Bhabha Atomic Research Centre, BARC, to cope with radiological emergencies in the public domain. These emergency response centres are responsible for detection and monitoring; as well as for the maintenance of an adequate inventory of monitoring instruments, protective gear, and well-trained staff. The emergency response centres under BARC also provide technical advice to the first responders and local authorities. Bhabha Atomic Research Centre trains personnel from various paramilitary forces, particularly the National Disaster Response Force and Central Industrial Security Force, in undertaking rescue and response in the event of a nuclear and radiological disaster. The effective management of such disasters requires coordinated efforts on the part of the Department of Atomic Energy and Space, other concerned central and state ministries and departments, response forces, scientific and technical institutes, professional bodies, non-governmental organisations, the corporate sector, and the community.

RADIATION PROTECTION AND RISK MITIGATION

Nuclear fuel cycle facilities must have elaborate physical protection arrangements in place to ensure their security. While the beneficial aspects of a nuclear program and the use of ionising radiations are fully exploited, their use should not cause risk to public health and the environment. The structural design and the structural barriers in nuclear facilities usually prevent the release of any radioactivity outside the plant area, and the public is not likely to be exposed to radiations. Every country that has nuclear capability and has nuclear facilities for generating power and for other peaceful purposes has a national regulatory body and stringent operating procedures to ensure the safety of the community and reduction of risk. In India, the AERB is the regulatory body for ensuring safety in the operation of these facilities and safe use, transport and storage of nuclear, and radioactive materials.

A reactor accident is prevented by the design philosophy of defence-in-depth, where several levels of protection and multiple barriers are constructed to prevent the release of radioactive materials into the environment. The application of the defence-in-depth concept in a nuclear facility ensures three essential safety functions. These include controlling the power, cooling the fuel, and confining the radioactive material. In case of an emergency, the radioactive material should not reach the public. This is done by including biological shields, safety systems, and interlocks.

Safety audits of operations and strict compliance of safety procedures help to mitigate the consequences of any potential accidents. Appropriate safety and security measures, strict accounting procedures, and quick detection and identification of devices go a long way in risk mitigation of nuclear and radiation-related disasters.

The authorities need to strengthen the prevention of possible illicit trafficking of radioactive sources and special nuclear materials. Appropriate procedures need to be put in place to ensure that radioactive materials do not fall into the hands of criminal elements or terrorists.

Exposure of a person to radiation may be external or internal and incurred through various exposure pathways. External exposure may be due to direct irradiation from a sealed source or due to contamination. The risk of radiation can also be from airborne radionuclides or radionuclides deposited on the ground or clothing and skin. Internal exposure, on the other hand, may result from the inhalation of radioactive material in the air, ingestion of contaminated food or water, or contamination of an open wound.

Radiation protection and risk mitigation from external exposure are provided by TDS—time, distance, and shielding. In effect, external exposure is reduced by limiting the *time* spent near the source of radiation, maintaining a *distance* by moving away from the source of radiation and *shielding* oneself from the source. The effectivity of the risk mitigation measures depends upon the type of radiation emitted and the nature of the shielding material. In contaminated areas, protective clothing helps to prevent external body contamination and appropriate respiratory protection helps to prevent internal contamination. Eating, drinking, and smoking should be forbidden in contaminated areas.

Physicians who take care of victims of radiation exposure should cover their own risk. A patient who has been exposed only to an external source of radiation and is not contaminated poses no radiation hazard to others, and no precautions are needed. If the patient is externally contaminated, proper procedures like wearing vinyl gloves and mask, covering the patient with a blanket or sheet, and washing hands help to prevent the spread of contamination and inadvertent ingestion by physicians, nurses or other paramedics. On the other hand, if the patient is contaminated internally, precautions are needed when dealing with excreta. However, the affected person exposed to an internal source of radiation does not represent a direct hazard to others unless the radiation dose was extensive, and involved gamma emitters.

RESPONSE TO A BOMB BLAST: WHAT TO DO

In the event of a bomb blast by a terrorist outfit, if the affected people are not injured by the initial blast, they should not panic and leave the area immediately on foot. The use of public or private transportation such as buses or cars should be avoided before competent authorities responsible for checking for contamination with radioactive materials have checked them. In case the blast has occurred outdoors, and the affected people are inside a building, it is best to stay indoors and close the windows and doors to avoid ingress of contaminated air. Even when one is outdoors during the bomb blast and is not affected by the initial blast, it is prudent to go inside the nearest building. Staying inside will reduce exposure to any radioactive material that may be present as dust at the scene of the bomb blast.

In case a person was within the radius of a few hundred metres from the site of the bomb blast, it is crucial to take precautionary measures. Any external exposure to radiation and radioactivity cannot be ruled out and needs to be taken care of. Clothes and shoes should be removed as soon as possible and placed in a plastic bag and sealed. Removing clothing will eliminate most of the external contamination from any radioactive materials deposited on them. Taking a shower reduces the amount of radioactive contamination on the body. This effectively reduces the total external exposure to radiation and radioactive material after that, medical advice should be sought.

Once emergency personnel monitor the scene and assess the damage, they will be able to inform the affected community if radioactive materials were involved in the bomb. They will also be able to advise regarding the health effects that can be expected in the event of exposure to any radiation as well as the future course of action.

It is not prudent to self-medicate and take any prophylaxes like potassium iodide tablets without being instructed by

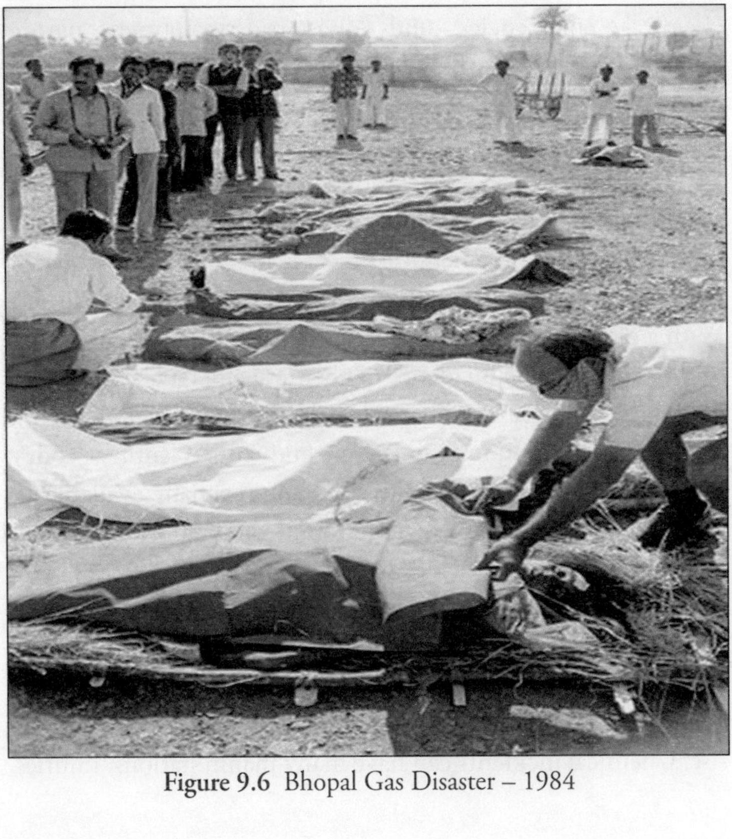

Figure 9.6 Bhopal Gas Disaster – 1984

competent authorities. These may be required only in the case of an accident in a nuclear power plant due to the release of radioactive iodine, but this too should be done only on the advice of the authorities.

Even if radioactive materials are not present in the bomb, following these steps can help reduce any injury from the chemicals that are present in the blast.

CHEMICAL HAZARDS

The growth of chemical industries has led to an increase in hazardous events associated with chemicals and Hazchems. Chemical accidents and deficiencies in safety management systems, as well as human errors, are the leading causes of chemical emergencies and disasters. Sometimes natural calamities like earthquakes and floods may also be causal factors of chemical disasters. Sabotage could be another reason for a chemical emergency.

The International Federation of Red Cross has estimated that between 1998–2007, there were nearly 3,200 technological disasters, including chemical incidents, with approximately 100,000 people killed and nearly 2 million people affected. With a global increase in the use of chemicals in various sectors of the economy, the incidence of chemical emergencies has risen over the last 70 years. Chemicals have played an increasing role in the world's economy since the mid 20th Century. Today, more than 15 million chemicals are commercially available, of which about 70,000 are in use around the world as fertilisers, weedicides, and insecticides as well as in the industries. It is expected that the use of chemicals will increase worldwide, particularly in developing countries and in countries with economies in transition. Accordingly, the potential occurrence of a chemical disaster or a chemical emergency is also likely to rise. Chemical incidents can have many manifestations, injuries, and effects requiring different response mechanisms. According to the Health Protection Agency of the UK, a chemical incident is an uncontrolled release or spread of a toxic substance resulting in harm to the public health and environment.

CHEMICAL DISASTERS: VULNERABILITY AND INCIDENCE

Chemical emergencies and disasters besides directly affecting the vulnerable community can also result in fire, explosion, and toxic releases. Wind speed and direction also play an essential role in the dispersion of toxic gas clouds. Vulnerability of the affected community is enhanced when the location of a severe hazardous industrial unit is in proximity to densely populated areas as was the case of the 1984 Bhopal gas tragedy—the worst chemical disaster in history that resulted in 3,800 immediate deaths and several thousand affected due to the release of the toxic gas, methyl isocyanate (MIC). The case study on Bhopal gas tragedy is appended in Appendix 11.

The frequency of chemical incidents due to hazardous chemicals has been increasing over time. The 1976 Seveso incident in Italy resulted in the release of dioxin from an industrial plant, the Bhopal gas leak from a tank in 1984, releasing MIC, resulting in 3,800 immediate deaths are some of the calamitous events which are considered as instances of major chemical disasters. The explosion of liquefied petroleum gas (LPG) terminal in Mexico City in 2000 and the explosion of the fireworks factory in Enschede, the Netherlands that same year were all accidents which resulted in significant losses.

In the past, there have been incidents of the deliberate release of chemicals, like the release of warfare agent in 1995 in Tokyo. Chemical disasters resulting from chemicals entering the food chain have also been witnessed, as was the case in the 2002 mass poisoning of kitchen utensils in Jabalpur, India due to the use of pesticide containers and in the case of inadvertent use of an insecticide in the preparation of sweets in the Philippines in 2005. A case of sodium bromide being confused as table salt was witnessed in 2007 in Angola, leading to major consequences. Although the frequency of chemical incidents has increased over time, the severity of the impact of industrial chemical disasters has decreased due to the growing ability to manage chemical emergencies and disasters.

CHEMICAL HAZARDS: CAUSES

The cause of chemical events varies from natural to anthropogenic. The latter includes events like an explosion of a factory, which stores or uses chemicals as was the case of an explosion in an oil storage facility in Hemel Hampstead in England in 2005. Contamination of food and water supply with chemicals occurred in a 2005 incident in which the plant explosion near the Songhua River in China led to a hundred tons of pollutants being released into the river, making the water unfit for consumption.

Anthropogenic chemical incidents are often caused by oil spills and leakages in storage units as well as during transportation, which is associated with chemical exposure. There have also been instances where irresponsible and illegal activities have led to exposure to hazardous chemicals, as in the case of a community in Senegal (including children) that was exposed to lead in 2008, resulting in lead poisoning. Similarly, dumping of toxic waste in the city of Abidjan, Cote d'Ivoire in 2006 caused several deaths and rendered thousands sick. Chemical incidents are also associated with natural hazards like volcanoes, earthquakes, landslides, and forest fires. Natural disasters can disrupt the chemical containment systems and causes chemical incidents, like tank rupture after flooding.

CHEMICAL HAZARDS: EFFECT

The effect of chemical incidents varies in different incident/accident scenarios. When the chemical hazard occurs in the form of outdoor release of gas and vapours like in the case of Bhopal gas leak, the effect due to inhalation exposure is more widespread. This is because the vapour or gas cloud moves downwind and disburses rapidly to a large population, depending upon atmospheric conditions and the heaviness of the gas. Usually, one or two chemicals are involved and are detected initially by reports of respiratory and eye irritation. The effect of the chemicals on the health, morbidity, and the mortality of the population are often calamitous and sometimes heritable. The environmental impact of toxic chemical is often high and widespread.

Release of aerosols in the air, both in liquid and solid form, can cause indoor and outdoor contamination over several kilometres, like in the Seveso chemical disaster in Italy. Inhalation exposure occurs shortly after emission. The material deposited on the soil and infrastructure remains until it is removed by wind and rain or cleaned intentionally. Exposure is limited to the accident site and its surroundings. There is also a concern about delayed effects in the case of carcinogenic substances.

Release of toxic chemicals into the surrounding environment other than air occurs when the toxic chemical comes in contact with soil, sediments, food, and water. In the case of release of noxious chemicals in a river, like in the event of benzene release in the Songhua River in China, the pollutants can spread downstream and make the water non-potable for several days. It is easier to avoid primary human contact with the chemical in this scenario as compared to airborne release. The secondary consequences of contamination of food and drinking water also hurt wildlife, fish, and whole ecosystems. The release of the chemical from surface water can percolate to the soil and subsoil water table.

Explosion and fire are frequently associated with calamitous chemical events as was the case in 1984, when a fire broke out in the Pemex LPG terminal in Mexico City. In many cases, the explosions have a short warning period, and the affected area is roughly circular around the explosion site. The significant injuries in such events include burns from thermal radiation and traumatic injuries due to the blast, including gas-filled organs, rupture of the eardrum as well as injuries from fragments, projectiles, and glass splinters that may occur due to structural damage.

A chemical event is sometimes detected when several people show consistent syndromes and symptoms of a disease as in the case of the mass exposure to a noxious chemical. The exposure to endosulfan that occurred in Jabalpur district in India in 2002 as well as the 2007 Bromide poisoning in Angola are some instances. The latter resulted in disease outbreak of an unknown aetiology near Luanda, the capital of Angola. The toxic aetiology included blurred vision, dizziness, weakness, and difficulty in speaking and walking. The problem with disease outbreaks is that they are often suspected as infectious diseases rather than symptoms that occur as a result of toxicity.

CHEMICAL AGENTS

Agent Orange is the code name for a powerful herbicide and defoliant which releases dioxins. It is widely used in herbicidal warfare programmes.

Blister agents (also known as vesicants) are chemical compounds that cause severe skin, eye and mucosal pain and irritation, and severe chemical burns, resulting in large, painful water blisters.

Blood agents or cyanogens are chemical compounds, which are carried by blood. The cyanides can inactivate the energy-producing cytochrome oxidase enzymes of cells in the body.

Carcinogen refers to a chemical substance, radionuclide or radiation that is an agent directly involved in the promotion of cancer due to its ability to damage the genome or to disrupt the cellular metabolic processes.

HAZCHEM are chemical compounds that can be used for mass destruction, causing severe damage to the health and property of society.

HAZMATs are any solids, liquids, or gases that can harm people, other living organisms, property, or the environment and may be radioactive, flammable, explosive, toxic, corrosive, biohazardous, an oxidiser, an asphyxiant, a pathogen, or an allergen.

Nerve agents are a class of phosphorous-containing organic chemicals, organophosphates that disrupt the mechanism by which nerves transfer messages to organs in the human body.

Psychic incapacitants are also called psychomimetic agents or hallucinogens that are represented by 3-quinclinidinyl benzilate (BZ), tetrahydrocannabinol (THC), fentanyl, and Lysergic acid diethylamide (LSD). They are mainly central nervous system depressants or stimulants, causing various physiological or mental incapacitations, leading to temporary disability.

Sarin Gas is an extremely toxic substance with a single application as a nerve agent used in chemical weapons. Production and stockpiling of Sarin was outlawed by the Chemical Weapons Convention of 1993.

CHEMICAL TERRORISM

Chemical terrorism is an act of violence using chemical agents to achieve professed aims. There are growing concerns as anti-national elements are increasingly finding chemical terrorism easy to adopt. They are not only adopting newer modalities but also becoming progressively aggressive. The main aim of terrorists is to intimidate the population or to seek attention. A terrorist attack involving chemical agents differs from a normal terrorist attack as it results in specific health effects and can cause fatal injuries, create panic, and affect the morale of the community. Various types of hazardous materials like chemical warfare agents, dual-use chemicals, toxic industrial chemicals, hazardous chemical wastes, agriculture chemicals, and other poisonous substances have harmful effects like panic reaction, chemical burns, injuries, and psychosocial trauma. They also cause immense damage to the environment.

Details of a few chemical warfare agents, their categorisation along with the individualities and related exposure symptoms are given in Appendix 13.

RISK REDUCTION AND MANAGEMENT FRAMEWORK

Risk and vulnerability assessment, surveillance mechanism and intelligence gathering are essential measures for managing chemical disasters and reducing risk. Detection, monitoring, early warning systems, safety, and security of chemical agents go a long way in reducing risk and losses in the event of a disaster. The regulatory environment for chemical disasters and chemical emergencies in India are given in Appendix 12.

Capacity building of first responders and emergency and medical functionaries is essential in order to reduce the severity of the disaster and to ensure that the affected can be saved and treated timely. Individuals and organisations also require capacity building to deal with chemical emergencies. Organisations need to assign specific responsibilities to minimise risk and to ensure a timely and effective response in the event of a chemical disaster. The training module should among other things include environmental chemistry, chemical exposures and their epidemiology, toxicology, risk, and exposure assessments as well as standard operating procedures for responding to reduce risk to the responders and the community.

It is wise to generate awareness among communities regarding local chemical sites, shelter and protective measure as well as safety procedures.

Early detection and alertness go a long way in reducing catastrophic impacts. Chemical hazards have both short term and long-term effects on public health, which need to be minimised. Often the polluter and the affected population are the most important in order to establish the occurrence and detection of a chemical incident. Assessment requires notification from the person responsible for the chemical release, and hence, the role of the polluter becomes crucial. A polluter fearing criminal or civil prosecution often fails to notify a chemical emergency.

Detection of a chemical event is also possible through sophisticated systems, observed environmental or health changes, airborne contaminant plumes, irritation of eyes and nose, death of wildlife, and other visible evidence of the chemical. Once a chemical hazard is detected, trained rescue and response authorities take charge based on the established guidelines and procedures. Appropriate local and regional public

Figure 9.7 Mock Drills help to Enhance Preparedness

health, environmental and incident management personnel, as well as specialised expert responders, are mobilised as soon as possible to deal with the chemical disasters.

The first response to a chemical hazard should be to terminate the release and prevent the spread of contamination, as well as to limit the exposure and risk. The media and public at large should be informed of the calamitous event as soon as possible. All exposed individuals should be registered, and their health investigations must be conducted. Chemical disaster victims need to be decontaminated immediately. This helps to remove and neutralise harmful chemicals on their bodies.

The framework of risk assessment and mitigation in chemical disasters across the world provides a responsibility chart of nodal agencies. In India, the nodal ministry for chemical emergencies is the Ministry of Environment. Appendix 14 provides a list of relevant nodal departments, ministries and organisations that can be contacted in the event of a chemical emergency.

TEN

CBRN II: Biological Disasters and Epidemics

Live organisms and toxins that lead to widespread diseases, disabilities or death among humans, animals, and plants cause biological hazards. Epidemics or pandemics of diseases and pestilence are natural biological disasters. Sometimes the accidental release of virulent microorganisms can also cause a biological disaster. The intentional use of biological agents in biological warfare and bioterrorism are anthropogenic hazards of a recent origin.

EPIDEMICS AND PANDEMICS

Epidemics

An epidemic is the outbreak of a disease affecting a disproportionately large number of people within a region at the same time. Epidemics can result in heavy mortalities in the short term. Epidemics of infectious diseases can lead to a depletion of the population with a corresponding drop in economic activity.

Infectious diseases have infested human communities and civilisations since the dawn of history. Major epidemics that have resulted in large scale losses have been those of cholera and diarrheal diseases, measles, malaria, and dengue fever. The epidemics of plague in Europe during the middle ages resulted in wiping out entire communities. In the early 20th century, communities in Vietnam under the French and in India under the British suffered an immense loss of human life through several epidemics. The loss of lives was tragic during the outbreak of plague in Surat, and it also generated an exodus. In Spain, the outbreak of influenza reached epidemic proportions between 1917–1918 and caused massive loss of life.

More recently, the Human Immunodeficiency Virus (HIV) and Acquired Immunodeficiency Syndrome (AIDS) epidemic in Sub-Saharan Africa has decimated large communities. Novel pathogens like the Marburg virus constantly emerge to pose challenges at the point of primary contact and in removed locations in the world. Infectious agents are evolving perpetually, often acquiring enhanced virulence and epidemic potentials. The outbreak of Chikungunya that started in 2005 is one such instance. To add to the complexities, there is a possibility of zoonotic diseases like avian influenza and swine flu emerging in an epidemic form across the animal-human interface. Furthermore, epidemics do not respect national borders in a global world and often escalate to the level of pandemics.

Pandemics

A pandemic is an epidemic of an infectious disease that spreads through the human populations across multiple continents or globally. Tracking biological agents is necessary so that they do not enter new regions and escalate an epidemic to the level of a pandemic. In the past, epidemics of cholera, smallpox, leprosy, measles, polio, and yellow fever have escalated to the scale of pandemics. Since international travel is a norm today, it is essential to take necessary steps to avoid the spread of biological agents. International organisations like the World Health

Figure 10.1 Cremation of Nipah Virus Victim Kerala – 2018

Organization, WHO, Food and Agricultural Organization (FAO), and the Centre for Disease Control and Prevention (CDC) play a vital role in ensuring that an epidemic does not become a pandemic. Pandemics become disasters when besides illness, they cause large numbers of deaths. Potential pandemics include new strains of influenza, for example, Severe Acute Respiratory Syndrome, SARS, and Middle East Respiratory Syndrome, MERS, against which humans currently do not have sufficient immunity.

Epidemics and pandemics can be airborne if air and droplets transmit the infection as is in the case of flu, measles, SARS, and MERS. They can also be waterborne as in the case of Cholera. Salmonella, Listeria, and Hepatitis A are instances of food-borne diseases that can cause epidemics and pandemics. Some epidemics and even pandemics are vector-borne as they are transmitted when a carrier mosquito, flea, or a tick bites a healthy person after having bitten an infected person first. Malaria, dengue, and plague are all vector-borne diseases. Some viral biological agents, like the HIV and Ebola viruses, are transmitted through blood transfusion, from a mother to a child in utero, and through sexual contact. Zoonotic diseases that can cause epidemics are transmitted between animals and human beings through direct and indirect contact.

BIOLOGICAL WARFARE

Advances in bacteriology, virology, and immunology in the late 19th century and early 20th century enabled the development of biological weapons that are capable of being used in biological warfare. Bioweapons or biological weapons include organisms or toxins found in nature that can be used to incapacitate, kill, or cause harm to humans as well as livestock, and crops. Biological agents, including strains of bacteria and viruses, can be used in biological warfare as weapons of mass destruction, in much the same manner as nuclear and chemical agents. Biological agents are microorganisms such as viruses, bacteria or fungi that infect humans, livestock or crops and cause an incapacitating or fatal disease. The characteristics of several common biological warfare agents, including the disease they cause, the mode of transmission, the infective dose, incubation period, duration of illness, the lethality of the agent, and the persistence of the concerned organism are tabulated in Appendix 20. The table also provides information regarding the vaccine that can be used and its efficacy in the case of each biological agent. The relative ease of production associated with biological agents coupled with the low cost and low level of delivery technology prompted the use of biological agents after the First World War. Their use peaked during the cold war.

BIOTERRORISM

Bioterrorism is the intentional use of microorganisms or toxins derived from living organisms to cause disease or death in humans, animals, or plants. Bioterrorism involves the use of biological agents such as anthrax. Terrorists use bioweapons mainly because they are easily accessible, have low visibility, and are easily delivered. Bioweapons lend themselves to terrorist attacks because they are highly potent and can go unnoticed or undetected. Symptoms of illness resulting from a biological agent do not appear immediately. There is a delay between the use of the agent and the appearance of the symptoms, which is known as the incubation period. The incubation period may last for days or even weeks, allowing terrorists to escape unnoticed from the site of the attack.

The Biological and Toxin Weapons Convention resolved to eliminate biological weapons of mass destruction. The use of some agents, such as anthrax by terrorist groups poses a grave threat. The threat of destruction posed by bioterrorism is nearly as high as that by natural biological agents that can cause an epidemic. In the case of bioterrorism, the spectrum of possible pathogens is narrow, while natural outbreaks can occur on account of a wide range of organisms.

Agro-terrorism is a form of bioterrorism that involves the malicious use of plant or animal pathogens to cause devastating diseases in the agricultural sector. There are no known cases of agro-terrorism. However, there is a possibility that agro-terrorism could be employed as an act of malevolence in the future. Although it was more of an accident than an agro-terrorist incident, the spread of the invasive weed *Parthenium hysterophorus*, also known as the Santa Maria fever, has had vast repercussions on human and animal health in India.

RISK MITIGATION

Through prompt detection of incipient outbreaks, protection against natural and artificial outbreaks of diseases in the form of epidemics and pandemics as well as through bioterrorism can be achieved. The infected people must be isolated as per well-defined protocols. Investigational and therapeutic countermeasures are to be taken after the potential outbreak. Slow-evolving epidemics do not cause upheavals in society and do not come under the crisis management scenario.

One Health Approach recognises that human health is connected to animal health in the environment. It is a collaborative, multisectoral, and transdisciplinary approach—working at the local, regional, national, and global levels—to achieve optimal health outcomes recognising the interconnection between people, animals, plants, and their shared environment. One Health approach is necessary because six out of every 10 infectious diseases in humans are spread through animals.

In India, the Nuclear, Biological and Chemical Warfare Directorate, the Defense Research and Development Organization, DRDO and Department of Atomic Energy, DAE develop detection and protection systems. They also develop and provide protective equipment for CBRN disasters. The Ministry of Health and Family Welfare is the nodal ministry that handles cases of biological disasters, just as the Department of Atomic Energy is the nodal ministry for radiation and nuclear disasters. The contact details and the websites for government offices, organisations, and agencies that can be contacted for more information regarding biological hazards and during a biological disaster are in Appendix 19.

PREVENTION OF EPIDEMICS AND PANDEMICS

Biological emergencies, including pandemics, and epidemics can be prevented by raising community awareness regarding water, sanitation, hygiene, public health issues, integrated disease surveillance, vector control measures, and stringent use of pesticides and insecticides. Enhancement of medical response capabilities plays a very crucial role in prevention, detection, and response to biological emergencies.

International organisations like the WHO, FAO, and the CDC play a vital role and prescribe guidelines for the prevention and control of epidemics within and across international borders. At the micro-level, a range of household and community measures can mitigate the risk of epidemics and pandemics. These include hygiene and sanitation practices like washing hands, access to clean water and vaccination. Compulsory immunisation should also be taken.

Maintaining personal hygiene helps to prevent the spread of diseases. It is essential to wash hands with soap and water before and after handling food in the kitchen as well as before and after eating. Bathing regularly is essential as it eliminates infectious spores and other biological agents that may have been deposited on the skin.

Besides personal hygiene, it is essential to keep the house, workplace, and surroundings clean. Special attention needs to be paid to the elimination of any stagnant water that can become a breeding site for mosquitoes and other vectors. Disposal of any domestic, human, or animal waste without contaminating soil and water is crucial. Flies are vectors of a large number of diseases. Waste that attracts flies and insects needs to be suitably disposed of at the earliest.

Eating food that is cooked well kills any food-borne bacteria. This is especially important while cooking meat, which is less likely to spread diseases if cooked well rather than rare or medium. When cooked food cools down to room temperature, it can develop harmful bacteria. It is best to eat prepared food immediately. Cooked hot food can be safely stored at 140°F or 60°C or if cooled down to near or below 33.8°F or 10°C. It is essential to refrigerate cooked food within two hours of its preparation.

Raw poultry, meat, eggs, and unpasteurised milk can be contaminated and needs to be cooked and reheated. Cooking and reheating them thoroughly at 158°F or 70°C kills pathogens.

Fruits and vegetable are to be thoroughly washed with clean water before eating. When shopping and storing food in the refrigerator, raw meat should be separated from fresh produce like fruits or vegetables to prevent cross-contamination. Salads should be carefully handled with clean hands and utensils. Milk and dairy products are safest when pasteurised

Hygiene in the kitchen is of paramount importance to reduce vulnerability. Kitchen utensils, tools, and equipment should be kept clean. The food should be covered to keep flies, rodents, and animals away. Washing hands with soap and water before handling food is of utmost importance. Kitchen surfaces and utensils that have been used to store or prepare raw meat, fish, and eggs should be thoroughly cleaned as bacteria from uncooked meat can be transmitted to cooked food and ingested.

It is imperative to use clean and safe drinking water as a preventive measure against many waterborne and other diseases. The water source of the community and the family should be prevented from contamination from animal droppings and wastewater. Water sources and overhead tanks in homes, offices, and schools should be maintained carefully. Risk factors of waterborne diseases include unprotected water sources, leaking septic tanks and latrines, contaminated surface water runoff entering wells and springs, animals using the same source as people, and foreign objects falling into the water source.

Vector control and early warnings to reduce the vulnerability of the community go a long way in reducing risk of vector-borne diseases. It is essential to prevent insect bites in order to reduce vulnerability to vector-borne disease. Carriers should avoid being bitten by mosquitos since they can spread the pathogen or disease-producing agents like a virus or bacteria, to a healthy person. It helps to sleep under insecticide-treated nets and fine mosquito nets to reduce exposure in malaria-endemic areas. All members of the family except babies younger than two months of age should use insect repellents as per the instructions on product labels. Insect repellants should not be applied over a cut, over irritated skin or on children's hands, eyes, and mouth. If a sunscreen has to be used, then it should be applied before applying the insect repellant.

Zoonotic disease spread can be prevented by ensuring that pet and farm animals and their habitats are kept clean. It is essential to wash hands with soap and water after touching animals and their habitat. Approaching unknown dogs should be avoided as they may be infected.

In order to avoid transmission of serious illnesses, one must never eat animals that are sick or have been found dead. It is also essential to drink only pasteurised milk and eat meat that is thoroughly cooked. Raw vegetables and fruits must be thoroughly washed before cooking and eating.

EPIDEMICS AND PANDEMICS: WHAT TO DO AFTER AN OUTBREAK

Enhancement of medical response capabilities plays a crucial role in detection and response to biological emergencies as well as in containment of an epidemic and pandemic.

After a warning is issued, it is essential to store a two-week supply of water and food and periodically check regular prescription drugs to ensure a continuous supply. Non-prescription drugs like pain relievers, stomach remedies, cough and cold medicines, fluids with electrolytes and vitamins should be stocked for emergencies. A typical list of medicines and other essentials that should be part of a first aid kit for emergencies at home, school, office or in other organisations is given in Appendix 21. This medical kit is valuable during all disasters—natural and man-made—that a family, school, or other organisation may face.

After the first few cases of an infectious disease are reported, risk can be reduced by using antiviral medications

Figure 10.2 Nipah Virus Mitigation – Kerala 2018 Kerala-2018

and by proactive surveillance, followed by quarantine. The local authorities should be notified in the event of any unusual incidence of sickness in humans or animals immediately.

In the case of an outbreak of vector-borne and zoonotic diseases, care should be taken to avoid contact with vectors. Long-sleeved clothing and regular use of insecticides and repellents help to protect from mosquitoes, which can spread Zika fever, yellow fever, chikungunya, and dengue. During a MERS-COV epidemic (an epidemic of the Middle East Respiratory Syndrome, also known as camel flu, a viral respiratory infection caused by the Coronavirus), it is prudent to avoid contact with camels. While handling sick animals or those found dead in the area, it is imperative to wear protective gear as they might be infected. It is essential to avoid contact with birds and poultry in locations with flu outbreaks. Contact with animals like bats and chimpanzees should be avoided in the event of viral hemorrhagic fevers and an outbreak of the Ebola virus since they are common carriers of the virus.

During the epidemic of a contagious disease, one should maintain a safe distance of about 1–2 m from infected people and avoid going to crowded places. Caregivers and family members of the affected people should monitor their fever and other symptoms. Personal protection equipment of caregivers includes masks, protective glasses, gloves, apron, and soap or alcohol-based disinfectants.

Some viruses can be transmitted via blood and body fluids, through cuts in the skin, cutaneous mucus, or a needle prick. Disinfectants need to be applied to exposed areas after washing them thoroughly with soap and water. It is important to use face masks to protect against respiratory infection during an epidemic of airborne diseases. Proper hygiene and sanitation, access to clean water and vaccination go a long way in avoiding infection during an epidemic. Compulsory immunisation should also be taken.

During an epidemic, purified water should be used. Purification of water through reliable methods like aqua tabs and chlorine tablets for the household, office, school, and other institutions go a long way in preventing the spread of waterborne diseases during an epidemic.

Young children, pregnant women, and the elderly need special attention during epidemics, as they are more prone to catching infections. Particular precaution needs to be taken to ensure that they are not exposed to the risk of catching an infection. They should be immunised at the very onset of the outbreak. Regular checkups and the requisite pathological tests should be done to ensure timely treatment in case they do get infected. Medical practitioners, doctors, nurses, and technologists need to work in close conjunction with the rescue teams and the local administration during a disaster. They need to be trained to enable them to work in the disarray and minimalist environment that prevails post-disaster.

The contents of a typical first aid kit as recommended by India's National Disaster Management Authority to help a family, office, or other organisation manage the affected, during disasters, and biological emergencies are detailed in Appendix 21.

In cases of infectious diseases, early diagnosis and timely quarantine of the infected people is required to contain the epidemic. It is imperative for medical personnel to have a mobile and readily available investigation and testing facility. In the event of an epidemic outbreak, it is advisable to have a comprehensive investigation kit to aid in early detection and diagnosis. An advisory has been prepared by the NDMA regarding the contents of a typical investigation kit that can be used for diagnosis during an epidemic. Details of the epidemic outbreak investigation kit are given in Appendix 22.

ELEVEN

Heatwaves, Cold Waves, Agrarian Disasters: Drought, Frost, and Pest Attacks

This section deals with a large number of calamities which are not dramatic in their incidence, but have an immense impact on human lives and livelihoods, especially amongst the rural and agrarian communities. They also impinge upon society's food security and cause colossal economic losses that adversely affect the economy. The increased frequency and intensity of extreme weather events such as droughts, floods, heat, and cold waves in the last two decades is attributed to global warming. Heat and cold waves, frost, and drought are also known to adversely affect the health and lives of livestock, animals, and human population.

DROUGHTS

The famous gut-wrenching picture titled *The Vulture and the Little Girl* showing a malnourished child being scrutinised intently by a vulture in drought-hit Africa is one of the most poignant images the world has of a drought-related famine. Kevin Carter had captured the Pulitzer Prize-winning photograph of a frail famine-stricken boy, earlier thought to be a girl in 1993 in South Sudan, several hundred meters from the UN feeding centre in Ayod. The word drought brings forth other images of parched fields, empty wells, and water tanks, as well as agrarian distress in rainfed areas.

Droughts occur because of extended periods of water shortage, and are often associated with reduced crop yields, malnourishment and loss of livelihoods. Drought differs from other natural hazards due to its slow onset. It evolves over months or even years with an indeterminate onset and end. Droughts influence vast geographic expanses and have been a part of climate variability for virtually all regions across the world since times immemorial. Drought conditions have been widespread in North Africa, West Asian countries, India and China, and are known to have occurred in North, Central, and South America. In 2002, India experienced its worst-ever drought in twenty years. The inter-region probability of drought in India varies from once in two years in western Rajasthan to once in 15 years in Assam. In the past, in rural India, the age of a person used to be pegged to the year in which there had been a severe drought.

DROUGHT: CAUSES

Droughts commonly occur in areas with meagre or no rainfall. Drought may be meteorological, agricultural, or hydrological. Meteorological drought is a situation when more than 10 per cent decrease in precipitation over the normal occurs in an area; while a hydrological drought occurs when a prolonged meteorological drought leads to depletion of surface and sub-surface water. Agricultural drought is a situation in which the soil moisture and rainfall are inadequate to support a healthy crop. The deficiency in precipitation over an extended period results in the depletion of soil moisture, which, in turn, reduces crop production.

Figure 11.1 Drought in Andhra – India

Figure 11.2 Drought in Rajasthan – India

Droughts are also affected by EI Nino in the Pacific Ocean, which is a phenomenon that affects many weather systems around the globe. The warmer waters of the western tropical Pacific Ocean shift eastward along the equator usually in mid-December. Typically, EI Nino and the Indian Monsoon rains are inversely related. During an EI Nino year, India usually suffers from a meteorological drought, especially in the rain-fed area. Six of the most extended droughts in India since 1871 have been EI Nino-triggered droughts.

Over the years, globally, droughts have become less frequent. However, their severity has increased. Moreover, drought is no longer a situation of mere scarcity or absence of rainfall. It can occur in regions with high rainfall as well, due to inefficient water resource management. Even in areas with sufficient rain, water scarcity conditions are prevalent because of overexploitation of the water resources in the area. Groundwater is the primary source of 90 per cent of drinking water and over 50 per cent of the water needed for irrigating crops. There is insufficient and ineffective rainwater harvesting; hence, limited recharge takes place.

DROUGHT: RISK, VULNERABILITY

Drought vulnerability is a product of a region's risk of water shortage, and the exposure of the community to the effects of water shortage. Droughts cause little structural damage but have wide-ranging economic, environmental, and social impact. The extent and intensity of the impact of drought vary with the management of water resources, the structure of the agricultural sector, and cereal reserves. Earlier, the impact of drought was mostly restricted to the agricultural sector, but today, there is a growing complexity of the effects of drought on all sections of an economy.

Today droughts have an adverse secondary impact on regional inequality, employment levels, school attendance, trade deficits, debt, and inflation. In the USA, droughts have had a significant impact on transportation, recreation and tourism, energy sector, forest fires, environment, and aggravating soil erosion. At the microeconomic level, a drought can result in loss of crops, food insecurity, water-related health risks and loss of income and livelihoods. In the absence of effective government intervention, droughts can lead to famine and starvation with a deleterious effect on households, communities, and entire villages.

More often than not, the coping mechanism resorted to during a drought is detrimental to the welfare of the family, as the family resorts to reducing and modifying consumption. School dropout rates increase, and children assist the family in household chores and bringing up younger siblings, while the able-bodied migrate or participate in relief works. Due to migration of the able-bodied in search of work, only the elderly and the children are left behind in the villages. Enhanced borrowings, mortgages, and disposal of assets become a norm amongst the vulnerable drought-affected communities.

DROUGHT: PREVENTION, MITIGATION, PREPAREDNESS, AND WARNING

Drought prevention and mitigation measures are related to integrated water management, soil conservation, watershed development, and forest management. Drought proofing is done before crops are planted, and when the crop is growing through an in-situ reduction in plant population and supplemental irrigation. Appropriate cropping patterns and the use of short duration variety quality seeds help in drought mitigation. Intercropping, mulching, and weed control help to reduce risk. Afforestation and plantation of hardy trees like casuarina and promotion of bio-diesel plantations, and fodder for cattle aid in the mitigation process.

Communities affected by drought, resort to several coping mechanisms to reduce their vulnerability. Diversification of activities helps to mitigate the problems of loss of crops and livelihood. While small farmers and landless labourers tend to migrate in search of work in severe drought situations, larger farmers diversify their crops to reduce the risk. Milk has proved to be a great boon in drought-prone areas of India that is covered by the three-tier Amul cooperative system. The income from milk production during a drought in Saurashtra, for instance, has provided security cover to small farmers and landless labourers.

Figure 11.3 Drought Assessment Karnataka – India

The Department of Agriculture Cooperation and Farmer's Welfare has put together a drought early warning, surveillance, and early response system. Agriculture is a state subject, and each state has a detailed drought manual with a contingency plan in case of late-onset of monsoons and dry spells. Development of crop contingency plans to meet drought situations is part of the Ministry's mandate. It also identifies and propagates the plantation of drought-tolerant grasses, shrubs, and trees in drought-prone areas along with water conservation measures.

Conservation of water at all times is vital. Often water is wasted in urban households with flagrant disregard until a drought brings home the message that every drop is precious. Conservation of water within urban homes through small changes in habits will go a long way in preserving civilisation, as every effort towards this end matters. Recently Chennai, for instance, has learnt to its consternation, that every drop of water matters. The residents depend upon water that is supplied by tankers, especially during the summer, as the reservoirs that feed the city's water supply system have started to dry up—a situation that is becoming apparent in other parts of the world. One of the simplest and effective ways is to turn off the tap while brushing teeth and not allowing the water to flow incessantly. In order to save water, a bath by bucket rather than a shower is more environment-friendly. It is a cardinal rule to avoid throwing water down the drain. Even if it is wastewater, it can be used to water indoor plants or the garden. Dripping taps must be repaired immediately. In most probability, all they may need is replacement of the washers. Plumbing should be checked for leaks and repaired if there are any. It is efficient to buy appliances that are more energy and water-efficient. Wherever possible, rainwater harvesting should be practiced. Small efforts on the part of the reader and urban communities will go a long way in saving water—a resource that belongs to the entire planet. These will avert droughts, which are occurring frequently more due to overexploitation of the existing water resources and inefficient water management than poor rainfall.

HEATWAVES

Heatwaves are a recent phenomenon. It is a period of abnormally high temperatures and excessive heat which has a widespread and severe effect on the health of the affected community and environment. Climate change has caused an increase in the average temperatures across the world, and has enhanced the possibility of severe heatwaves.

Globally, the combined average temperature over land and ocean in the last few years was 1.1°C above the 20th-century average. In recorded history, the 10 warmest years have occurred after 1997 and reflects on global warming. The year 2016 made history with a record raise in global temperature, shallow sea ice, enhanced sea-level rise, and ocean heat. The extreme weather and climate conditions have continued in the following years. Heatwaves are projected to increase in number, intensity, and duration in the current century, unless the global community wakes up to the reality of global warming and climate change, and takes significant steps to reduce greenhouse gas emissions and limit our collective carbon footprint.

HEATWAVES: CAUSE AND INCIDENCE

Heatwaves occur due to a combination of seasonal climatology, prevailing circulation, and long-term trends associated with global warming. The proportion of the earth's surface that experiences sweltering summers has increased from 1 per cent from 1951–1980 to 10 per cent during the last three decades

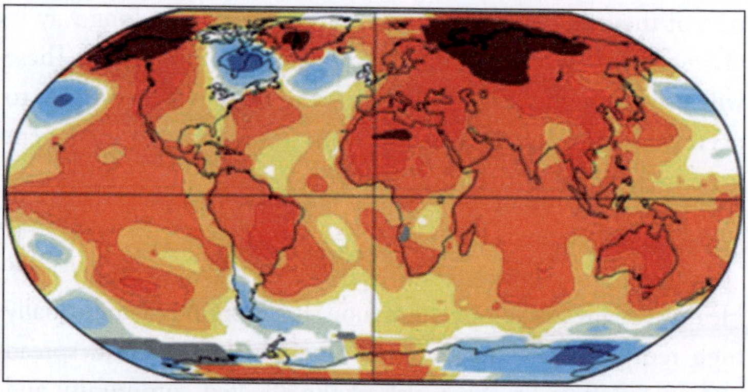

Figure 11.4 Global heatwave conditions in 2016.
Source: NASA

from 1981–2010. Record-breaking heatwaves have been witnessed across Australia, Argentina, China, and in Central Asia, large parts of Europe, Mexico, Japan, South Korea, and the USA in the current millennium.

In India, a severe heatwave occurred in 2010, which was followed by another one in 2014, which surpassed global temperature records since the 1880s. Heatwaves are known to be silent killers. Since 1992, over 22,000 people have died in India due to heat. In 2015, a severe heatwave occurred in the states of Andhra Pradesh, Telangana, Uttar Pradesh, Punjab, Odisha, and Bihar, resulting in the death of 2,300 people.

HEATWAVES: RISK AND IMPACT

During heatwaves, the water resources are the most severely impacted. In the USA, the summer of 2007 saw the largest known fish kill in the history of the Yellowstone National Park. Due to high water temperatures the trout succumbed in large numbers. Rising temperatures and the increasing frequency, duration, and intensity of hot spells pose a severe challenge to human safety. Heatwaves gravely affect the health of the community. Extreme heat can lead to dangerous conditions like heat stress and heatstroke.

The effects of heat on health is more severe in urban areas where residents are exposed to higher and nocturnally sustained temperatures due to the Urban Heat Island (UHI) effect. The UHI effect is mainly caused by heat-absorbing surfaces like buildings and paved surfaces, and exacerbated by reduced vegetation and limited tree cover in urban areas. The heat entrapped between buildings adds to the UHI effect. Pollution and lifestyles in urban areas, including excessive fuel combustion and air conditioning, increase the intensity of UHI. It is a catch-22 situation, where higher urban temperatures require greater use of energy during the summer, which, in turn, increases air pollution and greenhouse gas emissions, thereby spiralling higher temperatures.

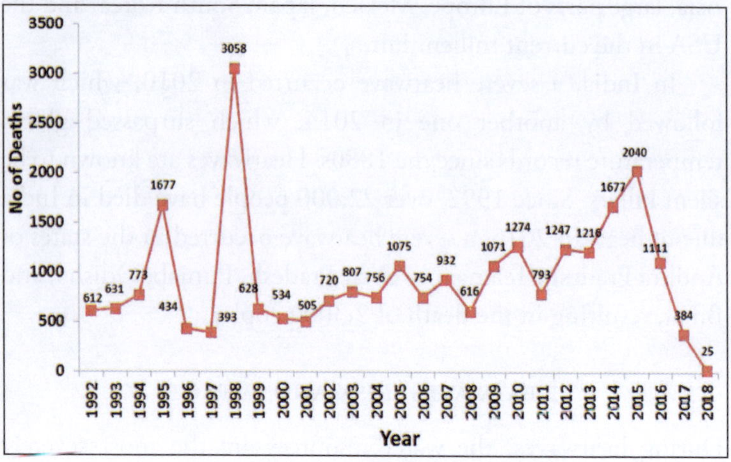

Deaths due to Heat Wave in India

HEATWAVES: MITIGATION AND PREPAREDNESS

Preparedness and early warning systems can help mitigate the effect of heatwaves. With increasing incidence and intensity and grave impact on health and mortality, considerable attention is being paid to heatwave risk mitigation. The reduced mortality in France during the heatwave in 2006 as compared to an event in 2003 is attributed to a more efficient early warning system that was established after the 2003 event.

In urban areas, heatwave mitigation measures like increasing vegetation and plantation, reduced use of air conditioners and constructing more open parks and lung spaces go a long way to reduce urban heat island effect. Effective pollution reduction is a substantial risk mitigation measure. Other steps that can be taken at household or workplace levels to reduce vulnerability to heat include the use of temporary window reflectors made of aluminium foil-covered cardboard that help reflect heat.

Drapes and shades can be used to cover windows that receive the morning or afternoon sun.

During summer months, it is essential to listen to local weather forecasts and stay aware of potential temperature rise. The elderly, children, sick and overweight members of the family and community are more likely to be affected by the heatwave and to become victims of excessive heat. They may need special assistance. One person in the family, office, school, or other establishments should be trained in first aid to be able to treat heat-related emergencies.

During heatwave and high temperatures, it is prudent to stay indoors and to limit one's exposure to the Sun. It is best to stay on the ground floor or lower floors, and drink plenty of water. The mantra to combat a heatwave is a well-balanced diet, light and regular meals, and drinking water to stay hydrated at regular intervals. Staying out of the Sun as much as possible and protecting the face and head by wearing a hat or covering with cloth is essential.

Children and pets should not be left alone in closed vehicles. During a heatwave, sick and overweight individuals are more likely to be affected. People with epilepsy, heart trouble, kidney, or liver diseases, and especially those who are on fluid-restricted diets or individuals with fluid retention issues, should consult a doctor before increasing their liquid intake. Medical and health issues like exhaustion, heat rash, sunburn, stress, heat exhaustion, syncope, and heatstroke can be avoided by reducing exposure to the Sun as much as possible and staying indoors. The symptoms of syncope are giddiness, drowsiness, vertigo, and fainting.

Heatstrokes can be potentially fatal and need immediate medical care. Heatstroke fevers can be as high as 104°F, and may cause delirium and seizures. A person can go into a coma, which can be potentially fatal. Reducing vulnerability during hot weather involves staying out of the sun, drinking water intermittently to keep hydrated, and wearing loose cotton clothes to allow for heat loss through perspiration.

COLD WAVE

A cold wave, a cold snap or a cold spell is a weather phenomenon that is distinguished by the rapid cooling of the air to a minimum temperature. The minimum temperature is dependent on the geographical region and the time of the year. Cold waves are extreme weather events that can severely affect and even prove fatal, especially for the very young, the elderly, and the infirm. A cold wave can also cause death of livestock and wildlife.

A cold wave develops when cold air masses are brought in over large areas. The precise criterion for a cold wave is determined by the rate at which the temperature falls, and to the minimum temperature, it can fall. Cold waves can be preceded or accompanied by significant winter weather hazards like blizzards or ice storms in some parts of the world. In middle Europe, this occurs mainly during winter months when cold air masses are transported from the polar region. The impact of a cold spell is more enhanced in places like Siberia, Alaska, and large parts of Canada that customarily get very cold.

The U.S. National Weather Service defines a cold wave as a rapid fall in temperature within a twenty-four-hour period that requires substantially increased protection to agriculture, industry, commerce, and social activities. In the USA, a cold spell is defined as the national average high temperature dropping below 7°C. A cold wave of sufficient magnitude and duration may be classified as a Cold Air Outbreak (CAO) or a CAO.

COLD WAVE: INDIAN SCENARIO

The IMD maintains that a region experiences a cold wave when it experiences a dip in temperature that is four degrees below the normal. A cold wave in the Indian subcontinent is predominately seen in the northern hilly regions and adjoining plains above the twenty degrees latitude. In winter, cold spells and cold waves occur mainly in the states of Jammu and Kashmir, followed by Himachal Pradesh, Punjab, Haryana, Bihar, Uttarakhand, and Uttar Pradesh. The low temperatures associated with cold dry winds that blow in from the north as transient westerly disturbances are the raison d'etre of cold waves in India. The westerly disturbances are usually associated with cloudy skies, sharp dip in temperatures at night, and unusual rain. Sometimes cold wave conditions are also reported from large amplitude troughs from states like Maharashtra and Karnataka.

Cold waves cause most of the winter rain and pre-monsoon rainfall across northwestern India. Excessive precipitation due to western disturbances can also cause crop damage, landslides, floods, and avalanches.

COLD WAVE: EFFECTS

Cold spells are associated with increased mortality rates in populations around the world. Most of the deaths occur due to hypothermia, especially in the case of the elderly, the sick, and the very young. In developed countries, more deaths occur during a heatwave than by a cold wave. The mortality rate is higher in lesser developed and developing countries. Globally, in these countries more people die during cold weather than hot weather, due to the rise in diseases like cold, flu, and pneumonia. Poverty also plays a role in increasing the vulnerability of the poor to cold spells.

Exposure to cold mandates higher caloric intake for all animals and humans. When a cold wave is accompanied by heavy and persistent snow, grazing animals often die by starvation, besides hypothermia, as they may be unable to reach their food sources. Cold waves are as deadly to plants as droughts. In the past, cold waves have caused famines. In mid-latitude zones, cold waves can kill plants during the early and most vulnerable stages of their growth. The unexpected freeze and frost brought by cold waves can cause crop failure, as plants succumb to the cold before they can be harvested economically.

Fires become a potential hazard during extreme cold. The air during a cold wave is denser and hence contains more oxygen. Consequently, in case a spark ignites a fire in an unusually cold atmosphere, it draws in more oxygen and is likely to develop or cause a more intense fire.

COLD WAVE: PREPAREDNESS AND RISK MITIGATION

Risk mitigation measures for the community include getting the homeless off the streets, and preparing temporary shelters for them, which can include public buildings. The shelters need to be stocked with food, water, and blankets. Hot soup kitchens and warm clothing for the more impoverished members of the community need to be provided. Hospitals need to be prepared for the admission of frostbite and hypothermia victims.

Vulnerable crops should be sprayed with water before a cold wave, as it protects the plants from freezing by absorbing the cold from the surrounding air. Suitable stocks of forage need to be secured for livestock to provide sufficient nourishment during the cold spell.

Preparedness for a cold wave involves dressing appropriately and layering clothing, as well as stocking up on food, water, and other necessities before a cold wave hits the area. It is also essential to stock candles, matches, flashlights, and portable fuel for cooking, along with wood and charcoal for fireplaces or wood stoves, and heaters like *angeethis* and *bukharis*. Using charcoal fires for cooking or heating within an enclosed dwelling is extremely dangerous due to the build-up of carbon monoxide, (which can give rise to the risk of carbon monoxide poisoning) and should be used sparingly and put off before sleeping.

Exposure to cold should be minimised especially for the elderly and the very young.

FROST

Frost is a weather condition in which the air temperature falls below the freezing point of water. Frost is common in temperate and colder climates. It occurs in the form of a thin white layer of ice that forms outdoors and mainly at night when the air temperature of a place falls below the freezing point of water. The ice crystals of frost form when water vapour in the atmosphere comes in contact with a solid surface, which has a temperature below freezing point. As a result, the water vapour in a gaseous state in the atmosphere changes into solid ice when it comes in contact with the solid surface, reaching its freezing point.

In temperate zones, frost appears on surfaces near the ground as fragile white crystals. The depth of frost crystals varies depending on the amount of time they have been accumulating and the concentration of the water vapour. Frost crystals may be invisible, transparent and translucent, or white and clouded. Frost appears white if a mass of frost crystals scatter light in all

Figure 11.5 Frost, Himachal Pradesh, India

directions. Frost appears in different forms like rime, crystalline, white, window, advection, and black frosts. Crystalline frost appears if the atmospheric air has low humidity. Window frost occurs on glass surfaces, and advection frost develops when a cold wind blows over cold surfaces. Black frost typically occurs without visible ice at low temperatures and very low humidity, while rime forms under supercooled wet conditions. Frost damages plants and crops that have evolved in warmer climates. In cold weather, the temperature sometimes falls low enough to freeze the water in the cells that make up plant tissue. This results in tissue damage, which is also known as frost damage.

In India, frost is a hazard associated with an immense loss of production and productivity. During winters, mainly in the northern and northwestern parts of the country, frost frequently impacts the growing rabi crop, sown between October and December. Frost may sometimes reduce production to such an extent that it can result in an agrarian crisis if there is no government intervention or security cover. Accordingly, frost has been notified by the Government of India as a natural hazard, which attracts relief measures.

PEST ATTACK

A pest is an animal or plant, which is detrimental to humans and their concerns like agriculture, livestock, forestry, and the environment. In broad terms, a pest is any living organism—animal, plant or fungus—which is invasive or troublesome to humans, other plants or animals, livestock or human structures. An organism can be a pest in one setting but beneficial, domesticated or acceptable in another. European rabbits that were introduced in Australia caused ecological damage beyond the damage they had inflicted in their natural habitat. Different types of weeds can also be useful for specific conditions. For instance, Paterson's Curse is often valued as a food source for

Figure 11.6 Pest Attack Maharashtra, India

honeybees and as a wildflower. However, the same plant can be poisonous to livestock.

Animal pests are groups of animals, which adversely affect the health of humans and cause damage to crops, livestock, and natural ecosystems. Animal pests adversely affect agriculture by feeding on crops or parasitising livestock. Codling moth that feeds on apples and a boll weevil that lives on the cotton plant are instances of pests that can destroy the entire crop. An animal can also be a pest when it causes damage to a wild ecosystem or carries germs as a vector within human habitats. Organisms which act as vectors and spread human diseases include rats and fleas, which are vectors of the plague. Mosquitoes are the vectors for malaria, while ticks spread Lyme disease.

Zoonotic diseases like the Ebola virus, MERS-COV, Swine flu, and Avian flu infect humans who come in contact with animals, including pets and other domestic and wild animals. Besides acting as vectors, animals may be infected with zoonotic diseases, and carry the infection across species to humans. Birds and poultry can cause a bird flu outbreak. Bats and chimpanzees are carriers of viral hemorrhagic fevers, and camels spread MERS-COV.

In order of economic importance, the animal groups that are identified as pests are insects, mites, nematodes, and gastropods. Agricultural and horticultural insect pests include aphids and other hemipteran pests, lepidopteran, dipteran, and coleopteran larvae, spider mites, locusts, crickets, ants, cockroaches, flies, and wasps. Termites, woodworm, and wood ants also cause immense structural damage. Bookworms, silverfish, carpet beetles, and clothes moths result in non-structural damage.

Plant Pests have a specific definition worldwide. The International Plant Protection Convention defines plant pests as '*...any species, strain or biotype of plant, animal, or pathogenic agent injurious to plants or plant products*'. Plants may sometimes be considered as pests as well, especially in the case of invasive species. An invasive species is not native to a specific location. The introduced invasive species tend to spread rapidly to such an extent that it damages the environment. It also affects human health, livelihoods, and the economy. Plant pests may be monophagous, oligophagous, and polyphagous depending upon the number of hosts they have.

Figure 11.7 Pest Attack Maharashtra, India

RISK MITIGATION

Risk mitigation measures in the context of pest regulation pertain to the management of species that harm human activities. It covers the entire range of tolerance, deterrence, management, and complete eradication of pests as an integrated pest management strategy. There have been historical records of pest control in agriculture. Cats were used to control pests like rodents in grain stores as far back as 3000 BC in Egypt. Ancient Egyptians and Indians used mongooses to control snakes and rodents. In Europe, by 500 AD ferrets were used for pest control. Agricultural pests were managed by cultural, chemical, and biological means.

Environmental pest control involves trapping and killing insects, rodents, and other pests. Poisoned bait and firearms are other forms of control. The most common method for controlling pests is the use of suitable pesticides. Historical records show that around 2500 BC Sumerians first used chemical pesticides. They used sulphur compounds as insecticides. The spread of the Colorado potato beetle in the USA was the possible beginning of the use of pesticides in the form of arsenic compounds in the West. In the 18th and 19th century, insecticides like pyrethrum and derris were commonly used. The discovery of synthetic insecticides like DDT and herbicides, in the 20th century, made the use of pesticides an integral part of agriculture around the world. Pesticide use in agriculture, along with chemical fertilizers has become essential to ensure a good harvest. The pesticide industry has grown across the world into a multimillion dollar business.

The excessive use of pesticides has become a matter of concern as it leads to health hazards along the food chain. Organically grown food and biological pest control are now viable alternatives. An attempt is now being made to reduce the use of pesticides in agriculture as much as possible. Pest resistant varieties of crops are now being propagated. Ploughing and cultivation of the soil before sowing as well as crop rotation reduces the pest burden and helps to limit the use of pesticides. Cultivation by ploughing exposes pests to predators like the black-headed gulls. Crop rotation helps to control corn rootworm and early season incidence of Colorado potato beetle by 95 per cent.

Biological pest control is an alternative to chemical pesticides, and a solution to plant and animal resistance to chemicals. The use of biological means to deal with pests, for example, the introduction of suitable predators or parasites are more environmentally friendly than the use of chemical pesticides. Biological pest control is a method of controlling insects and mites by using predators, parasites, and other non-chemical natural mechanisms. Ancient cave art depicts the use of ducks to consume pests in paddy fields in China. In China, colonies of weaver ants have been placed in citrus plantations to control caterpillars and beetles since 300 AD. The Indian Mynah was sent to Mauritius to control locusts, which could consume entire plantations. Trap crops are another form of biological control of pests. They are grown to attract pests and divert them from crops.

Risk mitigation measures for vector-borne diseases, where infection in humans spreads due to insect bites, include the control of mosquitos both indoors and outdoors through the elimination of stagnant water, which becomes a mosquito-breeding site. The prevention of insect bites through the use of repellants and mosquito nets goes a long way towards this end. Insecticides help in protection from vectors which spread malaria, Zika virus, yellow fever, dengue, and chikungunya. Another environment-friendly method to kill mosquito larvae is by putting Bacillus thuringiensis (Bt) bacteria into the water,which is suspected to be a mosquito breeding site, rather than using chemicals.

In order to avoid zoonotic diseases, avoiding contact with animals that might be infected is essential. Acute illnesses can be avoided if contact with pets and wild animals is reduced, and if unpasteurized milk and raw meat are not consumed.

In order to prevent pest attacks, books should be kept in a cool, clean, and dry, places and they should be inspected intermittently. Bookworms, including larder beetle and black carpet beetle, which attack leather-bound books, and moths that are attracted to cloth-bound books, can be treated with pesticides. Their spread can be controlled by freezing insect larvae at low temperatures. Termites are pests, which can extend underground and enter homes to infest built-up structures. Inspection, control, and extermination with the help of termiticides are measures to control termites.

Food items must be stored in sealed containers and discarded if they are infested. Since pesticides are not safe to be used near food items, alternate treatments of food should be adopted. Pasteurisation of milk kills all germs as does the cooking of food, including meat. Freezing food items for four days at 0°F or baking them for 30 minutes at 130°F are some of the treatments that are advantageous for food items before they are stored.

Epilogue

Hazards are not Disasters

As mentioned at the beginning of this book, disasters happen. Moreover, they happen to people like us. They happen because we do not possess enough knowledge about the possible hazards that may occur or those that beset certain situations. Hazards happen mostly because we do not know how to reduce the risk. They also happen because we do not have preventive measures in place in anticipation of it. They also tend to become a calamitous event because we do not have enough know-how to handle a hazard.

Hazardous events will continue to occur as we have little control over the occurrence of natural hazards. However, our acts of omission and commission will determine whether we allow ourselves and the community at large to be assaulted by anthropogenic or man-made disasters. It is also in our hands to determine the outcome of a natural hazard—for all hazards need not become disasters.

The impact of a hazard and the economic and human losses associated with it can be reduced through strategic risk mitigation measures and effective preparedness. Disaster risk is a function of the concerned hazard, the vulnerability of the community and population, the exposure of the concerned and their likelihood as well as the probability of their assets and economic activities likely to be affected by the hazard. Disaster risk also depends on the capacity of the affected population to manage and reduce the risk as well as strengthening its resilience.

It is indeed true that hazards that have caused disasters in the past will continue to impact humans, their assets, livelihood, and activities as well the environment. A natural hazard cannot be stopped, but effective risk mitigation measures and enhanced preparedness before the occurrence of the hazard can go a long way in reducing human, material, and environmental losses. The capacity building of individuals, families, and communities can strengthen resilience and enhance strength and capabilities to manage and reduce risk. Once a calamitous event takes place, the alacrity and effectiveness of the response mechanism is a critical element in saving lives. Post-disaster rehabilitation and building back better, besides bringing normalcy to the lives of the affected population, also ensures that the potential risk of the hazard in future is reduced.

Appendices

Appendix 1: Basic Disaster Emergency Kit

A basic family emergency kit may include the following recommended items:

- One gallon of water per person per day for at least three days
- At least a three-day supply of non-perishable food rations
- Battery-powered or a hand crank radio, and a weather radio
- Flashlight with extra batteries
- First aid kit
- Extra batteries
- Whistle to signal for help
- Dust mask to help filter contaminated air
- Wrench or pliers to turn off utilities
- Can opener for food
- Local map marking a pre-arranged post-disaster meeting place
- Cell phone with charger and a backup battery

****This list is illustrative and not exhaustive
The Author

APPENDIX 2:
ADDITIONAL ITEMS IN THE FAMILY EMERGENCY KIT

After a family discussion, you may also want to add some of the following items to the basic family emergency kit.

- Prescription medications for the ill and the elderly
- Non-prescription medications like pain relievers, anti-diarrhoea, antacids
- Reading glasses and batteries for hearing aids
- Infant formula, bottles, and warm blanket if there is a baby in the family
- Cash, traveler's checks or a debit card
- Important family documents, like copies of insurance policies, identification
- Sleeping bag or a warm blanket for each person
- A complete set of clothing with sturdy shoes for each family member
- Household chlorine, bleach, and medicine dropper to disinfect water
- A light aluminium fire extinguisher
- Sanitary napkins and other personal hygiene items
- Favourite toy, book, game or puzzle for children to reduce the trauma

Any other item the family may decide is important

****This list is illustrative and not exhaustive
The Author

APPENDIX 3: LIST OF MAJOR TSUNAMIS THAT AFFECTED INDIA

S. No.	*Year*	*Remarks*
1	326 BC	First recorded tsunami by Alexander the Great
2	1 April – 27 May 1008	Tsunami on the Indian coast because of a local earthquake
3	12 April 1762	Earthquake in the Bay of Bengal generated a tsunami wave of 1.8 m in coastal Bangladesh
4	19 August 1868	Earthquake 7.5M in the Bay of Bengal. 4 m tsunami wave run-up level at Port Blair, Andaman Island
5	31 December 1881	Earthquake of magnitude 7.9M in the Bay of Bengal, resulted in tsunami run-up level of 0.76 m at Car Nicobar, 0.3m at Dublat, 0.3 m at Nagapattinam, and 1.22 m at Port Blair in Andaman & Nicobar Islands
6	1883	Karaktau, volcanic explosion in Indonesia resulting in 1.5 m tsunami wave at Chennai, 0.6 m at Nagapattinam, and surges at Calcutta harbor
7	1884	Earthquake in the western part of the Bay of Bengal. Tsunamis at Port Blair and mouth of Hooghly River
8	26 June 1941	Earthquake of magnitude 8.1M in the Andaman Sea at 19.90 N, 92.5o E. No reliable data on the resultant tsunamis that affected the east coast of India. Although there are some unverifiable reports, no press reports of any tsunami-related damage from the east coast
9	27 November 1945	Makran Earthquake of 8.3M resulting in 12–15 m wave in Ormara, 13 m at Pasni, and 1.37 m at Karachi, Pakistan. In Gulf of Cambay of Gujarat, wave height of 11m was estimated, and 2 m at Mumbai, where boats were taken away from their moorings

S. No.	*Year*	*Remarks*
10	26 December 2004	An earthquake of high Magnitude (9.3M) generated giant tsunami waves in northern Indian Ocean. The Tsunami caused extensive damage to many coastal areas of Indonesia, India, Malaysia, Maldives, Sri Lanka, and Thailand. More than 200,000 people lost their lives in 14 countries in the Indian Ocean region

Source: National Disaster Management Guidelines (Management of Tsunamis)

APPENDIX 4: LIVES LOST IN SOME MAJOR TSUNAMIS

Year	*Place*	*Number of Lives Lost*
1692	Port Royal, Jamaica.	3,000
1703	Tsunamis in Honshu, Japan following a large earthquake	5,000
1707	38 ft Tsunamis in Japan	30,000
1741	Following volcanoes eruptions, 30 ft wave in Japan	1400
1775	The great Lisbon earthquake generated a wave up to 20 ft high that struck coastal Portugal, Spain and Morocco	50,000
1783	A Tsunami in Italy	30,000
1868	Tsunami in Chile and Hawaii	More than 25,000
1883	The eruption of the volcano Krakatau generates a massive wave that sweeps over shores of nearby Jawa and Sumatra	36,000
1896	The Sanriku Tsunami strikes Japan without warning, A wave estimated to be more than 70 ft high hits a crowd gathered to celebrate a religious festival	27,000
1896	Tsunami washes away part of the embankment and main boulevard of Santa Barbara.	27,000
1906	A devastating offshore quake submerged part of Tumaco, Columbia and washed away every house on the coast between Riover de, Ecuador, and Mkay, Columbia	1,500
1933	Tsunami, Sanriku Japan	3,000
1946	Alaskan earthquake generates a Tsunami that destroys North Cape lighthouse, killing five. Hours later the waves arrives at Hilo, Hawaii killing 159 people and causing enormous damage	
1946	Honshu, Japan Earthquake Tsunami	2,000

LIVES LOST IN SOME MAJOR TSUNAMIS

22nd May 1960	A wave reportedly up to 35 ft high kills 1,000 people in Chile and causes damage in Hawaii, the Philippines, and Okinawa, Japan as it sweeps across the Pacific	Approx. 2,000 (+3,000 persons missing).
28th March 1964	Good Friday earthquake in Alaska sent out a wave, swamping much of the Alaskan coast and destroying three villages. The waves killed 102 people in Alaska, 4 in Oregon, and 11 in California as it swept down the West	131
16th August 1976	Tsunami killed more than 5,000 people in the Moro Gulf region of the Philippines	8,000
19th August 1977	Indonesia	189
18th July 1989	Indonesia	540
12th September 1979	New Guinea	100
12th December 1979	Columbia	500
26th May 1983	Sea of Japan	Approx. 100
17th July 1998	An offshore earthquake triggered a wave that struck the northern cost of Papua New Guinea, killing 2,000 people and leaving thousands more homeless	2000

Source: National Disaster Management Guidelines (Management of Tsunami)

APPENDIX 5: MAJOR FIRE INCIDENTS IN INDIA

Case Studies: Different Scenarios

Fire in a tent: December 1995—Dabwali, Haryana—A very tragic incident occurred on 23 December 1995 in the small town of Mandi Dabwali that shook the entire state of Haryana. A fire broke out as a spark burnt down the tent in which schoolchildren and their parents were celebrating the annual day of a private school in Dabwali. 540 adults and children died in the fire caused by short-circuiting of the electric generator used to power the tented venue. Many were injured fatally in the stampede that followed, as parents and children rushed to leave the enclosure. The flammable tent made of rayon burnt to cinders within minutes, and there were no fire extinguishers. Due to the narrow lanes, fire tenders could not reach the venue on time either.

Uphaar Cinema fire: The Uphaar Cinema fire occurred on 13 June 1997 in a packed Cinema hall in Delhi. It was one of the worst fire tragedies in the NCR. The fire killed 59 cinemagoers who died mostly due to asphyxiation. 103 people were seriously injured in the resulting stampede, as the cinemagoers tried to rush through the narrow exit at the same time. The legal case against the owners and management of Uphaar reached finality after two decades. They were brought to book in 2018 for negligence in ensuring safety measures.

Odisha religious congregation: February 1997—A calamitous fire broke out during a religious congregation at Baripada Odisha. 206 devotees died while 148 were injured in the stampede.

School fire: July 2004—A tragic fire incident occurred at the Sri Krishna Higher Secondary School, Kumbakonam in Thanjavur district of Tamil Nadu. The children were caught unawares and were at a greater risk having received no instructions on fire safety. There was no evacuation plan, and the school had no fire safety measures. 94 children died in the event and many were injured.

Fire in factories: September 2005 and 2016—Three illegal firecracker factories in Khusropur village of Bihar caught fire and left behind 35 dead and 50 injured. Most were workers, including a few minors who were employed illegally.

A similar catastrophic explosion occurred in a fireworks factory at Mudalipatti, near Sivakasi in Tamil Nadu. It claimed 54 lives and left 78 severely injured.

A fire in a chemical factory in Dombivali in Thane, Maharashtra in 2016 burnt the factory to the ground and left 90 injured and 19 dead. Fire in a chemical factory is complex and difficult to put out.

Fire at a fair: April 2006—Meerut—During the Brand India Fair at Victoria Park in Meerut in Uttar Pradesh, a major fire broke out and killed 100 people. The post disaster analysis revealed several lapses on the part of the organisers.

Kolkata hospital fire: December 2011—In the AMRI hospital in Kolkata, 89 people, including patients, were killed by a hazardous fire, mostly due to suffocation caused by carbon monoxide spreading across the hospital premises.

Burning trains: The Nellore train fire in 2012—The Tamil Nadu Express caught fire and some of the bogeys were burnt to cinders along with 32 passengers who died a horrific death. 27 people were injured in the incident that occurred as the train neared Nellore. The Ladhowal train fire in Punjab and the fire in the Sabarmati Express in Gujarat are other tragic fire incidents that caused immense loss of life.

Multi-storied buildings on Fire: February 2013 and 2018—A major fire broke out in a multi-storied market complex in Kolkata in which 19 people were killed, and over a dozen critically injured. Five fire incidents occurred in Mumbai, India's financial capital, in a span of 20 days in 2018. Most of the casualties were due to breathing in noxious air and asphyxiation. Some of the affected suffered burn injuries and some sustained major injuries and even died while trying to jump out of upper stories. In August 2018, a fire broke out in an upper story of Crystal Tower, in Mumbai. The event resulted in four deaths and left behind 16 severely injured people.

Inferno in hotel: February 2019, Delhi—A fire started on the first floor of a hotel in the Karol Bagh market place in the early hours. The four-storey building was gutted and 17 of the 53 residents, including 2 foreign nationals, were killed. 25 were evacuated safely even as 2 people panicked and jumped out of the third and fourth floors of the hotel. There was a stampede-like situation on the staircase as the narrow emergency exit was locked. A few died while exiting, but most of the deceased died due to suffocation in their sleep. Several wooden structures in the hotel literally added fuel to the fire. The situation worsened because the water sprinkler system installed in the hotel was non-functional.

Death in classrooms: May 2019, Surat—A tragic fire incident took 21 young lives in Surat, a small town in Gujrat. The young teenagers mostly between 15–19 years were in high school, and attending preparatory classes for an architecture exam at a coaching center. The four-storied coaching centre had a narrow staircase and no fire safety systems. The centre had erected temporary class rooms on the rooftop with the walls and roof made up of flammable plastic materiel. A fire broke out at 3:30 PM on the ground floor and spread through the building, engulfing the upper floors. The victims on the higher floors were trapped. Some of them attempted to escape the inferno by jumping through the windows. Four of them died as they jumped off the building. The remaining 17 died inside the blazing building. 19 others were hospitalised in critical conditions. Although 19 firefighters with hydraulic platforms were pressed into service by the fire control room, it was too late.

– The Author

APPENDIX 6: FIRE SAFETY STATEMENT

(A Prototype)

The Fire Safety Statement of this building has been drawn up after a detailed safety risk assessment exercise. Please read the details given below and familiarise yourself with the fire hazards, the mode of warning, and the emergency escape routes:

- Fire hazards include: …
- Risks: …
- Safety measures to be taken for prevention: …
- Standard Operating Procedures on detection of smoke, heat or flame: …
- Mode of warning: …
- Emergency escape routes: …
- Manner of escape: …
- Important emergency contact numbers:
  - — Fire brigade
  - — Building superintendent
  - — Hospital
  - — Police
  - — Ambulance, others…

– Signed
Management

APPENDIX 7:
STATE-WISE BREAK-UP OF FLOOD-PRONE AREAS

(Area in lakh hectare)

S. No.	*Name of States / UTs*	*Area Prone to Floods as Assessed by RBA*	*Flood Prone Area as Reported by States*
1.	Andhra Pradesh	13.90	34.80
2.	Arunachal Pradesh	–	0.82
3.	Assam	31.50	38.20
4.	Bihar	42.60	68.80
5..	Chattisgarh		
6.	Delhi (NCT)	0.50	0.70
7.	Goa	–	–
8.	Gujarat	13.90	20.50
9.	Haryana	23.50	23.5
10.	Himachal Pradesh	2.30	2.31
11.	Jammu & Kashmir	0.80	5.14
12.	Jharkhand		
13	Karnataka	0.20	9.00
14	Kerala	8.70	14.70
15	Madhya Pradesh	2.60	3.37
16.	Maharastra	2.30	3.30
17	Manipur	0.80	0.80
18.	Meghalaya	0.20	0.95
19.	Mizoram	–	0.54
20.	Nagaland		0.09
21.	Orrisa	14.00	33.40
22.	Punjab	37.00	40.50
23.	Rajasthan	32.60	32.60
24.	Sikkim		0.20
25	Tamil Nadu	4.50	4.50
26	Tripura	3.30	3.30
27	Uttar Pradesh	73.36	73.40
28	Uttrakhand	–	–
29	West Bengal	26.50	37.16
30.	Pudducherry	0.10	0.50
	Total	335.16	453.58

APPENDIX 8:
AREAS WITH DRAINAGE CONGESTION AND WATER-LOGGING (ESTIMATES)

(in lakh ha)

State	*Irrigation Commis-sion*	*National Commission on Agriculture (1976)*	*Ministry of Agriculture (1984-85)*	*Figures as reported by States*
Andhra Pradesh	NR	3.39	3.39	3.39
Assam	NR	4.50	4.50	
Bihar	NR	1.17	7.07	9.41
Gujarat	NR	4.84	4.84	4.84
Haryana	6.5	6.20	6.20	6.20
Jammu & Kashmir	NR	0.10	0.10	0.10
Karnataka	0.07	0.10	0.10	0.10
Kerala	NR	0.61	0.61	0.61
Madhya Pradesh	0.57	0.57	0.57	0.57
Maharashtra	0.28	1.11	1.11	1.11
Orissa	NR	0.60	0.60	2.17
Punjab	10.9	10.90	10.90	10.90
Rajasthan	3.48	3.48	3.48	3.48
Tamil Nadu	NR	0.18	0.18	0.18
Uttar Pradesh	8.10	8.10	19.80	19.80
West Bengal	18.5	18.50	21.80	21.80
Delhi	NR	0.01	0.01	0.01
Total	48.40	59.86	85.26	89.17

APPENDIX 9: LANDSLIDES: NOMENCLATURE

- **Main scarp:** A steep surface on the undisturbed ground around the periphery of the slide, caused by the movement of slide material away from the undisturbed ground; the projection of the scarp surface under the displaced material becomes the surface of rupture.
- **Crown:** The material that is still in place, practically undisturbed and adjacent to the highest parts of the main scarp is termed as crown.
- **Head:** The upper part of the slide material that is along the contact between the displaced material and the main scarp is head.
- **Toe:** The margin of displaced material most distant from the main scarp.
- **Displaced material:** Material uprooted from its original position on the slope by movement in the landslide; forms both the depleted mass and the accumulation.
- **Surface of rupture:** The surface forming (or formed) the lower boundary of the displaced material below the original ground surface.
- **Original ground surface:** The surface of the slope that existed before the landslide took place.
- **Zone of accumulation:** The area of the landslide within that the displaced material lies above the original ground surface.
- **Zone of Depletion:** The area of the landslide where the displaced material lies below the original ground surface.

(*Source:* http://pubs.usgs.gov/circ/1325/pdf/C1325508.pdf)

APPENDIX 10:
A TYPICAL AVALANCHE WARNING

Time of Issue: 1630 hours

Fax Message

TO : Chief Secretary ……XYZ
INFO : Relief Commissioner…….XYZ
FROM : Ministry Of Home Affairs, New Delhi

NO. Dated, the 2019

Avalanche Warning

As per Snow & Avalanche Study Estt. (SASE), letter No. ………. dated .... 2019, Avalanche Warning valid for next 24 hrs from .... 2019 (1700 hrs) to .... 2019 (1700 hrs)

S. No.	*District*	*Danger Level*	*Altitude Range (m)*
A. Jammu Division			
1	Poonch	3 (Yellow)	Above 2000 mtr
2	Rajouri	3 (Yellow)	
3	Reasi	3 (Yellow)	
4	Ramban	3 (Yellow)	
5	Doda	3 (Yellow)	
6	Kishtwar	3 (Yellow)	
7	Udhampur	1	
B. Kashmir Division			
1	Anantnag	1	Above 2000 mtr
2	Kulgam	3 (Yellow)	
3	Badgam	2 (Yellow)	
4	Baramulla	4 (Orange)	
5	Kupwara	4 (Orange)	
6	Bandipora	3 (Yellow)	
7	Ganderbal	3 (Yellow)	

S. No.	District	Danger Level	Altitude Range (m)
C. Laddakh Division			
1	Kargil	3 (Yellow)	
2	Leh	4 (Orange)	
D. Himachal Pradesh			
1	Chamba	4 (Orange)	Above 2000 mtr
2	Lahaul-Spiti	4 (Orange)	
3	Kullu	4 (Orange)	
4	Kinnaur	4 (Orange)	
5	Shimla	2 (Yellow)	
E. Uttarakhand			
1	Uttarkashi	3 (Yellow)	Above 2000 mtr
2	Chamoli	4 (Orange)	
3	Rudraprayag	3 (Yellow)	
4	Pithoragarh	4 (Orange)	

Note: People are advised not to venture in avalanche prone areas during warning period.

Danger Level	*Degree of Danger*	*Description*
1	Unlikely	Generally safe conditions. Snowpack on slopes, if any, is generally stable with isolated instability. Movement is generally safe. Rare avalanche activity is possible with high external loading e.g. tremors, explosives or movement in formation zones.
2	Low	Partly unsafe conditions. Small size triggering is possible on few extreme slopes. Valley movements are generally safe. Movement on slopes with care.

Danger Level	*Degree of Danger*	*Description*
3	Medium	Unsafe conditions. Triggering is possible from the most avalanche prone slope and may reach the valley in medium size. Avoid movement on slopes. Routes should be selected with care. Valley movement with precaution. Evacuate from unprotected settlements on/near the avalanche paths.
4	High	Highly unsafe condition. Triggering is possible from all avalanche prone slopes and may reach the valley in large size. Suspend all movements. Airborne avalanches likely. Evacuate from all settlements on/near the avalanche paths.
5	All round	Extremely unsafe condition. Numerous large avalanches are likely from all possible avalanche slopes even on moderately steep terrain. Airborne avalanche likely and may follow unexpected paths. Evacuate from avalanche prone areas.

In view of the above, the State Governments are advised to keep a close watch, monitor the situation in their areas regularly and take appropriate precautionary measures. District authorities be advised accordingly. It is also requested that MHA may be kept informed about any developments in this regard at MHA control Room.

Control Room Officer
MHA Control Room

APPENDIX II: CASE STUDY

Chemical Disaster: The Bhopal Gas Tragedy

On a cold winter night in December 1984, Bhopal, the capital of Madhya Pradesh in Central India faced one of the most tragic chemical disasters in recent times. A gas leak created by a strong exothermic reaction in the Union Carbide India (UCI) plant affected the 900,000 sleeping inhabitants of the city.

Hazard: Gas leakage from the Union Carbide India Plant, Bhopal

Occurrence: 2 and 3 December 1984 from 11:00 PM to 1:00 AM

Backdrop: The Union Carbide Plant, which produced pesticides, was looking to achieve self-sufficiency in agriculture production. Due to crop failures and the famine in the 1980s, farmer's debts decreased the demand for expensive insecticides like Sevin, which was produced by UCI, and the plant was in the process of dismantling and shifting to another country. The UCI plant at that time was operating at a quarter of its production capacity.

Event: On 11:00 PM, an operator at the UCI plant noticed a small gas leak. He also noticed that the pressure under storage tank 610, which contained 40 tons of Methyl isocyanate (MIC), had increased. MIC, a very reactive chemical, was used in the preparation of Sevin. The leak occurred due to water getting mixed with the chemical. The water was used to clean internal pipes of tank 610 with the MIC already in it. The pressure and heat kept building up, and at around 1:00 AM, the safety valve of the tank gave way, and 40 tons of MIC gas was released into the air. Due to the changing winds, the plume spread to a large area in the city of Bhopal.

The situation was further aggravated by the fact that tank 610 could not be cooled, as the coolant for the refrigeration unit had been drained out for use in another part of the plant. To make things worse, the safety devices, gas flare system and the vent gas scrubber, which were designed to neutralise any potential toxic discharges from tank 610 had been turned off.

Impact: More than half a million inhabitants of Bhopal were affected, and people from densely populated and more impoverished neighbourhoods around UCI plant were more severely affected.

- 3,800 people died on the same day
- 10,000 estimated deaths in the first few days by the plume from the UCI plant
- 15,000 to 20,000 premature deaths occurred in the subsequent two decades
- Thousands injured

Key Issues: The Bhopal gas tragedy was a combination of technological, organisational, and human errors. The release of large amount of water in a tank containing a highly reactive chemical (MIC), non-functioning of the refrigeration unit, and the switching off of the safety devices proved to be lethal errors and led to a tragedy of high magnitude. Lack of knowledge concerning which gas was involved and appropriate course of treatment required resulted in the increase in the number of deaths. Lack of community's awareness as well as emergency preparedness for a potential calamitous chemical event on a large scale further aggravated the situation. Furthermore, economic pressures faced by the industry and communities can also influence the likelihood and severity of chemical incidents.

– The Author

APPENDIX 12: CHEMICAL TERRORISM AND CHEMICAL DISASTERS REGULATORY ENVIRONMENT: LEGISLATIONS AND RULES IN INDIA

1. The Environment (Protection) Act, 1986 (amended 1991)
    - The Environment (Protection) Rules, 1986 (amended 2004)
    - The Manufacture, Storage and Import of Hazardous Chemicals Rules, 1989 (amended 2000)
    - Hazardous Waste (Management, Handling and Transboundary Movement) Rules, 2008
    - The Environment Impact Assessment Notification, 2006
    - The Chemical Accidents (Emergency Planning, Preparedness and Response) Rules, 1996
    - Bio-medical Waste (Management and Handling) Rules, 1998 (amended 2000)
2. The Factories Act, 1948 (amended 1987)
    - State Factory Rules
3. The Inflammable Substances Act, 1952
4. The Motor Vehicles Act, 1988 (amended 2001)
    - The Central Motor Vehicles Rules, 1989 (amended 2005)
5. The Public Liability Insurance Act, 1991 (amended 1992)
    - The Public Liability Insurance Rules, 1991 (amended 1993)
6. The Petroleum Act, 1934
    - The Petroleum Rules, 2002
7. The Insecticide Act, 1968 (amended 2000)
    - The Insecticide Rules, 1972 (amended 1999)
8. The National Environment Tribunal Act, 1995
9. The Explosives Act, 1884 (amended till 1963)
    - The Gas Cylinder Rules, 2004

- The Static and Mobile Pressure Vessels (Unfired) Rules, 1981 (amended 2002)
- The Explosives Rules, 1983 (amended 2002)

10. The Explosive Substances Act, 1908
11. The Drugs and Cosmetics Act, 1940 and various Rules framed thereunder
12. The Position Act, 1919
13. The Weapons of Mass Destruction and their Delivery Systems (Prohibition of Unlawful Activities Act, 2005)
14. The Defense of India Act, 1971 and the Rules framed thereunder
15. The Civil Defense Act, 1968
16. The Water (Prevention and Control of Pollution) Act, 1974 and Rules, 1975
17. The Air (Prevention and Control of Pollution) Act, 1981 and Rules, 1983
18. The Chemical Weapons Convention (CWC) Act, 2000
19. The Disaster Management Act, 2005

APPENDIX 13: CHEMICAL TERRORISM AND CHEMICAL DISASTERS

Chemical Warfare Agents			
Agent Classification	*Individualities*	*Exposure Symptoms*	*Examples*
Nerve agents (Anticholinesterases)	Nervous system outbreak Can enter body through inhalation or skin.	• Pinpoint pupils • Runny nose • Drooling • Coughing • Tightness in chest • Muscle twitching • Nausea • Convulsions • Coma • Death	• Tabun Odour: None/fruity • Sarin Odour: None/fruity (used in Tokyo subway attack in March 1995) • Soman Odour: None or camphor (mothballs) • VX Odour: None/Sulphur
Blister agents (Vesicants)	Skin irritation and can also be inhaled. Rapidly absorbed into skin.	• Tearing up or itching of eyes • Runny nose • Hoarseness or hacking cough • Initial redness of skin, followed by blisters • Skin effect varies with agent	• Mustard Gas Odour: Garlic • Lewisite Odour: Geraniums

Chemical Warfare Agents			
Agent Classification	*Individualities*	*Exposure Symptoms*	*Examples*
		• Mustard gas: no immediate effect • Lewisite: immediate pain	
Choking agents (Lung-damaging agents)	Respiratory tract breakdown	• Coughing • Irritated eyes, nose, throat • Shortness of breath • Pulmonary oedema • Frothy secretions	• Chlorine • Chloropicrin • Phosgene • Diphosgene • Mustard • Lewisite • Isocyanates
Blood agents (Cyanogen)	Blocks circulatory system and has a rapid onset	• Occur immediately • Strong stimulated breathing • Loss of consciousness • Convulsions • Apnoea • Headache	• Hydrogen Cyanide Odour: Bitter almonds • Cyanogen Chloride Odour: Bitter almonds

APPENDIX 14: CHEMICAL DISASTERS

India: Important Websites

Ministry / Institute / Agency	*Website*
Council of Scientific and Industrial Research	http://www.csir.res.in
Defence Research Development Organization	http://www.drdo.org
Department of Atomic Energy	http://www.dae.gov.in
Department of Economic Affairs	http://www.finmin.nic.in
Department of Road Transport Highways	http://www.morth.nic.in
Directorate General Factory Advice Service and Labour Institute	www.dgfasli.nic.in
Disaster Management Institute, Bhopal	www.dmibpl.org
Indian Institute of Chemical Technology	www.iictindia.org
Indian Institute of Management, Ahmedabad	http://www.iimahd.ernet.in
Indian Institute of Technology, Delhi	http://www.iitd.ac.in
Industrial Toxicology Research Centre, Lucknow	www.itrcindia.org
Ministry of Agriculture	http:/agricoop.nic.in
Ministry of Chemicals and Fertilizers	http:/chemical.nic.in
Ministry of Commerce and Industry	http:commerce.nic.in
Ministry of Defence	http://mod.nic.in
Ministry of Finance	http://finmin.nic.in
Ministry of Health and Family Welfare	http:/mohfw.nic.in
Ministry of Home Affairs	http://mha.nic.in
Ministry of Labour and Employment	http://labour.nic.in
Ministry of Petroleum and Natural Gas	http://petroleum.nic.in

Ministry / Institute / Agency	*Website*
National Chemical Laboratory, Pune	www.ncl.res.in
National Civil Defence College	http://ncdcnagpur.nic.in
National Disaster Management Authority	www.ndma.gov.in
National Environmental Engineering Research Institute, Nagpur	http://neeri.res.in
National Institute of Occupation Health, Ahmedabad	www.nioh.org
National Safety Council, Mumbai	www.nsc.org.in
United Nations Environment Programme/Division of Technology, Industry, and Economics	www.uneptie.org
United Nations Development Program	www.undp.org.in
World Environment Centre	http://www.wec.org

APPENDIX 15: RECOMMENDATIONS OF UN FOR TRANSPORT OF DANGEROUS GOODS

Rules for Movement			
Air	*Ship*	*Road*	*Rail*
International Civil Aviation Organization (ICAO), Montreal www.icao.int	International Maritime Organization (IMO), London www.imo.org	United Nations Economic Commission for Europe (UNECE), Geneva www.unece.org	Office for International Rail Transport (OCTI), Berne www.otif.org
Technical Instructions for the Safe Transport of Dangerous Goods by Air (T1)	International Maritime Dangerous Goods Code (IMDG)	European Agreement concerning the International Carriage of Dangerous Goods by Road (ADR)	Regulations concerning the International Carriage of Dangerous Goods by Rail (RID)

APPENDIX 16: RADIATION DOSE LIMITS

All nuclear facilities, including those handling radioactive sources, follow the dose limits given by ICRP in its 1991 report, ICRP-60. With minor modifications, these recommendations have been accepted by the Atomic Energy Regulatory Board (AERB), in India and are in force since 1991. The dose limits prescribed by ICRP in its report for application in occupational exposure are summarised below:

Application	*Dose*	
	Occupational	*Public*
Effective dose	20 mSv per year averaged over defined period of 5 years	1 mSv in a year
Annual equivalent dose in the		
(i) lens of the eye	150 mSv	15 mSv
(ii) skin	500 mSv	50 mSv
(iii) hands and feet	500 mSv	–

Psychosocial Effects

Common post-disaster disorders include anxiety, acute organic brain syndrome, post-traumatic stress disorder—with symptoms like flashbacks, nightmares, irritability, depression, numbness, acute burst of fear, panic, or aggression.

Source: National Disaster Management Guidelines
Nuclear and Radiological Emergencies

APPENDIX 17: IONISING RADIATION: TYPES AND PENETRATION POWER

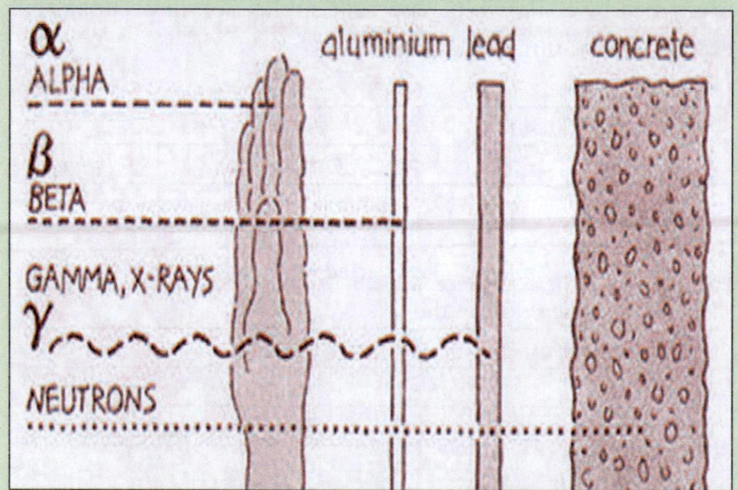

Source: Radiation and Radiation Protection International Atomic Energy Agency and World Health Organization

APPENDIX 18:
EFFECTS OF NUCLEAR RADIATION

Radiation effects on health include somatic effects, which manifest immediately during the life time of an individual.

Hereditary effects may appear in the future generations.

Somatic effects may be in the form of radiation sickness, death of the individual, and damages to radiosensitive organs.

Deterministic effects include hematopoietic syndrome, gastrointestinal syndrome, Central Nervous System (CNS) syndrome, pneumonitis, cataract, sterility, skin erythema, and skin burns.

Effects of Radiation

Dose (Gy)	*Effects*
Upto 1.5	No short-term effects.
1.5-2.5	Nausea and vomiting within 3–6 hours, lasting up to 24 hours. Symptoms reappear 10–14 days after irradiation and last for 4 weeks.
2.5-3.5	Nausea and vomiting within 1–6 hours, lasting for 1–2 days. Symptoms reappear 1–2 weeks after irradiation and last up to 6 weeks. Fatalities: up to 30 per cent.
3.5-6	Nausea and vomiting within 1–6 hours, lasting for 1–2 days. Symptoms reappear 1–4 weeks after irradiation and last up to 8 weeks. Fatalities: 30–90 per cent within 2–12 weeks.
6-10	Nausea and vomiting within 15–30 minutes, lasting for 2 days. Fatalities: 90–100 per cent within 1–6 weeks.
10-25	Nausea and vomiting within 5–30 minutes; no latent period at higher doses. Fatalities: 100 per cent within 4–14 days.
>25	Immediate nausea and vomiting. Fatalities: 100 per cent within a day or two.

APPENDIX 19: IMPORTANT WEBSITES FOR MORE INFORMATION ON BIOLOGICAL DISASTER

United Nations Children's Fund	www.unicef.org
World Health Organization	www.who.int
International Health Regulations	www.who.int/csr/ihr/en
The Australian Group	www.australiagroup.net/en/biological_agents/html
Indian Veterinary Research Institute	www.ivri.nic.in
Ministry of Home Affairs	http://mha.nic.in
Ministry of Health and Family Welfare	http://mohfw.nic.in
Ministry of Agriculture	http://agricoop.nic.in
Ministry of Defence	http://mod.nic.in
National Disaster Management Authority	www.ndma.gov.in
Council of Scientific and Industrial Research	http://www.csir.res.in
Defence Research Development Organization	http://www.drdo.org
Department of Biotechnology	www.dbtindia.nic.in
National Institute of Virology	www.icmr.nic.in/pinstitute/niv.htm
National Institute of Epidemiology	w.icmr.nic.in/pinstitute.nie.htm
National Institute of Communication Diseases	www.nicd.org
Indian Council of Agricultural Research	www.icar.org.in
National Institute of Cholera and Enteric Diseases	www.niced.org
Public Health Foundation of India	www.phfi.org
Vector Control Research Centre	www.pon/nic.in/vcrc
Centers for Disease Control and Prevention	www.cdc.gov
National Bureau of Plant Genetic Resources	www.nbpgr.ernet.in
Disaster Management Institute	www.dmibpl.org
Armed Forces Medical Services	www.indianarmy.gov.in/dgafms/index.htm

APPENDIX 20:
CHARACTERISTICS OF BIOLOGICAL WARFARE AGENTS

Disease	*Human to Human Transmit*	*Infective Dose (Aerosol)*	*Incubation Period*	*Duration of Illness*	*Lethality (approx. case fatality rates)*	*Persistence of Organism*	*Vaccine Efficacy (aerosol exposure)*
Anthrax	No	8,000–50,000 spores	1–6 days	3–5 days (usually fatal if untreated)	High	Very stable spores. Can remain viable for > 40 years in soil > 100 days in humans	As recommended and approved by National Regulatory Authority
Brucellosis	No	10–100 organisms	5–60 days (usually 1–2 months)	Weeks to months	>5 per cent if untreated	Very stable	No vaccine
Cholera	Rare	10–500 organisms	4 hours–5 days (usually 2–3 days)	≤ 1 week	Low with treatment, high without treatment	Unstable in aerosols and fresh water; stable in saltwater	No data on aerosol
Glanders	Low	Assumed low	10–14 days via aerosol	Death within 7–10 days in septicaemic form	>50 per cent	Very stable	No vaccine

Disease	*Human to Human Transmit*	*Infective Dose (Aerosol)*	*Incubation Period*	*Duration of Illness*	*Lethality (approx. case fatality rates)*	*Persistence of Organism*	*Vaccine Efficacy (aerosol exposure)*
Melioidosis	Low	Assumed low	1–21 days (up to years)	Death in 2–3 days in septicaemic form (untreated)	19–20 per cent for severe disease	Very stable; survives indefinitely in warm, moist soil or stagnant water	No vaccine
Plague	Moderate Pneumonic	100-500 organisms	1–7 days (usually 2–3 days)	1–6 days (usually fatal)	High unless treated within 12–24 hours	For up to 1 year in soil; 270 days in live tissue	3 doses not protective against 118 LD50 in monkeys
Tularemia	No	10-50 organisms	1–21 days (average 3–6 days)	≤ 2 weeks	Moderate if untreated	For months in moist soil or other media	80 per cent protection against 1–10 LD50
Smallpox	High	Assumed low (10–100) organisms	7–17 days (average 12)	4 weeks	High to moderate	Very stable	Vaccine protects against large doses in primates
Venezuelan equine encephalitis	Low	10–100 organisms	2–6 days	Days to weeks	Low	Relatively unstable	TC 83 protects against 30–500 LD50 in hamsters

Disease	*Human to Human Transmit*	*Infective Dose (Aerosol)*	*Incubation Period*	*Duration of Illness*	*Lethality (approx. case fatality rates)*	*Persistence of Organism*	*Vaccine Efficacy (aerosol exposure)*
Viral haemorrhagic fevers	Moderate	1–10 organisms	4–21 days	Death between 7–16 days	High to moderate depends on agent	Relatively unstable depends on agent	No vaccine
Botulism	No	0.001 μg/kg is LD 50 for type A	12–5 days	Death within 24–72 hours; lasts months if not lethal	High without respiratory support	For weeks in non-moving water and food	3 dose efficacy 100 per cent against 25–250 LD 50 in primates
Staph enterotoxin B	No	0.03 μg/ person incapacitation	3–12 hours after inhalation	Hours	< 1 per cent	Resistance to freezing	No vaccine
Ricin	No	3-5 μg/kg is LD50 in mice	18–24 hours	Death within 10–12 days for ingestion	High	Stable	No vaccine
T-2 Mycotoxins	No	Moderate	2–4 hours	Days to months	Moderate	For years at room temperature	No vaccine

Source: National Disaster Management Guidelines (Management of Biological Disasters)

APPENDIX 21:

FIRST AID KIT

Recommended Contents for a First Aid Kit

S.No.	*Item*	
1.	Activated charcoal (For poisoning emergencies)	20
2.	Adhesive strip bandages in assorted sizes	2
3.	Adhesive tape (leucoplast)	2
4.	Alcohol (rubbing 70%)	100 ml
5.	Alcohol- wipes	10
6.	Antacid tablets	20
7.	Antibiotic ointment (Soframycin)	1
8.	Antiseptic spray	1
9.	Bandages (elastic)	2
10.	Bandages (crepe)	2
11.	Blanket (woollen)	1
12.	Blood pressure instrument	1
13.	Burn spray	1
14.	Calamine lotion	100 ml
15.	Cotton swabs	20
16.	Disposable latex or vinyl gloves	10
17.	Eye pads	10
18.	Face mask for CPR (adult)	2
19.	Face mask for CPR (child)	2
20.	First aid guide	1
21.	Flashlight	1
22.	Gauze pads (sterile vaseline)	10
23.	Hot-water bottle	1
24.	Oxygen cylinder, lightweight aluminium 110 lit, (optional)	1
25.	ORS sachet	5
26.	Pain spray	1
27.	Paper drinking cups	5
28.	Safety pins	10
29.	Scissors (stainless steel) 12.5 cm	1
30.	Soap	1
31.	Slings (elbow, shoulder)	5
32.	Sugar or glucose solution	100 gm
33.	Thermometer-oral	1
34.	Torch	1

APPENDIX 22: EPIDEMIC OUTBREAK INVESTIGATION KIT

• Disposable storage vials (5ml)	• Rubber bands
• Disposable sample collection vials	• Ziploc plastic bags
• Stool culture bottles	• Absorbent material (tissue papers, cotton wool, newspapers)
• Throat swabs	• Labels
• Blood culture bottles	• Glass-marking pens
• Viral transport mediums	• Adhesive tapes
• Cary Blair mediums/Stuart's transport mediums	• Scissors
• Vacutainers (plain and EDTA)	• Scalpel/blades
• Disposable syringes and needles (5ml)	• Spatulas
• Tourniquet	• Forceps
• Gloves	• Loop holders
• Masks (triple-layer surgical mask)	• Pasteur pipettes/pipettes and pipette aids (rubber teats)
• Disposable gowns	• Rapid diagnostic kits
• Puncture-proof discarding bags (disposable)	• Sodium hypochlorite concentrates (4 per cent)
• Spirit swabs/alcohol swabs	• Hand disinfectants
• Band-aids	• Stationery (writing pads, pens, pencils, erasers, sharpeners, etc.)
• Vaccine carrier with icepacks	• Calculator
• Spirit lamp/gas lighter	• Torch with spare batteries/ rechargeable batteries.
• Matchboxes	• Laboratory request forms
• Test tube racks	• OT test kit
• Centrifuge tubes	• Epidemiological survey formats
• Lancets	• Epidemiological reporting formats
• Slides and cover slips	• Outbreak investigation guide/ module

Selected entomological equipment such as:

- Aspirator and flashlight for indoor/outdoor mosquito collection
- WHO susceptibility kit for adult and larvae with reagents
- Bioassay kit
- Kit for outdoor mosquito collection
- Ladle battles for keeping larvae, strainer, dropper, trays and funnel net for wells
- Vector dissection equipment:

○ Pyrethrum spray (0.02 per cent) with flit gun	○ Physiological saline
○ White bed sheet to spread on floor	○ Dissecting microscope
○ Dissection needle	○ Staining equipment and material
○ Petri dishes	○ Filter paper
○ Cover slips for slides	○ Mosquito net

Synoptic keys for identification of vector
Any other, as per the requirements of the outbreak.

Source: National Disaster Management Guidelines
Medical Preparedness and Mass Casualty Management

APPENDIX 23: CAPACITY DEVELOPMENT FOR DROUGHT MANAGEMENT

Department	*Specific Areas for Capacity Building*
Agriculture	Agriculture practices, farming methods, Agriculture inputs, Extension services, Seeds supply, Demand management of seeds for contingent crop planning and promotion of I.D crops, Mechanization of Agriculture, Promotion of Drought resistance crops, Water conservation
Agro-Industries	Training of rural youth for custom hiring, farm mechanization, post-harvest, value addition, etc.
Animal Husbandry	Animal rearing, Poultry, Fisheries, Horticulture, Improving the areas under cultivation in fallow lands (CPRs) for fodder production. Promotion of chaff cutters to avoid wastage
Banking	Strengthening of SHG – Bank linkages, Loans for farming & allied activities, Risk coverage
Forest	Value addition of forest products, Alternate, livelihoods, Afforestation Programmes, Prevention of soil erosion, Pollution control
Ground water	Ground water conservation, water supply storage and distribution, Awareness creation through participatory ground water monitoring. Recharging dried up Ground water system, Increase water use efficiency
Health	Awareness on sanitation, health and hygiene, Nutritional status, Socio-psychological aspects, Counselling
Horticulture	Popularization of dry-land horticulture and micro-irrigation technique, training of rural youth. Self-employment schemes
Insurance	Coverage of all rain-fed crops, Risk coverage for less than average low yield/ low productivity/ and farmer-friendly mechanism

Department	*Specific Areas for Capacity Building*
Irrigation	Creation of awareness about availability of water in advance for crop planning. Improving irrigation efficiency
Panchayati Raj	Awareness, preparation and implementation of action plan for drought proofing in participatory mode. Supply of drinking water from safe source. Gruel centres in year of drought
R&D	Awareness creation about drought proofing mechanism, fore-warning documentation, training, research, etc.
Disaster Management/ Revenue (Relief)	Drought declaration, Criterion for Drought declaration, Drought monitoring and evaluation, Electronic database creation and management for taking up drought proofing measures
Rural Electrification	Coverage to all areas, Correct voltage regulation, Assured power supply with proper voltage during day time without any interruptions

References

Occupational Safety and Health Administration. (2002). *Hazardous Chemicals in Labs* [PDF file].

NIOSH Numbered Publications – Criteria Documents. National Institute for Occupational Safety and Health (NIOSH) Publications.

Hazard Evaluation System and Information Services (HESIS) Publications. California Department of Public Health (CDPH).

Understanding Toxic Substances: An Introduction to Chemical Hazards in the Workplace. (2008).

Caution – Avalanches! Ed. Swiss Federal Institute for Snow and Avalanche Research SLF, Davos, 2005 Documentation of Mountain Disasters, Eds. J. Kienholz H. and Loipersberger A., International Research Society INTERPRAVNT, Klagenfurt, Austria, 2002.

Guidelines for Legislated Landslide Assessments for Proposed Residential Development in British Columbia, The Association of Professional Engineers and Geoscientists of British Columbia, March 2006.

National Disaster Management Authority. 2009. *National Disaster Management Guidelines: Management of Earthquake*. Government of India.

National Disaster Management Authority. 2009. *National Disaster Management Guidelines: Medical Preparedness and Mass Casualty Management*. Government of India.

National Disaster Management Guidelines. 2009. *Management of Floods, National Management Authority*. Government of India.

Spiker, E.C., Gori, P.L. 2003. *National Landslide Hazards Mitigation Strategy – A Framework for Loss Reduction*. Circular 1244. United States Geological Survey.

Ferguson, S.A., LaChapelle, E.R. 2003. *The ABCs of Avalanche Safety*. Mountaineers Books.

UN-ISDR Global Survey of Early Warning Systems, United Nations, 2006.

The World Bank and the United Nations. 2010. *Natural Hazards, Unnatural Disasters, Economics of Effective Disaster Prevention*. Washington, DC: The World Bank.

Mega Disaster in a Resilient Society – The Great East Japan (Tohoku Kanto) Earthquake and Tsunami of 11th March, 2011 – Synthesis And Initial Observations, International Environment and Disaster Management Graduate School of Global Environment Studies Kyoto University 25th March, Japan 2011.

De U.S., Dube R.K., Prakasa Rao G.S. 2005. 'Extreme Weather Events over India in the last 100 years'. *J. Ind. Geophys. Union*, 9(3): 173–187.

Department of Planning Commission. 2006. *Disaster Management for the Eleventh Five-year Plan (2007-2012)*. New Delhi: Government of India.

The Report of the High-Power Committee on Disaster Management in India, National Centre for Disaster Management, Indian Institute of Public Administration.

Disaster Reduction in United Nations 2011, Roles mandated areas of work of Key United Nations entities (ISDR).

United Nations Development Programme. 2004. *A Global Report: Reducing Disaster Risk – A Challenge for Development*. (BCPR).

Fordham, M. 1998. 'Making women visible in disasters: Problematizing the private domain'. *Disasters* 22(2):1261–43.

Fothergill, A. 1996. 'Gender, Risk, and Disaster'. *International Journal of Mass Emergencies and Disasters*. 14(1):33–56.

Oxfam UK. 2004. *A Little Gender Handbook for Emergencies (Or Just Plain Common Sense)*, Oxfam UK, Humanitarian Department.

Available through: Oxfam: http:// homepage.oxfam. org.uk/ emergencies/ed_general/scipio/gender_handbook.htm.

Morrow, B., Phillips, B. 1999. 'Women and Disasters'. *International Journal of Mass Emergencies and Disasters*. 17(1).

Central Ground Water Board, Ministry of Water Resources. 2000. *Guide on Artificial Recharge to Ground Water*, New Delhi: Government of India.

Kumar, M.D. 2003. 'Food Security and Sustainable Agriculture in India: The Water Management Challenge'. Working Paper 60, International Water Management Institute, Colombo.

Agha Kouchak, A., Farahmand, A., Melton, F.S., Teixeira J., Anderson, M.C., Wardlow, B.D., Hain, C.R. 2015. 'Remote sensing of drought: Progress, challenges and opportunities'. *Reviews of Geophysics.*,_53(2): 452–480.

Srinivasarao, Ch., Venkateshwarlu, B., Sikka, A.K, Prasad, Y.G., Chary G.R., Rao K.V., Gopinath, K.A., Osman, M., Ramana, D.B.V., Maheshwari, M., Rao, V.U.M. 2015. *District Agriculture Contingency Plans to Address Weather Aberrations and for Sustainable Food Security in India*. Hyderabad: Central Research Institute for Dryland Agriculture.

Gupta, A.K., Tyagi, P., Sehgal, V.K. 2011, 'Drought disaster challenges and mitigation in India: strategic appraisal'. *Current Science*. 100(12): 1795–1806.

Van Loon, A.F. 2015. 'Hydrological drought explained'. *WIREs Water*. 2(4): 359-392.

National Disaster Management Authority. 2010, *National Disaster Management Guidelines: Management of Drought*. New Delhi: Government of India.

IMD, 2013. A preliminary report on heavy rainfall over Uttarakhand during 16-18 June 2013. Govt. of India, Ministry of Earth Science, Indian Meteorological department, Lodi Road, New Delhi, July 2013.

National Disaster Management Authority. 2008. *National Disaster Management Guidelines – Management of Cyclones*. Retrieved from: http://www.ndma.gov.in/images/guidelines/cyclones.pdf

Odisha State Disaster Management Authority. 2013. *India Cyclone Phailin in Odisha October 2013: Rapid Damage and Needs*

Assessment Report. Retrieved from: http://www.osdma.org/Publication.aspx?vchGlinkld=GL005

SAARC Disaster Management Centre, New Delhi. http://saarc-sdmc.nic.in/index.asp

Agarwal, A. 2007. *Cyclone Resistant Building Architecture* (1st ed.). United Nations Development Programme.

Baker, L. 1988. *Brick* (1st ed.). Thrissur: Center for Science and Technology for Rural Development.

Baker, L., Chandra, N. 1992. *Earthquake* (1st ed.). Centre for Science and Technology for Rural Development.

National Information Center of Earthquake Engineering. 2004. *Guidelines for Earthquake Resistant Non-Engineered Construction* (1st ed.). Kanpur: NICEE.

Desai, R., Desai, R. D. 2008. *Manual on Hazard Resistant Construction in India* (1st ed.). Ahmedabad: United Nations Development Programme.

Department of Agriculture and Cooperation, Government of India. Crisis Management Plan, 2016.

Government of Uttarakhand, 2013. Uttarakhand Disaster Recovery Project (P 146653) (The World Bank Assisted), Environment and Social Management Framework. Draft Report, October, 2013. http://dmmc.uk.gov.in/files/pdf/Final_ESMF2.pdf

Government of Uttarakhand, 2013. Uttarakhand Disaster Recovery Project (P 146653).

Whom to Contact for What in India

FOR ADDITIONAL INFORMATION ON DISASTER MANAGEMENT

- Website of Ministry of Home Affairs (MHA) www.ndmindia.nic.in
- Website of National Disaster Management Authority (NDMA) www.ndma.gov.in
- Website of National Disaster Response Force (NDRF) www.ndrf.gov.in
- Website of National Institute of Disaster Management (NIDM) www.nidm.gov.in

WHOM TO CONTACT FOR FORECASTS AND EARLY WARNINGS

- **Chairman**
  Central Water Commission
  Tele: 011-26715351
  Email: chairman-cwc@nic.in
- **Director**
  Flood Forecast, Monitoring Directorate
  Tele: 011-26182836
  Email: sharadchandra-cwc@nic.in

- **DG**
  India Metrological Department
  Tele: 011-24611842, 24611792
  Email: kjramesh2607@gmail.com; dgmmet@gmail.com
- **Scientist—G & Head Services**
  India Metrological Department
  Tele: 011-24616051,43824229, 24652484
  Email: m.mohapatra@imd.gov.in
- **Scientist—'H', Director/Head**
  Snow & Avalanche Study Establishment
  Tele: 0172-2699801
  Email: director@sase.drdo.in
- **Director**
  Indian National Centre for Ocean Information Service
  Tele: 040-23886001
  Email: director@incois.gov.in
- **Director General**
  Geological Survey of India
  Tele: 033-22521779, 22521775
  Email: dg.gsi@gov.in

WHOM TO CONTACT FOR RESCUE AND RELIEF FOR EACH STATE

Relief Commissioners & State Emergency Operation Centres (SEOCs) of the states/union territories

- **Andhra Pradesh**
  Spl. Commissioner Disaster Management,
  Managing Director (DM)
  Phone: 0863-2377099
  Fax No.0863-2444186
  Email: commr_relief_rev@ap.gov.in
  SEOC Phone: 08645-246600, 247185
  Email: seoc-apsdma@ap.gov.in

- Arunachal Pradesh
  Secretary, Disaster Management
  Phone: 0360-2214094, 2215581, 2212446
  Email: arun01ddm@gmail.com
  SEOC Phone: 8974987127, 9436074396
- **Assam**
  Addl. Chief Secretary, DM & Relief Commissioner
  Phone: 0361-2237006, 2237221, 2237273
  Email: tsmassam@gmail.com, asdmaghy@gmail.com, e-rdmassam19@gmail.com
  SEOC Phone: 0361-2237219
  Email: statedmcontrolroomassam@gmil.com
- **Bihar**
  Principal Secretary, Disaster Management
  Phone: 0612-2215600, 2217786, 2294201, 2215600
  Email: secy-disastermgmt-bih@nic.in
  SEOC Phone: 0612-2217305/301, 2217786
  Email: secy-disastermgmt-bih@nic.in
- **Chhattisgarh**
  Secretary, Revenue & DM
  Phone: 0771-2510209, 2221269
  Email: revenue.cg@nic.in, cgrelief@gmail.com
  SEOC Phone: 0771-2221242, 2223471
- **Goa**
  Secretary, Revenue/Relief Commissioner
  Phone: 0832-2419415, 2419414
  Email: secedu-sect.goa@nic.in
  SEOC Phone: 0832-2419446, 24194097
  (2419550-Flood time)
  Email: secyrev.goa@gov.in
- **Gujarat**
  Director of Relief & Addl. Secretary
  Revenue Department
  Phone: 079-23251509, 23259502, 23251506

Email: cor-rev@gujarat.gov.in
SEOC Phone: 079-23251900, 23251617, 23259219
Email: revcontrol1@gujarat.gov.in, revcontrol2@gujarat.gov.in

- **Haryana**
  Addl. Chief Secretary
  Financial Commissioner & Revenue DM
  Phone: 0172-2711925, 2713590
  Email: fcr@hry.nic.in
  SEOC Phone: 0172-2545938
  Email: sdmaharyana@gmail.com
- **Himachal**
  Addl. Chief Secretary, Revenue Department
  Phone: 0177-2621195, 2622269
  Email: revsecy-hp@nic.in
  SEOC Phone: 0177-2628940
  Email: sdma-hp@nic.in, seocshimla@gmail.com
- **Jammu Kashmir**
  Relief Commissioner DM
  Phone: 0191-2586218, 2506463
  Email: jkrelieforganisation@gmail.com; jksdma@gmail.com
  SEOC Phone: 01942303399, 0194- 2477261
  Email: jksdma@gmail.com, farooqashah61@gmail.com, director.sdma@jk.gov.in
- **Jharkhand**
  Principal Secretary, Home & Disaster Management
  Phone: 0651-2400220, 09431104455
  Email: dmjharkhand@gmail.com
  SEOC Phone: 0651-2446923
  Email: sec-home-jhr@nic.in
- **Karnataka**
  Principal Secretary
  Disaster Management and Revenue Department
  Phone: 080-22032995, 22253707
  Email: secy.dm@gmail.com

SEOC Phone: 080-22340676
Email: sodmrevenue@gmail.com

- **Kerala**
  Addl. CS of Revenue Department and
  Relief Commissioner
  Phone: 0471-232922, 2331645
  Email: prl.secy.revenue@gmail.com, revenuedmdk@gmail.com
  SEOC Phone: 0471-2364424, 2323127
  Email: seoc.gok@gmail.com
- **Madhya Pradesh**
  Principal Secretary, Revenue & Relief Commissioner
  Phone: 0755-2550988
  Email: reliefcom@mp.nic.in; psrevenue@mp.gov.in
  SEOC Phone: 0755-2441419, 4926892
  Deputy Secretary: 0755-2441574
  Email: eocmp@radiffmail.com
- **Maharashtra**
  Addl. Chief Secretary
  Relief & Rehabilitation Relief Commissioner
  Phone: 022-22025274
  Email: acs.r&r@maharashtra.gov.in
  SEOC Phone: 022-22027990
  Email: controlroom@maharashtra.gov.in,
  dm@maharashtra.gov.in
- **Manipur**
  Addl. Chief Secretary, Relief & Disaster Management
  Phone: 0385-2450038
  Email: secymanipurdm@gmail.com; khanmh64@yahoo.co.in
  SEOC Phone: 0385-2443441
- **Meghalaya**
  Addl. Chief Secretary,
  Revenue & Disaster Management
  Phone: 0364-2223045, 2225669, 2591992, 2225669
  Email: pwingty@yahoo.co.in, ttdkhar.2007@rediffmail.com

SEOC Phone: 0364-2502098
Email: sdmadeptt007@gmail.com

- **Mizoram**
  Secretary, Disaster Management and Rehabilitation
  Phone: 0389-2323224, 2325710
  Email-mizoramdmr@gmail.com; comsecymiz@gmail.com, fanail@ias.nic.in
  SEOC Phone: 0389-2342520
- **Nagaland**
  Home Commissioner cum Relief Commissioner
  Phone: 0370-2270068, 2270050
  Email: homecommissionernagaland@gmail.com
  SEOC Phone: 0370-2291120, 2291122
  Email: seoc.nsdma@gmail.com
- **Odisha**
  Special Relief Commissioner and Commissioner cum Secretary DM
  Phone: 0674-2534180, 2536721, 2536740
  Email: srcodishagov@gmail.com
  SEOC Phone: 06742534177
  Email: srcodishagov@gmail.com
- **Punjab**
  Special Secretary Revenue
  Phone: 0172-2740173(O), 2741762, 2743854
  Email: secy.r@punjab.gov.in
  SEOC Phone: 0172-274990
  Email: daily.monsoon.report@gmail.com
- **Rajasthan**
  Secretary
  Disaster Management & Relief and Civil Defense
  Phone: 0141-2227509
  Email: relief-rj@nic.in
  SEOC Phone: 0141-2227296, 2227084,
  2385776, 2385777

- **Sikkim**
  Commissioner cum Secretary Disaster Management
  Phone: 03592-202664
  Email: skmlrdm@gmail.com
  SEOC Phone: 03592-201145
  Email: sdma01@gmail.com
- **Tamil Nadu**
  Additional Chief Secretary
  Commissioner Revenue Administration
  Phone: 044-28523299, 28593988, 28447701
  Email: com-ra@nic.in, ksatyagopal@gmail.com
  SEOC Phone: 044-28593990
  Email: tnstateeoc@gmail.com
- **Telangana**
  Special Chief Secretary (Revenue)
  Phone: 040-23452768, 23450779
  Email: commr_dm@telangana.gov.in
  SEOC Phone: 040-23454088
- **Tripura**
  Principal Secretary Revenue, Relief, Rehabilitation & Fire Service
  Phone: 0381-2419520
  Email: barun.sahu@gmail.com
  SEOC Phone: 0381-2416045, 2416241
  Email: scrtripura@gmail.com; seoctripura@gmail.com
- **Uttar Pradesh**
  Relief Commissioner/Secretary Revenue
  Phone: 0522-2238200 / 2236305
  Email: rahat@nic.in, upsdma@nic.in
  SEOC Phone: 0522-2237515, 2235121
  Email: rahat@nic.in
- **Uttarakhand**
  Additional Secretary DM & Finance
  Phone: 0135-2712000, 2719425, 2711439

Email: savinbansal@yahoo.co.in
SEOC Phone: 0135-2710334, 2710232
Email: seoc.dmmc@gmail.com

- **West Bengal**
  Principal Secretary DM & Civil Defense
  Phone: 033-22501003, 22143674
  Email: ps.dmd-wb@nic.in
  SEOC Phone: 033-22143526
  Email: wbdmeoc@gmail.com, eoc.dm-wb@gov.in
- **Andaman & Nicobar**
  Principal Secretary DM & Rehabilitation & Relief
  Phone: 03192-233364
  Email: secyfin@and.nic.in; psandaman@gmail.com
  SEOC Phone: 03192-234287, 2388808
  Email: statecontrolroom@gmail.com
- **Chandigarh**
  Relief Commissioner, Deputy Commissioner cum Controller Civil Defense
  Phone: 0172-2700109, 2700053
  Email: dc-chd@nic.in
  SEOC Phone: 0172-2704048
- **Dadra & Nagar Haveli**
  Collector & Relief Commissioner DM
  Phone: 0260-2642721, 2213329
  Email: dmc-dnh@gov.in; dmc.dnh.ut@gmail.com
  SEOC Phone: 0260-2642106
- **Daman & Diu**
  Collector & Relief Commissioner DM
  Phone: 0260-2230698, 2230049
  Email: collector-daman-dd@nic.in; dycollg-dmn-dd@nic.in, dmc.dnh.ut@gmail.com, collector-dnh@nic.in
  SEOC Tele: 0260-2231377, 2230049

- **Delhi**
  Principle Secretary cum Divisional Commissioner DM
  Phone: 011- 23962825, 23931269, 23914805
  Email: divcom@nic.in
  SEOC Phone: 011-23831077
  Email: ddma.delhi@nic.in
- **Lakshadweep**
  Collector & Chairman DDMA
  Phone: 04896-262256, 263180, 262384, 2622235
  Email: lk-coll@nic.in
  SEOC Phone: 04896-262279, 262258
- **Pondicherry**
  Commissioner Relief Cum Rehabilitation &
  Secretary Revenue
  Phone: 0413-2330700, 2233306, 2299501
  Email: dcrev.pon@nic.in; secyrev.pon@nic.in
  SEOC Phone: 0413-2253407, 2233218

WHOM TO CONTACT IN THE NDRF FOR RESCUE

- **At Headquarters in New Delhi:**
  HQ DG NDRF, New Delhi-110066
  Phone: 011-26107953, Fax: 011-26105912
  Email: hq.ndrf@nic.in
- **For Assam and the North East at Guwahati:**
  Commandant 1st BN NDRF, Guwahati, Assam
  Phone: 0361-2840027, Fax: 0361-2840284
  Email: ndrf01@yahoo.com.in
- **For West Bengal and Eastern India at Kolkata:**
  Commandant 2nd BN NDRF
  Kolkata, West Bengal
  Phone: 033-25264394, Fax: 033-25263077
  Email: 2ndndrf@gmail.com

- **For Odisha and Bihar at Mundali:**
  Commandant 3rd BN NDRF, Mundali, Odisha
  Phone: 0671-2879710, Fax: 0671-2879710
  Email: 3rdndrfmundali@gmail.com
- **For Andaman & Nicobar, Kerala, Lakshadweep, Puducherry at Tamilnadu:**
  Commandant 4th Bn NDRF, Arrakonam, Tamilnadu
  Phone: 04177-246269, Fax: 04177-246594
  Email: rb-6th@cisf.gov.in
- **For Goa and Maharashtra at Pune:**
  Commandant 5th Bn NDRF, Pune, Maharashtra
  Phone: 02114-231245, Fax: 02114-231509
  Email: 5bnndrf@gmail.com
- **For Daman Diu, Rajasthan and Gujarat at Gandhinagar:**
  Commandant 6th Bn NDRF, Gandhinagar, Gujarat,
  Phone: 079-23201551, FAX- 079-23202540
  Email: comdt.6ndrf@nic.in
- **For Chandigarh, Himachal Pradesh, Punjab and Jammu & Kashmir at Bhatinda:**
  Commandant 7th Bn NDRF, Bhatinda, Punjab
  Phone: 0164-2246030, Fax: 0164-2246570
  Email: 7thbnndrfbathinda@gmail.com
- **For Delhi, Haryana, Uttarakhand, Uttar Pradesh at Greater Noida:**
  Commandant 8th Bn NDRF, Greater Noida, UP
  Phone: 0120-2766013, Fax: 0120-2766618
  Email: eighthndrf@yahoo.com
- **For Bihar & Jharkhand at Patna:**
  Commandant 9th Bn NDRF, Bihata Patna, Bihar
  Phone: 06115-253942, Fax: 06115-253939
  Email: ndrfpatna@gmail.com
- **For Andhra Pradesh, Telangana, Karnataka at Vijayawada:**
  Commandant 10th Bn NDRF, Vijayawada, Andhra Pradesh
  Email: commandant125@rediffmail.com

Phone: 09419217790, Fax: 01955-252646

- **For Madhya Pradesh and Uttar Pradesh at Varanasi:**
  Commandant, 11 th Bn NDRF, Varanasi, UP
  Phone: 0542-2501201, Fax: 0542-2501101
  Email: up-11ndrf@gov.in
- **For Assam, Arunachal Pradesh, Manipur and Nagaland at Itanagar:**
  Commandant, 12th NDRF, Itanagar, Arunachal Pradesh
  Phone: 0360-2277109, Fax: 0360-2277106
  Email: bn12.ndrf@gov.in

For More Information about Dirty Bombs see the following websites:

- **World Health Organization:**
  http://www.who.int/ionizing_radiation/en
- **International Atomic Energy Agency:**
  http://www.iaea.org/worldatom/Press/Focus/RadSources/Radiolog_devices.html
  http://www.iaea.org/worldatom/Press/Focus/Nuclear_Terrorism/
- **U.S. Nuclear Regulatory Commission:**
  http://www.nrc.gov/reading-rm/doc-collections/fact-sheets/dirty-bombs.html
- **Centre for Disease Control and Prevention:**
  http://www.bt.cdc.gov